A Place for God

W9-BOB-285

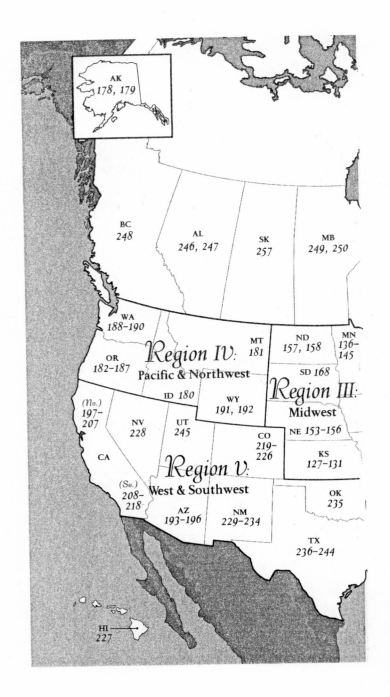

AK
178, 179

BC
248

AL
246, 247

SK
257

MB
249, 250

WA
188–190

Region IV:
Pacific & Northwest

MT
181

ND
157, 158

MN
136–145

OR
182–187

SD *168*

Region III:
Midwest

(No.)
197–207

ID *180*

WY
191, 192

NV
228

UT
245

CO
219–226

NE *153–156*

KS
127–131

CA

Region V:
West & Southwest

(So.)
208–218

AZ
193–196

NM
229–234

OK
235

TX
236–244

HI
227

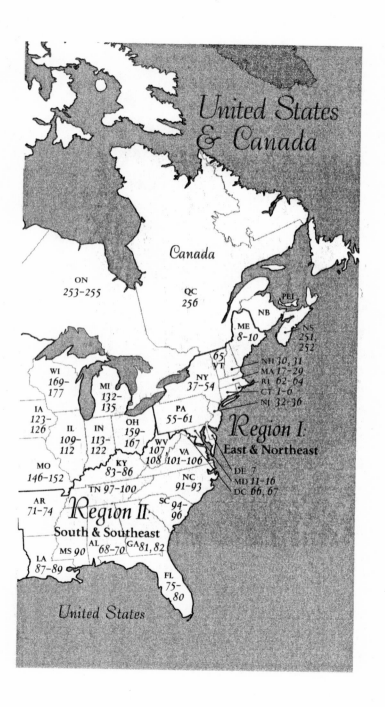

United States
& Canada

Canada

ON
253–255

QC
256

PEI

NB

ME
8–10

NS
251,
252

WI
169–
177

MI
132–
135

65
VT

NY
37–54

NH 30, 31
MA 17–29
RI 62–64
CT 1–6
NJ 32–36

IA
123–
126

IL
109–
112

IN
113–
122

OH
159–
167

PA
55–61

Region I:
East & Northeast

MO
146–152

KY
83–86

WV
107,
108

VA
101–106

DE 7
MD 11–16
DC 66, 67

AR
71–74

TN 97–100

NC
91–93

Region II:
South & Southeast

SC 94–
96

MS 90

AL
68–70

GA 81, 82

LA
87–89

FL
75–
80

United States

A Place
for God

A Guide to Spiritual Retreat
and Retreat Centers

Timothy Jones

I M A G E B O O K S
D O U B L E D A Y
New York London Toronto Sydney Auckland

AN IMAGE BOOK
PUBLISHED BY DOUBLEDAY
a division of Random House, Inc.
1540 Broadway, New York, New York 10036

IMAGE, DOUBLEDAY, and the portrayal of a deer drinking
from a stream are registered trademarks of Doubleday, a division
of Random House, Inc.

Scripture taken from the Holy Bible, New International Version®
NIV®. Copyright © 1973, 1978, 1984 by International Bible
Society. Used by permission of Zondervan Publishing House. All
rights reserved.

Book design by Donna Sinisgalli.

Illustrations by Laura Hartman Maestro.

Maps by Doug Johnson.

Library of Congress Cataloging-in-Publication Data
Jones, Timothy K., 1955–
    A Place for God: a guide to spiritual retreats and retreat
centers / Timothy Jones.
        p.   cm.
    Includes bibliographical references.
    1. Retreats.   2. Retreats—United States Directories.
3. Retreats—Canada Directories.   I. Title.
BV5068.R4J66 2000
647.94—dc21   99-29733
                                                                      CIP

ISBN 0-385-49158-1
Copyright © 2000 by Timothy Jones
All Rights Reserved
Printed in the United States of America

Contents

List of Maps

Acknowledgments

Many persons assisted me in this work. In particular, I thank Anne Luther and the staff of Retreats International in Notre Dame for help in locating retreat centers.

I thank the scores of people who provided information about their monasteries or retreat centers, including Father Eric Lies.

I thank several people who wrote descriptions of a number of the retreat centers: Abram Jones, Sharon Goin, and especially Kristin Searfoss.

And as always, I am grateful for the work of my agent, Margaret Langstaff of Literary Management Group, and the skilled, enthusiastic efforts of the team at Doubleday, especially Eric Major, Andrew Corbin, and my editor, Dr. Mark Fretz.

Spiritual Retreats

⤳

In Search of Quiet Places

I begin with a frank admission: It's not always easy to get away to go on a retreat. We often feel so harried that we can barely imagine leaving our whirl of responsibility behind, even for a short time. "Pulling away from the grind and creating space for quiet," a doctor and medical school professor once confided to me, "aren't my strong points." And if we did get away to a retreat center or monastery guest house, would we fit in? Aren't these the haunts only of the saintly and highly spiritual?

Whatever our questions, many of us also wish for something different. When we think about it, we *like* the idea of unhurried time with our thoughts. Sometimes, when the press of office deadlines or the clamor of the household leaves us quietly frantic, we daydream about time just to *be*. The chance to walk a wooded trail, prayerfully brood over a major decision, rub shoulders with spiritually centered people, or have uninterrupted time to simply think about God awakens a kind of holy wanderlust.

In the push and pull of contemporary living we

realize we have lost—maybe never possessed—a quietness of soul, a calm unassailed by the day's stresses. When we do slow down, or at least pause for a moment, we realize we yearn to make room for Something More. And we want refreshment more profound than what we get from a weekend at a resort or a day at the shore. We want to be replenished *spiritually*. Even church going doesn't always completely nourish our souls. We long for vacations that heal. Such are the longings that nudge us or drive us to retreat.

Across the continent, a movement is afoot. People flock to monastery guest houses and retreat centers in record numbers. An estimated 1.2 million Catholics went on retreats at spiritual life centers across the country in 1997. That says nothing of the host of Protestants, members of other faiths, or seekers with no affiliation at all. Anne Luther, executive director of Retreats International, a network and kind of clearinghouse for hundreds of centers across the country, says fifteen years ago, most retreatants were priests and perhaps a few sisters from Catholic orders. Now, whatever the denomination, programs at retreat centers around the country are flourishing. A recent *Time* magazine article declared, "[M]onasteries and convents, usually regarded as strange or the stuff of medieval myth, are besieged with would-be retreatants and booked months in advance."[1] While organized church retreats have long been a staple of religious life, the influx of individual retreatants intent on spiritual growth is a new thing. And while the desert fathers in the fourth century and medieval pilgrims from the twelfth century on went on what could be called retreats, there is something decidedly contemporary about this new movement. Spiritually restless Americans look at a centuries-old tradition and begin to long to integrate it into decidedly modern lives.

Not that all the retreat centers abound with modern conveniences. Many of these places apart are rustic affairs for the pioneering soul. The isolated monastery of Christ of the Desert in New Mexico looks like a throwback to simpler days of kerosene lights and wood stoves. (The road leading to the 6,500-foot-elevation grounds, says the brochure, is winding, steep, and narrow; during the rainy season tire chains are definitely advised.)

But most, while typically modest, offer the modern retreatant the comforts of modern life. Many centers sit amid mildly rolling hills or on quiet suburban street corners, advertising accommodations akin to any Motel 6 or Howard Johnson's.

And retreat centers dot the landscape of practically every locale. Their proliferation in the twentieth century, spurred by the work of religious orders and varied denominations, means that at least a handful of the hundreds of North American retreat centers and monastic guest houses can be found in every state; most metropolitan areas boast several. Many are linked to Catholic monasteries (80 percent are affiliated with a religious order), some are run by denominations or parachurch ministries, and others simply spring up when someone feels called to put out a shingle. Many seem starkly quiet while others, like the guest house at the Archabbey at Saint Meinrad, Indiana, sharing grounds with seminaries, have all the bustling activity of a college campus. A quiet atmosphere of devotion and worship seems to pervade them all.

That quiet lies behind much of the current resurgence. Deep down many of us suspect that Ladislaus Boros was right when he said, "Everything true and great grows in silence." Wouldn't the projects and decisions and relationships in our lives benefit from more quiet, less distraction? What John Oman called the twin perils of flurry and worry plague us daily. And while our lives are full (read *crowded*), they seem somehow *less* than they could be. They resemble a page crammed with too much type—and the margins get narrower all the time. More and more we have to squint to read the meaning of our lives. So we seek soul respite, vacations that open our lives to deeper dimensions.

It is precisely here that *A Place for God* can help. Whether you find a mountaintop hermitage overlooking the Pacific near Big Sur, California; a cluster of cedar-log cabins in the wooded lake land of northern Wisconsin; the opportunities for canoeing on Texas's Frio River at the Presbyterian Laity Lodge; or an oasis of monastic hospitality on Chicago's South Side, the options for getting away are more diverse—and inviting—than you likely have imagined.

Consider this book a travel guide to a territory of inward adventure, spiritual renewal, and holy leisure. It intends to gather sound insight, practical suggestions, and road-tested information to guide you to just the patterns and places your soul needs.

Almost a third of the pages that follow explore the joys of going on a retreat, encouraging a reader who is interested but still hesitating, and giving guidance to the person who is ready to go. The rest of the book catalogs more than 250 retreat centers, representing all fifty states and most Canadian provinces, along with all the pertinent information you will need to have a fruitful experience. It is all designed to be useful to you wherever you find yourself—whether you are an experienced retreat goer or a first-timer. My goal is to make going on a retreat not just a wistful reverie but a beckoning reality that seems eminently doable and compellingly within reach.

It is not always easy to get away, about which I will say more later. But to go on a spiritual retreat, to leave behind the scenes of work and family, may be less intimidating or out of reach than you think. And it may make all the difference in the world for you, as, you will soon see, it has for me, as it has for many.

❧

A Vacation for the Soul

I'm amazed that it took me so long to go on a personal spiritual retreat. For years I had heard of the practice, one with a pedigree stretching back centuries in spiritual tradition. People I respected raved about the benefits. And I knew I sometimes wanted more than sightseeing and visits with distant relatives. I dreamt about a vacation for my cramped soul. I needed a holiday that actually had something holy about it.

But in all, it took ten years for me finally to turn my itch for a spiritual getaway into a reality— ten years from my first halfhearted attempts to my actually going. Had I known then what I know now, I never would have taken so long.

When I began my first efforts, I was juggling two jobs, struggling to meet a book deadline, and anxious about a career change I was laying plans for. I felt called to the hundred and one worthy things I pursued but restless. My schedule seemed both to intensify my need to get away and put it out of reach.

Still, friends told me about a Mennonite couple who ran a retreat center amid acres of Michigan woodland, not far from my Indiana town. Their reports tantalized me. *I need this,* I told myself. I would walk the hiking paths of the woods in silence, eat from a well-stocked refrigerator, dip into a library of books on prayer, and simply find rest for my soul. No agendas. No deadlines. And plenty of spiritual elbowroom. The couple who ran the center would get me started on my time there, and then get out of the way. In the tradition of Elijah, Moses, Jesus, Anthony and the desert fathers, Thomas Merton, and countless other spiritual models, I would find a quiet place for a combination of soul work and spiritual rest. I would be like Henry David Thoreau trekking "to the woods because I wished to live deliberately, to front only the essential facts of life, and see if I could not learn what it had to teach." Going away in itself would refresh me, I thought, to say nothing of the spiritual atmosphere of a woodsy hermitage. I would, like the sixth-century saint, Benedict, and the many others who followed his path through the centuries, recover for a time a more sane rhythm of work and rest, activity and retreat. And though I had small children at the time, my wife urged me to go: "We'll do fine by ourselves for a couple of days," she said.

The way was clear. I called and reserved my spot.

Then I noticed something odd. As the date to leave approached, my feelings grew more mixed, more uneasy. I could name reasons: The pace at work seemed to increase. The deadline for a chapter of the book I was working on loomed larger. Even without getting away for a couple of days I knew I could not get my work done. But what finally held me back was even more mundane: On the day I was to leave I woke up to a dusting of snow on the ground. I knew I could brave the cold. I could have driven the few hours without any great risk, but the weather report tipped the scale of my ambivalence—to the side that said, *Don't go*. I balked. I called and canceled. It seemed more responsible to stay put and simply slug away. Going on a retreat had the feel of a luxury, a whim or option. I never made it to the hermitage in the Michigan woods.

Over the years, I thought about trying again. I moved to Tennessee and learned that the Abbey of Gethsemani, the Kentucky monastery of the renowned monk and writer Thomas Merton (a kind of hero for me), was only three hours away. *I would love to go,* I thought. But still I hesitated. I was up to my ears in publishing projects, a new job, the same pressures. But finally, one summer, for reasons I can only guess, I decided the time had come. I booked a retreat at the abbey several weeks in advance and eagerly awaited the August day when I could finally go.

Yet once again something conspired against my going. Days before I was to leave, my wife's father, hospitalized from a heart attack, took a turn for the worse. He had scant days, if not hours, to live. Of course my wife and I dropped everything—including any plans for a retreat—jumped in our Plymouth Caravan to head for Illinois, and within a few days, we laid my father-in-law to rest. My retreat was not to be.

This time, however, I felt new determination. Once home, I wasted no time in rescheduling.

And so one Friday in early October, I finally made it. I arrived at the Kentucky haunt of Merton and mystics and monks too numerous to know or name. I found myself tasting the delights of solitude and silence and reverence that I had longed for and only dreamt about, only imagined. I had waited and tried for years, but here I was. With no regrets.

Hosts of people are discovering, as I did, the joy of retreat. Part of it has to do with our society's recovery of interest in all things spiritual. While the soul's life was once the quiet murmur of anonymous believers, spirituality shows up in corporate boardrooms and party conversations. Kathleen Norris's 1996 book, *The Cloister Walk,* chronicling her nine months living among the monks at Saint John's Abbey in Minnesota (a retreat center listed in the directory that follows), remained on the bestseller lists for twenty-seven weeks, giving glimpses of a way to revive a sagging life. Suddenly religious communities, even the cloistered variety, seem to offer something valuable, something worth traveling to. Seekers once satisfied with a week in Provence have begun asking directions to places with an aura of spirituality. It's not that people want to become hermits, just that they long for that quietness amid too-busy lives. "Get Thee to a Monastery," was the title of a recent *Time* article on the phenomenon, and the writer asked, "Why the interest in these sanctuaries, amid a pop culture in which nuns and monks are usually depicted as demanding and dry or who, in their softest incarnations, wonder, 'How do you solve a problem like Maria?'?"[1] If our culture's spiritual fascination lapses into "angel" channeling and sightseeing at pagan tourist sites, it also includes trips akin to the medieval pilgrimages to the Holy Land. We look for what counts, wanting to keep our lives from being a hamster cage wheel where we go through the motions but rarely pause to reflect. We want not to miss God's whispers amid the noisy clutter. We hanker after sabbaticals that offer a sense of Sabbath, for restful pauses that help us make the routine meaningful.

And so hundreds of thousands of Americans go to hard-to-find, isolated centers serving cafeteria-style food with functional, no-frills furniture and sometimes severe strictures on talking. If there hangs about spirituality a trendy superficiality, we also can sense an ancient gravity and a disciplined desire, even if it takes making a kind of pilgrimage. Even if it takes giving up scarce leisure time.

The phenomenon will not surprise those with a historical sense. The idea of retreat has roots in time-tested and soundly biblical traditions. Retreat has for centuries been a way to recover vital aspects of life lived with God and others. An ancient discipline suddenly seems wonderfully worth reclaiming. Hidden, quieter benefits, such as I will explore in chapters to come, suddenly seem essential.

That is what I found when I finally made it to the Abbey of Gethsemani: a wonderful sense of having arrived—in the marrow of my soul.

Not surprisingly, I had some adjusting to do when I first arrived. The normal stresses of disengaging from home and family and work still nibbled at the edges of my newfound freedom. While I knew I was in an inviting, restful place, I faced the normal distractions of settling in. I was a bit anxious about finding my way to a cafeteria that was not terribly well marked, for instance. And while I wanted to join the monks for the services in their "daily office" where they prayed and chanted the Psalms, I knew I would, to some extent, have to fumble through while I mastered the service leaflet. For all I wanted to absorb what I was witnessing and feeling, I had to deal with a bit of monastic culture shock. It felt wonderful but strange.

Soon my anxieties began melting in the steady quiet and reverent atmosphere. As coming chapters will demonstrate, a retreat can mean many things. The benefits range wide. But that October, as fall trees gently shed their colorful leaves, mostly I discovered the joy of simple encounter with God, unencumbered with so many of the distractions of my normal life. I found the truth of what Emilie Griffin says about spiritual disciplines: They are "ways to truth, stepping stones from our furious activity into God's calm and peace. When we have crossed over on the stepping stones, we escape into the life of grace."[2] The sheer beauty of the abbey church, towering both stark and majestic above the rolling hills and valleys, repeatedly caught my attention wherever I walked. I began to grow quiet within. That afternoon of my arrival I wrote in my journal what I was beginning to experience:

I write atop what the locals call a "knob," a hill, that overlooks the abbey church and grounds. Rolling Kentucky farmland, bathed in vivid sunlight, surrounds me. The wind is blowing lightly. The silence of this place is not an absence, but more a gentle, healing presence. As I scaled this hill I felt as though the cares of my world were being gently peeled away with each step. I feel such wholeness, such quiet, happy warmth.

My journal is full of other sights and sounds: I wrote of my guest room in the south wing of the monastery (once a part of the monastic enclosure) and the room's tall, graceful window. The view opened on to a patch of vivid blue sky and the walls of the white stucco church. Soon I would hear bells knelling on the hour and half hour— not to hurry me or mark time so much as to hallow it. They knocked on the door of my consciousness, even at night while I slept, to remind me of a deep call to prayer that too often I forget. That day and evening and the next morning, I went to the simple, unadorned prayer services at the monastery church. I heard the chanting of the monks reverberating in unison's simplicity through the cool sacred space of the church, playing second to no symphony. My stumbling through the service booklet and trying to hit the right notes could not matter. No, I was caught up in something wonderfully beyond myself.

As I prayed and watched the monks during vespers, I felt a clean simplicity shorn of fluff and flashiness. There was a rock-bottom steadiness to it all that filled me with satisfaction. I kept thinking of Merton's exulted descriptions of monastic worship in his autobiography, *The Seven-Storey Mountain*, descriptions that now had the reality of flesh and blood and wood and stone. The silence, the strictures on talking, took getting used to. But the severity of the silence was tempered by the hundreds of acres of lake country and rolling farmland. It was easy not to miss much my normally wordy world. Rather than chafing at the moratorium, I was able, at least for the three days I was there, to bathe in the quiet.

That first afternoon I went for a walk in cedar and pine and black oak woods, coming across a mirror-still lake. The heavens did not open up and the scrim separating this world from the next did not vanish. I have no headlines to report of what I saw or felt. But throughout the weekend the winding woodland paths continued to open me to a world of reflection and quiet. Indeed, the whole time had a kind of burnished inner glow. Once home, I felt refreshed for days, even when again immersed in the routines of work and home. A quiet warmth carried me along. I resolved to return, to not wait so long when I felt my world closing in around me.

The variety of retreat experiences vary widely, as I would discover on visits to other places, as I would discover by corresponding with hundreds of other quiet places in the research for this book. The monks at Gethsemani belong to the Trappists, a strict, no-nonsense order that adds to the typical monastic vows of chastity and obedience severe limits on speech.

But it's a bit different at the Archabbey at Saint Meinrad in Indiana, where I retreated some months later. From the time you drive into the town, you can see the massive brownstone church of Romanesque architecture (the primary style of the early Middle Ages) creating an imposing profile, declaring that nothing will make this structure budge. Driving into the monastery itself is more like arriving at a campus, which in fact adjoins the compound. There is more bustle, motion, and activity than at Gethsemani. An extrovert might prefer the more lively pace. Even worship carries a different flavor. The newly renovated church is bright and airy, walls painted with creams and yellows. The sounds of buzz saws (for building renovation) and riding mowers are likely to be in the air. Guests mingle with students and the sounds of conversation. Tourists stop by, some intent on visiting the Abbey Press bookstore on an edge of the abbey compound. But still, there is that barely definable ethos of quiet holiness. I came away replenished. And I made a fast friendship with one of the monks, an eighty-something gentle bald man with a twinkle in his eye and a flair for calligraphy. I was touched by a different way of life that inspires me still. When I'm tempted to think I need to add accessories to my life by way of fame and fortune, I think of the quiet monks, praying and loving and worshiping day in, day out, year in, year out.

Other places I have visited over the years offer a Protestant flavor, an evangelical ethos that keeps me focused on the truths of Christian faith. The Navigators' Glen Eyrie Retreat and Conference Center in Colorado is just such a quiet, hallowed place. Some years ago I went there for a weeklong workshop given by Richard Foster, author of the bestselling *Celebration of Discipline.* The retreat drove home to me the heritage of spirituality in the Bible. We sang of solid truths in contemporary worship songs and traditional Gospel hymns. Glen Eyrie offers personal renewal retreats in a holy atmosphere without the monastic flavor of a Catholic monastery. Retreatants can hike the trails that wander through the towering rock formations, waterfalls, lush lawns, and hidden valleys of oak and pine. For all the comforts of inn-style rooms and paved roads, abundant wildlife and clear mountain air make for a rugged outdoor experience, a time for connecting with the Creator and the soul he has implanted in each of us, a soul restless until it finds its rest in his quiet presence.

Vacations for the soul, pilgrimages of the spirit—that is what I have been exploring, and now make a part of my spiritual disciplines. It's a glorious alternative to packing into tour buses or braving long lines at airline check-in desks for the latest resort hot spot. And what I find while I am away continues to pervade and transform my daily life, as Gospel values and a new simplicity find room to take root and grow.

⋙

Reasons to Go

Once I asked a friend what made him take his first retreat. "I got to know a man," he told me, "who seemed to have unusual resilience and energy. I liked that and knew I didn't have it. So I asked him what made for the difference. He told me that he regularly went away for a personal retreat. And that planted a seed in my thinking. Then, when I hit a crisis in my life, when I felt desperate for guidance from God, I knew it was time to go, to learn from my friend's example."

People are discovering that the din of daily life can drown out what one ancient spiritual sage called a still, small voice. The weight of duty can flatten us and squeeze us dry of energy. Only getting free from the press of distractions lets us recover our senses. Only as we pull apart for a time can we allow God to put us back together again.

The attractions that make North Americans beat a path to retreat centers are as old as human-kind. Religious figures from every age and culture have gone off to woods or mountaintop to seek a more centered life. In the uncluttered geography of the out-of-the-way place, they grasped what perhaps God had been trying to get across all along. No wonder the pivots in the long story of God's doings with the people of Israel appeared in places far removed from the madding (and maddening) crowd.

And so spiritual history brims with examples of retreat. We see, for example, Abram counting stars in a remote desert night sky just before he heard God's promise to bless him with descendants. Or Elijah knocking his knees in a distant mountain cave before he finally heard God's whispered guidance. And then, much later, we see Jesus facing the devil's temptations after the Holy Spirit drove him into a wilderness. They all knew desert or back road as a catalyst to confrontation with the living God. "Fierce landscapes," to use Belden Lane's term, sheared them of the encumbrance of familiar comforts and opened them to encounter and insight. "I am now going to allure [my people Israel]," said the Lord through his prophet Hosea. "I will lead her into the desert and speak tenderly to her" (Hosea 2:14).

This pattern is no more graphically demonstrated than in the fourth-century migration of those who came to be known as the desert fathers and mothers. They streamed into the deserts of Egypt, Palestine, Arabia, and Persia. They fled the lulling and dulling effects of the pagan and marginally Christian cities in order to open up their souls. They believed, as Thomas Merton wrote, "that to let oneself drift along, passively accepting the tenets and values of what they knew as society, was purely and simply a disaster."[1]

Their approach strikes us now as extreme and exaggerated. Surely their athletic asceticism took fanatical lengths. (Simon Stylites, who spent twenty-three years atop a sixty-foot-high pillar, seems hardly like a patron saint for today's seekers after "soulfulness.") But what speaks still is their determination. We sense that the idea, shorn of its excesses, has something right about it for us.

We can also see that going on retreat does not dictate holing up in a cabin or joining a religious order, only realizing that faith can sometimes grow best when we leave behind the crowding demands of overcommitment. We put ourselves beyond the reach of cell phones and needy associates or demanding bosses. "Retreat, then," writes Philip Zaleski, "is life stripped bare, boiled to the bones, pared to first and final things."[2] We go to great lengths (or at least on a two-hour drive) to keep daily life from smothering the soul. But as you do, you can re-collect a scattered life and focus on the one who calls and seeks and invites us to communion.

How will the pattern of getting away occasionally enrich our lives? What will a retreat help you do?

Discover a Climate of Grace

Going on a retreat may at first seem like an austere undertaking. Get serious about going, and anxiety about how you will "fit in" begins to rumble in the pit of the soul. We are accustomed to conceive of the spiritual life in lofty terms, reserved for the holy elite, perhaps, but not for us. But we soon find, if we go, that retreat can lead us into a supportive community and, ultimately, the arms of a gracious God.

A man came from Toronto, alone, to take a retreat at the Abbey at Gethsemani in Kentucky. "How did you get here?" one of the monks asked him. "Well, I took a plane to Louisville. Once at the airport I held up a sign that said, ABBEY OF GETHSEMANI, hoping for a lift. Within two minutes I had a ride, but only to New Haven."

"Why didn't the man who drove you take you all the way to the abbey?" the monk continued. "It's only a few more miles."

"He told me he was a Vietnam vet and was still having trouble with drugs and alcohol. He was afraid to come all the way. He didn't want to get too close to a monastery."

Sometimes we think the air of a retreat house is rarefied with holiness. We picture imaginary impurity detectors. We fear we won't be "good enough" to set foot within. Not only does this forget that retreat centers operate by a centuries-old Benedictine counsel to welcome all seekers, it ignores that we live and move and have our being through the Lord's favor. A retreat unfolds not by our wondering if we "measure up" but instead by living by the promise of growth that led us there in the first place. And we are saved by grace through faith, Paul the apostle told his first-century hearers in his Ephesians letter in the New Testament, not heroic works of righteousness. Which means we set out on a retreat leaning on the mercies of the Lord we seek. We go not through grit or our own determination or our self-won sanctity. It is Christ's saving work, not ours, that fits us for life and for prayer. And that makes any spiritual undertaking—retreats included—an ever-open invitation.

And practically speaking, the atmosphere of our continent's hundreds of retreat centers is usually informal. Participating at worship services is rarely required, and if retreatants spend their time sequestered behind closed doors or walking the acreage, the staff usually bless it. "People come here and think they're supposed to sit in chapel all the time," says Brother John Thomas, a monk at Holy Cross Monastery in New York's Hudson River Valley. "You're trying too hard; that's spiritual constipation. God is bigger than that."[3]

And what we find will usually pleasantly surprise. One person came to a retreat intending "to be searched, to make hard decisions." But on the third day he heard from God, "You have come here to be loved."[4] One woman found early in her retreat a simple sentence from the medieval writer Julian of Norwich that carried her along for her whole time away. "The best prayer," wrote Julian, "is to rest in the goodness of God knowing that that goodness can reach down to our lowest depths of need."[5] That single insight formed the woman's praying for the week. It was enough. And more than enough.

Open Your Soul to an
Encounter that Refreshes

A simple desire for communion with God certainly helps account for the burgeoning guest lists of retreat houses. At root is a longing—a spiritual hunger for Someone whose traces and loving reminders we often brush past. This contact with the divine will not likely come, people realize, from another week of work or even a day with friends at the shore. "Society is like the air," wrote philosopher George Santanyana, "necessary to breathe, but insufficient to live on." Even other people, as C. S. Lewis suggested, are not sufficient for our own bliss. We know why, when we stop to think. We have within us a God-shaped hole that only God can fill. We stay restless, always seeking, without God.

To lives cluttered to the point of distraction, a retreat can beckon with the promise of divine encounter. We sense that something can happen in our seeking of God that heavily peopled schedules and routines hinder. John Mogabgab writes of the common experience of being at a party and trying to attend to more than one conversation at a time. It is frustrating and unsatisfying for all concerned. Unfortunately, he says, a similar circumstance seems to confound our desire to become attentive to God. A clamor of voices around us and inside us divides our attention. But during a retreat, he writes, "we can slowly discern God's loving voice calling out to us amid the crowd." We find God's gentle reminders more compelling than the shouts of those who are looking for us. "It is a voice that touches our depths and calls forth the hidden wholeness that is ours because we are Christ's," Mogabgab concludes.[6]

Find Yourself in Solitude

Sometimes absenting ourselves from a tangled situation for a day or two is far from frivolous escape but the better part of wisdom. Perhaps Pascal was right when he theorized that all the problems of the world can be tied to people's inability to sit quietly in a room. We need a creative distance from others, from relationships that would enmesh us and even entrap us. "We cannot see things in perspective," wrote Thomas Merton, one of the twentieth century's spiritual giants, "until we cease to hug them to our bosom."[7] The same is true for our relationships and daily occupations and preoccupations. Workplaces, after all, can become too much a person's universe. Daily responsibilities may come gradually to absorb all our focus. We don't realize it. But standing apart, walking away, driving to a quiet place loosens the false ties that blind us. "One day when I was off work," one man recalls, "I decided to pray. I was walking along, praying, and suddenly all kinds of ideas for changes in my life came to me. I met a kind woman who wanted to date me, put a deposit on an apartment close to church, and I registered to go back to school for my master's degree. In the end, I decided that these changes were too hard. I went back to a destructive relationship with my old girlfriend and then descended into the worst time of my life. But I always wondered if that day would have been a turning point if I'd kept the prayer going."

Solitude, whatever momentary panic it elicits in us, brings great benefits. Sometimes we see the meaning of life and other people better from afar. Type on a page, after all, becomes unintelligible when we stick our nose a mere inch away. The words come into proper focus only when we set the page at the proper distance. Only then can we decipher the words' meanings. A retreat in the mountainous woods an hour from home or even at a friend's vacant house down the road can do something similar. We find ourselves given perspective. We find a new freedom from the tyranny of urgency that drives us madly from one demand to another. Getting apart gives us a new angle of view that saves our sanity. We may even find, as Thomas Merton writes in *Thoughts in Solitude,* a new integrity. For if we live always and only under the pressure of others around us, of deadlines and obligations, our true self may get lost. "When [people] are merely submerged in a mass of impersonal human beings pushed around by automatic forces," he wrote, "they lose their true humanity, their integrity, their ability to love, their capacity for self-determination."[8] But solitude changes that.

Paradoxically, getting away helps us more deeply appreciate the people we rub shoulders with. We do not retreat into solitude thinking that only by escaping other people will we find spiritual wholeness. No, we go into solitude in order better to love others. Our absenting ourselves allows us more profound immersion in the world. It provides a climate where we can become more ourselves. "And now, Lord," Søren Kierkegaard prayed, "with your help I shall become myself." As we become our *true* selves, the persons God created us to be, we end up with more to give others, not less.

This helps explain the extreme but nevertheless instructive way the desert fathers saw what they called detachment. They knew that only with distance could they resist the pressures that mold society. At all cost they wanted not to drift along with cultural currents and end up shipwrecked. So they held up as a goal becoming an "outsider." A brother asked Abba Poemen, in a story that illustrates this, "How should I be in the place where I live?" Poemen said, "Have the mentality of the stranger in the place where you live so you don't too readily express your opinions and you will be at peace." To be a stranger to society was not to run from responsibility as much as it was to recognize that we cannot rightly live when we give others more than their due.

For most of us, spaces of quiet do not automatically present themselves. The very push and pull of the people in our lives makes it hard to get away when we need it the most. "It feels like I have no elbowroom," someone once confessed to a friend, moving his elbows and arms akimbo like he was trying to create space just thinking about his schedule. He knew he would have to buck the forces that constantly crowded out reflection. He felt like the character Sally in Richard Ford's novel *Independence Day*. She says to her boyfriend, the protagonist of the book, Frank Bascombe, "Life seems congested.

. . . Something's just crying out to be noticed, I just don't know what it is. I just feel things are congested and I'm missing something."[9] When we neglect solitude, we suffer a kind of congestive soul failure.

But solitude revives us. It may keep us from giving so much that we give out. Certainly we must at times be utterly available to others. Surely we go into all the world with compassion and missionary zeal. But there must be just as certainly times when we let the urge to clear a space for God take precedence. Going on retreat reminds us that any healthy life moves through seasons, even when it comes to our obligations. We strategically withdraw our energy and attention from all the people who, in one way or another, demand our attention or require our focus. We honor that voice within that says "Enough!" Not to evade reality but to better plumb its varied depths.

For many of us with jobs, ailing relatives, clingy toddlers, or attentive spouses, this retreat from their needs may seem callous. But every so often we hear within a whispered invitation to go away and find a place to be alone with God. Sometimes it's more than a whisper but a cry. And if we are not too backed into a corner or on the road hurriedly making the next appointment, we hear it. We will realize that the solitude of a retreat will provide an interval of stillness and gentle concentration, a pause in the constant and unremitting demands that will make us more than we would otherwise be. We will seize a chance to do more than respond to others, but be addressed by what C. S. Lewis called that stronger, quieter Voice.

Nurture Silence that Helps You Listen

It's a commonplace that we live in eardrum-jangling times. "The world is immersed in a 'noise culture,'" remind the monks of the Monastery of Christ of the Desert in New Mexico. "Here in the monastery, we hope to help you turn off the 'noise' in order to tune in to God." And that indeed appears as an attraction: to hear more than the constant chatter of our data-heavy lives. To find a way through and above the sea of words.

When we complain about the noise of our daily lives we usually don't mean just the decibels of neighbors' loud music or the trucks that roar down our streets. Just as distracting are sounds and words that pile up in our wordy world. Access to sound and information has so multiplied that many households have CD players in every bedroom, more than one TV, and a phone never more than a few steps away. And when we are on the road, cell phones and laptop computers and "personal digital assistants" never let us go long without an interrupting sound. "We do all manner of things to cope with the noise and the pace," writes Robert Benson in *Living Prayer*. "We get speed-dial and voice-mail systems and beepers and E-mail so that we can keep conversations going with dozens of people we have no time to talk to. We put phones in our cars so that we can do business while we listen to cassettes of the books we do not have the time to read, so that our daily commute from the places we moved to for peace and quiet doesn't turn into wasted time."[10] But timesaving devices do not save *us*. They leave us as frazzled as before, heads spinning and ears weary. Information overload does not make us wise, nor do the many words heal or instruct our souls. We feel scattered, unsettled, unfocused. "And when information bombards us faster than we can assimilate it," writes a *Newsweek* reporter, "we miss out on more than the surplus. . . . [A]n overwhelmed mind has trouble absorbing anything."[11]

And we often battle a kind of inner static, a sensation of interior voices driving us on or deep needs haunting our awareness. Every waking moment, it seems, we talk and listen to someone: ourselves, the people around us, or God. And we rarely manage to listen to others or talk to God with much attentiveness. Instead, an inner tape of "oughts" and "what ifs" and "must dos" drowns out everything else. We live in the grip of what Quaker writer Douglas Steere called the constant plans and distractions of our "surface self." Our inner ears become so desensitized by the constant volume of inner and outer noise that we have trouble hearing anything. "God does not cease to speak," wrote seventeenth-century spiritual writer François Fenelon, "but the noise of the creatures without, and of our passions within, confines us and prevents our hearing." For a faith that argues that God guides and communicates, this is problematic indeed.

But going on retreat allows us to come to an

inner settling. The Eastern Orthodox writers, the monk and recording artist John Michael Talbot once told me, use the image of a pond to make the point. If the surface of the water is always agitated, we will never see below to the bottom. Only when it is still do we see with clarity, and find our image reflected on its mirror face. And at the beginning, when we first look, we may see cans and boots and garbage that need to be cleaned out—a kind of refuse of the soul that requires attention. And then the water stirs up and gets agitated, until again we allow it to settle. Until again the water grows still and we can see again—through to its depths. Until again we can see ourselves on its placid surface.

In 1 Kings there is an intriguing story about Elijah, fleeing from Ahaz and Jezebel, burned out, fearing for his life. It was a tumultuous time in his life and the life of his nation. But he broke from the clamor and controversy. We read, "The Lord said, 'Go out and stand on the mountain in the presence of the Lord, for the Lord is about to pass by.' Then a great and powerful wind tore the mountains apart and shattered the rocks before the Lord, but the Lord was not in the wind. After the wind there was an earthquake, but the Lord was not in the earthquake. After the earthquake came a fire, but the Lord was not in the fire. And after the fire," concludes the story, "came a gentle whisper" (1 Kings 19:11–12). His soul finally quieted, Elijah heard.

The poet Kathleen Norris tells of working as an artist in elementary schools. Sometimes she used an exercise, a kind of experiment, regarding noise and silence. "When I raise my hand," she told kids in the classrooms, "you make all the noise you can while sitting at your desk, using your mouth, hands, and feet." It took the kids a while to really let loose, but eventually their stomping and shouting made a real racket.

Then they were to be silent. "Don't hold your breath and make funny faces," Norris had to say, "as this is how third-graders typically imagine silence." Then she said, "The only hard thing is to sit so still that you make no noise at all." Some were scared, unsettled by the eerie power of silence. But once they got the hang of it, most of the kids loved the stillness, amazed at how quiet they could be.

Norris would then ask them to describe their experiences on paper. Their efforts to write about noise used predictable images ("a herd of elephants"), but silence, she said, liberated their imaginations: "Silence is a tree spreading its branches to the sun," wrote one child. And then one girl in a tiny North Dakota town said this, a phrase worth pondering by the wisest adult: "Silence reminds me to take my soul with me wherever I go."[12] So we need a break from noisy lives. Silence allows us to carry our faith more profoundly to the scenes of work and play when we do return.

Experience the Renewing Power of Rest

The urge to retreat also has to do with a hunger for replenishing rest.

Ours is a culture bent on doing. People like the exhilaration of accomplishment. Our first impulse when presented with a situation—any situation—is to act. The last thing we think of is to stand back to reflect. This can-do quality certainly comes with advantages. But it also means there is often a wearying urgency to the lives and work of many people. Workplaces become production mills. Even our time away from work has a kind of drivenness: errands to run, children to drive to games, chores around the house that stare us down when we sit in an easy chair. The demands wear on us and the rigors weigh us down.

Something deep within us cries out for something more. We wish we did not live from item to item on our ever-present mental to-do lists. We would like to agitate less, enjoy more. This is precisely what we "practice" when we go on retreat. "Taking a spiritual retreat," says one thirty-something woman from Colorado, "is like fasting, not from food, but from activity. It's time to seek God, to help me find my center and get quiet again in my soul."[13]

Monk, writer, and social critic Thomas Merton tells of a time at his hermitage in the woods when he simply stopped to absorb the sound of rain around him: "The rain I am in is not like the rain of cities. It fills the woods with an immense and confused sound. It covers the flat roof of the cabin and its porch with insistent and controlled rhythms. And I listen, because it reminds me again and again that the whole world runs by rhythms that I have not yet learned to recognize, rhythms that are not those of the engineer."[14] Merton discovered the power of nondoing, not analyzing. He allowed himself to be greeted by the simple and restful sounds of something he need not orchestrate but simply enjoy.

So we go and allow ourselves a spiritual break. One woman went to a retreat center, burned out, anxious about a life in disarray, and one of the sisters asked a simple question: "What's one thing you can do for you today that you can't do at home?" The woman said, "Take a nap and a bath." "Well," replied the sister, "let's start there."[15] A starting place—and a valid one—that was.

This business of rest may seem strange, at first. We are not sure we really want to cease our restless striving. We are not sure it is even *right*. Inner voices keep them from ever taking a break, even for a day or two or a long weekend. Modern societies, such as ours, tend to define people by what they *produce*, or even what they *consume*. Our lives, every day of them, must *count*. We seem, as someone once said, addicted to our own significance. No wonder the thought of leaving behind our calendars, family duties, or office responsibilities induces quiet panic. And even leisure time leaves us unrenewed. We take our drive and zeal even into our vacations, placing heavy expectations for renewal and distraction. Or perhaps "time off" becomes an escape into mind-numbing oblivion—anything to give us a break from the push and pull. But there nags a realization that hours of mindless TV or other shallow diversions do not restore what our schedules ravage.

Amid such confusion comes a gentle invitation: "Come to me, all you who are weary and burdened, and I will give you rest. Take my yoke upon you and learn from me, for I am gentle and humble in heart, and you will find rest for your souls. For my yoke is easy and my burden is light" (Matthew 11:28–30). In place of our exhaustion, Jesus offers us rest.

A man named Chris Maxwell was rereading an article he had written in which he quoted Jesus' invitation to rest, his promise that his burden would be light. Chris discovered to his bemusement that he had misspelled one word he had frequently included. "As I wrote of Christ's comments about His yoke being easy, three times I used the word 'joke' instead of 'yoke.' Not a very funny joke for a perfectionist!" Then it hit Chris that frequently we view Jesus' promise as just that: a joke, or at least something that cannot be taken too seriously.

And certainly Christian faith and daily life have a very active side. This is another argument our mental tape plays when we think about leaving responsibilities behind for a time for rest and renewal. Jesus went about doing good, the book of Acts reminds us. Somehow our picture of fruitful life has much of the feel of the activist and tireless worker. But we also know that for Jesus ministry was never mere activity, never ungrounded activism. Even though a swirl of motion and need often greeted him, all he did flowed from a different spring. For all the activity of Jesus' ministry, still, we see, "very early in the morning, while it was still dark, Jesus got up, left the house and went to a solitary place, where he prayed" (Mark 1:35). Locked within the loud words of activity and people seeking him out is a simple verse that points to the grace-full replenishment that fed Jesus' work and ministry. We are to build, work, try. But we are not fully ourselves—or

God's—when we day by day bounce from one demand to another, living only in response to work pressures and others' drivenness. Something beyond us and hidden within us feeds our labor as well. "Only he who obeys a rhythm superior to his own," wrote Nikos Kazantzakis, "is free." The sheer nonproductiveness of going on retreat promises relief to lives that sometimes seem like agitated runs on hamster cage wheels.

Herman Melville tells a wonderful story in *Moby-Dick*. The harpooneer, he lets us know, is a key member of the crew of the whaling boats of the nineteenth century. But in the heated pursuit of the whale, everyone—*everyone*—in the little boat strains to pull the oars of the "vibrating, cracking craft," bobbing and careering, all the while each man clinging to his seat to prevent being tossed into the water. And the harpooneer, the very one who should be poised and ready to strike, has to pull the foremost oar. "But however prolonged and exhausting the chase, the harpooneer is . . . expected to set an example of superhuman activity to the rest, not only by incredible rowing, but by repeated loud and intrepid exclamations." And when the time comes to throw the dart, when he finally hears, "Stand up, and give it to him!" the harpooneer "now has to drop and secure his oar . . . seize the harpoon from the crotch, and with what little strength may remain, he essays to pitch it somehow into the whale." No wonder, Melville concludes, "that out of fifty fair chances for a dart, not five are successful; no wonder that so many hapless harpooneers are madly cursed and disrated; no wonder that some of them actually burst their blood vessels in the boat." Then this key line: "To insure the greatest efficiency in the dart, the harpooneers of this world must start to their feet from out of idleness, and not from out of toil."[16]

Retreat provides us a sanctified idleness out of which we start to our feet. Any person who has studied the creative process knows that there comes a time, after scrutinizing all the possibilities and angles, that incubation, a kind of passive waiting, is a key stage. And it is true with Christian life that we sometimes cease our labors in order to gather our forces, and let God renew and refill. Even God, after all, rested on the seventh day of creation.

Find a Proper Rhythm

Our bodies operate by unseen but vital rhythms. Our heart beats in time. We breathe on hidden cue. Our brain waves oscillate according to patterns. Everything we do and feel is affected by rhythm. No less with the soul, with our inner rhythms and outer activities.

E. M. Forster suggests in his novel *Howards End* that we could stand to do more to connect the inner and outer parts of our lives. The businessperson, he writes, "who assumes that this life is everything, and the mystic who asserts that it is nothing at all, fail, on this side and on that, to hit the truth." Nor do we come to a proper understanding by a compromise of the two approaches. "Truth, being alive, was not halfway between anything. It was only to be found by continuous excursions into either realm." A friend puts it simpler: "I love quiet, but only for part of a day. I like to go back and forth from recluse to socialite."

This is why spiritual writers often speak of rhythm. "There is a time for everything, and a season for every activity under heaven. . . . [A] time to scatter stones and a time to gather them" (Ecclesiastes 3:1, 5). There is a time for hunkering down and a time for getting away. Retreat provides the kind of "excursion" Forster spoke of.

This pattern is more basic to life than we may realize. Who of us doesn't benefit from breaks in the routine, from strategic pauses like coffee breaks or lunchtimes that allow us to regather our wits at work? Even our nightly recourse to the bed is testimony to the essential quality of rhythm to healthy living.

I think of a time when I was a pastor of a struggling church in Texas, hounded by pressures and fearful of the future; I drove a couple of hours to a university for a couple of days of reading and prayerful reflection on my work. I stayed in student housing, took walks, browsed and grazed in the library. It was a precursor to my time at the Gethsemani monastery, a kind of whetting of the soul's appetite. Still later, as a calling to writing crystallized, I attended a three-day writers' workshop hours away from my home. I was immersed in a new world in order to come away with something I could not get by plugging along in my habitual place.

Now, day in, day out, I take "retreats" of another sort several times a week; I run in the neighborhood, take a quiet cup of tea in the morning before the day gets "cranking," follow an occasional urge to step out of the house and go for a walk under a night sky. Every now and then my wife and I leave the kids at home and take in a movie. I take at least one vacation with the family during the year. All these ways of varying our pace and getting away partake of our elemental need for another different and varied way of being in the world.

It is part of the rhythm I am discovering that keeps me healthy, that allows my soul to join in the rhythms of God's creative work all around me.

Every life, I believe, contains the longing for solitude, rest, rhythm. Which means each person already has within reach the raw elements of retreat. Everyone can discover the benefits. Perhaps not at the level of a three-day jaunt to a log-cabin hermitage in the Rockies. Perhaps not by way of a long silent retreat in a monastery set amid acres of hilly Kentucky farmland. But the *pattern* of retreat—taking a breather, getting away to get in touch with deeper realities—that takes place in any healthy life. Everyone needs the alternation of putting out and taking in, of pulling back in order to find energy to keep going. Life gets out of sync otherwise. To balance the noise of modern life we need the enriching power of at least occasional spaces of quiet. We season our times with others with times apart.

And so going on an "official" spiritual retreat beckons with promise. Somehow, perhaps after waiting or trying and chickening out at the last minute more than once, there we sit in front of a phone, phone number in hand, ready to reserve a spot, realizing a release from the stress and a time to reconnect with God is just what we need. We may be like the woman who signed up for a retreat and then canceled. And then signed up again. And again. She wavered and then finally made it. Even though we hold back, finally the desire overcomes our fears. We hear a gentle invitation from God, or perhaps a frantic cry from our frazzled soul, and we go. We discover that the point is not perfection but beginning where we are. Not feeling we must already be a fully formed spiritual expert, but starting out on the journey.

Chapter 3

❧

Three to Get Ready

Like many people, I enjoy traveling, even on the occasional business trip. But as departure time approaches, my anxiety increases. Something in me wants to keep procrastinating; last-minute worries make me fuss and find detail after detail to keep me home. The hardest part has to do with my actually walking out the door on time. Sometimes I even make it to the departure gate running, breathless, in danger of missing my flight.

Such feelings can likewise affect our feelings about a retreat. They may eat away at the joys of getting away. Or even keep us from going at all. For all we might want to go, we have to confront our hidden desires to stay, to refuse to let go of the routine. Just as important, we need to gear up to make the most of what we are about to enjoy.

How then do we prepare? While the next chapter will look at practical matters—what to take (and even more important, what *not* to take), why you shouldn't plan much of an agenda for the first day or so—here we lay groundwork for leaving well and going in the best possible frame of soul. The most important preparations have to do with our hearts. Here are three things to tend to as you prepare to go:

Let Go of What "Has" to Be Done

Many of us talk about schedule as the big obstacle to going. We assume it's the press of work, the constancy of family needs, the urgency of what we do for others that hold us back. But I suspect even more daunting is our subtle fear that if we absent ourselves from our world for a few days, something choice will happen without us. Or we fear that something needing doing won't get done. Behind this, even more subtly, may be a fear that we won't be needed. "What we say, is," writes spiritual-life writer Richard Foster, " 'I want to be available to help whenever there is a crisis or problem.' But what really concerns us is that people will get along quite well without us!"[1] We like to feel indispensable. Going on retreat reminds us that the world runs by forces that have little to do with our little selves and microagendas. Getting away forces the recognition that we are not CEO of the world. It means giving up some control, and in a world that sometimes seems chaotic, that may be frightening indeed.

A part of us, too, wants the satisfaction of wresting achievement out of our lives by sheer dint of will. We savor accomplishments, not divine favor. "There are two ways of finding something that is lost," writes Gil Lahav. First, by accident, he says. Or second, "by swearing, grunting, and tearing the house apart. Although far more time-consuming, the second method is much more satisfying. Searching long and hard for something creates a restless suspense, a tension that is wonderfully relieved when the lost item is finally found. Finding a lost object in this manner strengthens the belief that we are in control of our lives."[2]

But for all we like the idea that we live self-made lives, every day we must admit with the Psalm writer, "This is the day *the Lord* has made" (Psalm 118:24). We watch for what God is already about. We leave room for divine accidents. We open our clenched fingers to place the details into Hands larger than our own. Going to a faraway place for spiritual work means losing a small slice of our active lives. It requires relinquishing some control. Our lives, after all, are less our own than we usually think. No one can predict that today will be all that we plan it to be. Who can say with perfect confidence that tomorrow will be what we envision?

That recognition, of course, may bring discomfort. The act of giving up control of our lives, even for a span of time, unnerves us. We do not easily let go of things we habitually grasp; nor do we eagerly admit our insufficiency. Withdrawing means we must forfeit, at least for a time, a compulsive need to achieve or accomplish. That requires a certain determination. It takes practice.

Adding to the discomfort is the suspicion that withdrawing from the crush of activity leads to inefficiency. In a world of demanding children, lonely senior citizens, and people with AIDS, to sit and not *do* seems self-indulgent. Even the word "retreat" itself often carries unhappy connotations. "Retreating" seems tantamount to escaping responsibility or giving up, like a cavalry turning heel in defeated disarray. It feels a little like surrendering. And in our personal lives we are keenly aware of mortgage payments, daily commutes, and supper dishes. The mere thought of getting away for a retreat causes a reaction—a reflex tugging from our round of routine responsibilities. What will happen to our long list of to-dos?

One of the first and best ways to get ready, then, is to remember our place in the scheme of things. We resolve that we will not (because we cannot) be all things to all people. We give up on trying to be and do it all. We learn, through sheer grit or gentle grace, to let go. We practice the discipline of disengagement from the thousand and one details that compel our attention through the week in order to be free to engage something even bigger. And we are often surprised what we find when we do. And *Who* finds us, and leads us forward. "When we reach the limit of our own resources," reflected one retreatant, "the Spirit can help us at last."

Continue to Cultivate Quiet in a Noisy World

I know of a woman who insists on keeping a TV on through the night, even while she sleeps. It's not that she enjoys what she hears and sees as she drifts off, but she is widowed, she battles the effects of overeating, and being left alone with her thoughts leaves her anxious.

Most of us are at least a little intimidated by silence. A travel article once told of the road leading to the Arctic Circle through the northern Yukon, how the silence was so profound that one could hear the rustling of the hairs in the ear canals. But that is not all we "hear" in pure silence; we also hear the chattering of our busy minds, our endless plans, our submerged regrets, our agitated anxieties that make it impossible for us to rest in stillness and quiet.

It does not help that our circumstances do not encourage quiet. People who produce radio and movies and advertisements all seem eager to fill in our silences. Their distractions compete, sometimes mercilessly, for our attention. Much conspires against our pondering anything in stillness. And we don't always help the situation. "The American is an enterprising [person]," writes one journalist, "who will take elaborate precautions against the embarrassment of being left alone with his thoughts. Rather than sit and look idly at the sky he will run twelve miles in the rain; on weekends in the country he arranges as many picnics and sporting events as might be necessary to prevent him from being surprised by an uninvited silence."[3]

Silence, then, is rarely handed to us. And it seems that we are constitutionally made to talk and fill our lives with the comforts of sound. But some-

times we get restless with the words. We know we
need something more than noise. We realize that
the constant din keeps us from hearing.

And so we become willing to live another way, a
way that allows for space to think and pray. "In
quietness and confidence is our strength," the Old
Testament prophet Isaiah declared. It serves us well
to "practice" silence in daily ways before we are
confronted with days of it. We cultivate new habits
right away, in daily life, in order to appropriate the
advantages of retreat. We create at least small spaces
of quiet and reverence in our busy schedules, pre-
paring for a longer drink at the well of silent retreat.
And then we look ahead to a longer space of listening silence that allows God eventually to get
through.

Pray with Wild, Wide-Open Relinquishment

In many arenas—retreating no less than others—
we may think we should roll up our sleeves and
charge in. But there needs to be a kind of sanctified
open-endedness as we go. Wrote C. S. Lewis, "Many
things—such as loving, going to sleep, or behaving
unaffectedly—are done worst when we try hardest
to do them."[4] He might have included going on
retreat. We cultivate discipline, yes, but we do well
not to strive too much. We are better helped by a
kind of creative relaxation, an attitude that comes
from trusting that the God who leads us on pilgrimage will bring us to where we need to be. We
approach the time of retreat, in other words,

prayerfully. We open ourselves to God and let God be the prime mover. We are going on a spiritual retreat, after all, out of more than a desire to become less frazzled but also out of a desire to become more aware and alert to God. Deep within is a longing to be met, loved, guided, wherever that might lead.

The Celtic saints of earlier centuries made much of the idea of *peregrinatio*, a difficult-to-translate word that suggests an open-ended journey. It was not uncommon for medieval Irish monks to set out with no destination; they left with only the simple impulse to go and seek, guided by the Holy Spirit. Unlike the pilgrimages to shrines common to medieval lore, writes Esther de Waal, "there [was] no specific end or goal such as that of reaching a . . . holy place that allows the pilgrim at the end of the journey to return home with a sense of a mission accomplished." Rather, the idea was to learn to live as travelers, pilgrims, "guests of the world," as sixth-century Irishman Saint Columbanus put it.[5] There was to be a creative openness, even if that meant living in a kind of exile so as not to hold too tightly to one's ambitions and spiritual itinerary. The idea was to leave behind the known and safe to find a truer basis for security. This was a largely inner journey.

We may begin full of certainty about what we need or what God needs to do for us, only to be surprised. We may come with tasks to tick off a list, only to discover a deeper, truer reason for coming. We may expect to conquer a fear, only to learn that we instead need to confess a hatred. We may find our carefully laid agendas blown away by the wind of God's Spirit, moving us in directions we could not have foreseen.

To spend time away acknowledges that another source lies at the root of who we are and where our lives lead. We open our lives to a God we may have been trying to keep at a comfortable distance. We turn to a God bigger than our plans. And we remember that this God has been at work in the world long before we came and will be long after. "You did not choose me," Jesus told his followers, "but I chose you and appointed you to go and bear fruit—fruit that will last" (John 15:16). If our job is not to work as though all hinges on us, but to join with what that great God is already doing, a retreat should have more the feel of an adventure than a strictly scheduled tour. We look for what God is doing, where he is leading, and then we follow. Such an outlook is, in general, a sane perspective for living; it is essential for going on retreat.

The Christian writer and scholar C. S. Lewis once spoke of our growth in spiritual depth and holiness as a construction project, one with twists we might not anticipate at the outset. He wrote,

> Imagine yourself as a living house. God comes in to rebuild that house. At first, perhaps, you can understand what he is doing. He is getting the drains right and stopping the leaks in the roof and so on: you knew that those jobs needed doing and so you are not surprised. But presently he starts knocking the house about in a way that hurts abominably and does not seem to make sense. What on earth is he up to? The explana-

tion is that he is building quite a different house than you thought of—throwing out a new wing here, putting on an extra floor there, running up towers, making courtyards. You thought you were going to be made into a decent little cottage: but he is building a palace. He intends to come and live in it himself.[6]

In the space that we find for our retreat, God will, God willing, come there, too, and live in that time and place. And make himself known. And make known to us things we would never otherwise have heard.

꒦

When It's Time to Go

It is one thing to acknowledge the appeal of a retreat; quite another to actually pull out of the driveway. Whatever our enjoyment of reading about going on retreat, whatever our careful preparations of
mind, body, and soul, there comes a time for deciding—and going. And that, many people find, requires yet more steps.

For one thing, getting away requires a certain
determination. While sometimes we will feel we can
hardly wait, hesitations may haunt us. As in many
areas of life, we feel a push-pull, a mix of "I want
to" and "I'm not sure." I think of a friend who
volunteered to chaperone her sixth-grade daughter's class trip to Cumberland Caverns. Joyce had
always had a fear of caves but she thought, *How bad
could one overnight trip be?* The prospect of time with her
daughter clinched it.

Once there, once actually in the cavern, her role
was to bring up the rear of the eighty-five twelve-
year-olds. As the trail narrowed, they had to walk
single file on a dark path. Then the walkway nar-

rowed even more—to a less-than-two-foot-tall tunnel wide enough for Joyce barely to squeeze through. "I saw it would be like pushing myself through a tube," she recalled. The prospect sparked in her a panic attack: a racing heart, a wave of nausea, and a sudden feeling of *This is more than I can stand.*

Another chaperone came to her rescue. "I've been through this tube before," he said. "At the other end the tunnel opens into a spacious room."

And that allowed Joyce to get in, arms and head first, and begin to wriggle and squeeze through. She kept at it. "Soon I felt the lip of the tube's other end. Someone grabbed my wrists and pulled me out, the same way you pull a facial tissue out of a box."

And finally, there she was—in the big room. "I had this wonderful sense of space. The air felt cooler. I could breathe. I had come through."

Make a Decision

It may seem obvious, but with the difficulties of getting away being what they are, the first step in going is to *resolve* to go. Not to decide, as the saying goes, is to decide, especially when daily duties accumulate and cry out for attention.

Deciding to go means confronting our tendency to think we cannot. "Finding time for retreat," writes Emilie Griffin, "is as difficult as finding time for prayer in an ordinary, overscheduled day. Whether the time be days or minutes, the issues are the same. Is retreat one of our priorities? Does God have a place in our scheme?"[1] That subtle stubbornness will not necessarily vanish once our reservation is made. We prepare to stay determined.

You may even need resolve for the time you actually go. One man, Philip Zaleski, found himself anxious. "This would be my first overnight stay in a monastery, and I had no idea what to expect. What if I didn't fit in? What if the monks turned out to be creepy? What if my wife needed me at home? . . . By the time the great day had arrived, I was a nervous wreck. Driving up to the monastery gates, my stomach flip-flopped and a jackhammer pounded in my skull. I grabbed my bags, walked halfway up the flagstone path to the front door, then turned around and retreated to my car. There I was seized with disgust at my cowardice and turned back again. Halfway up, and again I reversed. I must have spun around five or six times; any monks watching from within might have thought me an eccentric Sufi, practicing his whirls in the Massachusetts snow. Finally, I steeled myself and knocked."[2]

When carrying through on our inclination to go, it may help to recall why we are going in the first place. One woman, finally able to break away from her routine for a vacation by the ocean, realized, "My life [back home] in Connecticut lacks this quality of significance . . . because there is so little empty space. The space is scribbled on; the time has been filled. There are so few empty pages in my engagement pad. . . . Too many activities, and people, and things. Too many worthy activities, valuable things, and interesting people. For it is not merely the trivial which clutters our lives but the important as well."[3] Her life had grown full—with mostly good things, as it turns out—but nevertheless over-loaded. So, like her, we tell ourselves again that only by creating space and intentional quiet will events and objects and people and projects gain their proper place. Only by adding margins of space will we become all we should be.

Or we may remind ourselves of the spiritual barrenness of our lives as we know them. We look hard at the emptiness of a life full of things and projects but desolate in soul matters. We give rein to our famished hunger for spiritual substance and sustenance. One woman, working a high-pressure job with long hours and frequent travel, realized, as she said, "I felt far away from the spirit of silence and prayerful discipline." More than anything, she realized, she longed for "a chance to grow closer to God." So she decided to spend a day in prayer at a retreat house in Long Island, New York. "It wasn't a planned retreat being offered by some well-known retreat leader," she wrote. "Instead, it was my own day of disciplined prayer." She began the day by attending a morning prayer service at a church. She heard a passage of the Bible she resolved to reflect on during the day stretching ahead. "As I drove out of New York City," she wrote, "onto the Long Island Expressway, I felt a sense of high excitement and release. I was doing something very freeing. I was giving the Lord a whole day of myself. I was giving myself a whole day of the Lord."[4] That beckoning sense of God's fiery, wonderful, life-giving presence will keep us on the path to go, on the road that finally leads to spiritual renewal.

Finally, we decide by realizing again our responsibility for our own spiritual nurture. Salvation is a gift, but it is also something we say yes to. And while our relationship with God flows from God's grace, his initiative, his saving love, neither do we sit passively by. We certainly do not leave our growth in the things of God to others. "So don't sit around on your hands!" writes the New Testament writer of Hebrews (in Eugene Peterson's rendering). "No more dragging your feet! Clear the path for long-distance runners so no one will trip and fall, so no one will step in a hole and sprain an ankle. . . . And run for it!"[5] We say, "I will do it." And all the while we invoke God's help. We pray that God clear the path ahead, free us from the duties that seem to make the way impossible, and then we move forward with expectancy.

Gather Information

While the spiritual dynamics are important, a bit part of deciding to go also entails some purely practical issues.

There is, for example, the question of where to go. A retreat requires nothing more elaborate than a quiet place. It can happen even in your own home, provided you are able to turn on the answering machine, avoid the temptations to fold laundry, and create within it the solitude and silence necessary for undistracted prayer. Or a remote cabin in the woods (or a tent you pitch in the wilderness) can likewise provide an appropriately rugged setting. However, there is something to be said for a guest house or retreat center in the literal sense. As the directory that follows shows, retreat centers stretch across the continental North American landscape in astonishing abundance. They offer cabins, hermitages, or dorm-style rooms. And many of these quiet places have an indefinable sense of the holy pervading them.

The matter of place has spiritual implications. Abraham, after all, built an altar in the place where God appeared to him, a place to which he returned. Jacob marked the place where God had appeared to him in a vision of a heavenly ladder, erecting a stone that he anointed with oil. And many of us can recall a certain place that holds a significance that goes beyond the mere assemblage of rock or brick or pine grove. My friend John Franklin led a retreat at a run-down YMCA camp in New Zealand. It was an isolated place, an isthmus of not much more than pine trees and sand dunes. To the north and to the south was the Pacific Ocean in its ever changing colors, but the buildings were run-down. The bunk rooms had felt-tipped obscenities and other adolescent position statements written all over the walls. The bathrooms and the kitchen were basic. But the place was holy. The retreat had a wonderful sense of "shoes-off, walking-in-the-sand simplicity. It was as though Jesus was there with us," John recalls. "With Jesus we cooked fish on the beach. We broke bread. We left footprints in the sand. We marveled at his closeness in this unpretentious place while our unpretentious hearts burned within us as we spoke of what he was doing in and among us." So the matter of where we go carries some significance. A Sunday afternoon spent swinging in our backyard porch hammock may seem restful, but it is not the same as finding a place that communicates holiness by its very purpose.

With so many options, you might want to simplify matters and begin with a place within easy driving distance. Especially if this is your first foray, the familiarity and ease of choosing something local may make the going that much simpler. And should you decide to return, you will have established a relationship with an accessible center, becoming familiar with its offerings, staff, and grounds.

On the other hand, you may opt for a change of scenery—literally. The flatlands of Kansas may make the craggy wilderness of Colorado mountains look inviting indeed. Or your town's urban sprawl makes you eager to breathe in the scents of meadowland and forest. Or you think that nothing less than stark desert will allow you an uncluttered experience of God. (Some will remember that in Mark's Gospel the Spirit "drove" Jesus into the desert [Mark 1:12, NRSV].) In this matter of terrain, the sheer variety of retreat settings provide you with many options. While the purpose of going is not sightseeing, pleasant surroundings come as a bonus. Travel expenses typically mount as distance increases, but all the same, a retreat is bound to cost less than a similar junket for sightseeing purposes.

Perhaps even more important than the physical landscape is the spiritual climate of your destination. There are spiritual "personality types" in most of the retreat centers; many are Catholic, for instance, as Catholic orders (and the influence of an early monk named Benedict) have created a long tradition of providing hospitality for guests seeking guidance. Some centers are heavily flavored by aspects of Christianity unique to Catholicism, while others intentionally offer a more ecumenical tone. Some retreat centers are tied to Protestant denominations, others to parachurch organizations. The Quakers' Yokefellow Institute in Ohio has a different flavor than does the Southern Baptist Conference Center in Colorado. You may also find that some Christian centers offer classes or retreats in spiritual practices (such as Yoga) that make the eyebrows of conservative believers raise. You need not feel you agree with everything that each retreat center offers, but you may find it helpful to avoid a place, at least at the beginning, where a theology or practice seems so foreign as to annoy or distract.

Then there is the question of when to go. Not only must you consider your own calendar, but that of the schedules of the place to which you want to go. Some retreat centers are booked months in advance, requiring a substantial wait from the time you first place a call to inquire. Beyond that, centers will sometimes dictate other time restrictions. The Trappist Abbey of Gethsemani in Kentucky, for example, reserves the first and third full weeks of each month for women, the remainder of each month for men. Retreats there generally run either from Friday to Sunday or Monday through Friday, with shorter stays possible.

How long to stay? While one day apart may seem like a good beginning (and certainly better than nothing), many retreat guides suggest that only a retreat of at least two or three days allows the retreatant to truly engage the quiet and healing rest. A few offer only daylong retreats while others suggest minimum stays, such as Nada Hermitage in Colorado, requesting at least a week's residence. "Not a whole lot happens on that first day," says Father Matthias Neuman, OSB, of Saint Meinrad Archabbey in Indiana. "The person tends to spend time getting caught up on sleep, establishing a separation from the stresses of work, getting hostility out of the system. It's on the second or third day that issues begin to emerge." On the other hand, you may find value in scheduling a first retreat in such a way that you get a taste but don't feel obligated to order the full course. One clergyman I know periodically schedules himself for a weeklong retreat, only to return after a few days when the silence begins weighing too heavily. Others find that the time goes by all too quickly. And the need for solitude may be different for a single person than for a working father with a houseful of rambunctious children. All of these unique circumstances provide matters for prayerful experimentation.

What to pay also presents practical questions, especially for those on a modest budget. Most of the retreat centers listed in this book are nonprofit charitable organizations. As such they tend to suggest donations for guests' stays, typically in the range of thirty-five to fifty dollars ·for a twenty-four-hour period (including meals). Most will offer hospitality for guests with tighter purse strings unable to pay the recommended amount. And most would welcome a donation beyond the minimum, as well. Others charge a flat rate, still almost always considerably cheaper than typical stays at hotels with restaurant meal bills.

You may also want information about special circumstances. The vast majority of retreat centers receive both men and women, for example. But a handful do not. Some offer accommodations for married couples; others only for guests who come alone. Special dietary needs can often be accommodated in many retreat centers, even those with cafeteria-style eating, but not without prior contact. Those who are physically limited will want to ask about handicap access (noted in the directory where information is available).

Finally, other questions have to do with how you spend your time once there. Will the grounds allow you room to roam on quiet walks? Is worship an integral part of the retreat community's daily and weekly rhythms? What kind of "preached retreats" (where formal content is provided) are offered? And will there be someone on hand who can provide spiritual counsel, or even guide you through a series of personal meditations, a kind of holy homework that has you exploring a spiritual classic or pondering verses of the Bible? Upon request, many retreat centers offer personalized spiritual counsel for the time you are there (sometimes known as a directed retreat), usually for a modest suggested donation, while others, concerned to preserve the quiet focus of the center's community life, provide minimal counsel.

Make the Call

Once you have sorted through the possibilities of where to go, calling or writing form the next step. The retreat centers listed here encourage inquiries. You can also request a brochure or explore a Web site (roughly a third of the centers listed in this book have Internet access). You may even want to schedule an exploratory visit to get a feel for the place. While the purpose of a spiritual retreat may seem lofty, that does not negate the need for common sense and practical questions. Have ready a list of unanswered questions. And, if you are ready actually to go, have a calendar in hand! Nothing beats setting a date for getting you out the door and on the road.

❧

Packing and Other Fine
(but Crucial) Points

Some years ago my wife and family and I made plans to spend Thanksgiving with my wife's parents, who lived five hours away in Illinois. I had said to Jill earlier in the days before departure that I might take along some of my notes for the college centennial history book I was writing. It was to be a family holiday, but I thought I might find an odd moment here or there to slip away to a back room and go over my research. Jill wasn't excited, but said nothing.

Then, just before we left, Jill saw my laptop computer and gathered books and papers, ready to be packed into our Honda. "Are you taking your work along with you?" she asked with a slight edge in her voice. I stammered something about our earlier conversation. "Let me rephrase that," she said. "You're not taking your work along with you, are you?" I protested that I could get up in the wee hours, before the boys or Jill's parents were awake, and get in a couple of hours of work. Jill said nothing, her silence communicating loudly.

Finally I said, "Okay, I won't bring it along. I'll leave my work here."

And I found myself suddenly flooded with relief. I was amazed, expecting an internal struggle about leaving behind my work. Instead I suddenly felt like there was stretching before me great space and wonderful freedom. I looked forward to playing games with the boys, having time to sleep late, read a novel, visit with relatives without the pressure of a book needing writing. As it unfolded, things happened during that three-day holiday that would not have happened had I cluttered it with looming tasks and tempting work.

A trip carries with it an array of decisions about what to take, a retreat no less than any. It is not like packing for a sightseeing jaunt, where grabbing a map and sorting through changes of clothes suffice. Fortunately, arrangements today come simpler than those laid on pilgrims in medieval times, when travelers to shrines or the Holy Land had to obtain permission from a priest, clear up debts, make full confession, and draw up a will. Still, certain preparations will help. Decisions made while getting ready can have impact on what happens once you arrive.

Begin with an Unhurried Spirit

It may seem obvious, but what we most need to take along with us is a quiet heart, an open mind. The stress of packing, settling the dog at the kennel, saying good-bye to the kids may make us forget that the point is to move into an uncluttered, undis-tracted, *simpler* mode of existence. To get ready for such an experience, we do well not to rush around at the last minute before leaving. Instead, we allow time and space for the details that any leave-taking requires. The idea is not to squeeze every second out of a retreat, rushing off so we can have all the time possible once we arrive, but rather to permeate our activities with an unhurried eagerness. We can savor even the getting ready. We see it as a kind of ready-ing of the soul that parallels the physical prepara-tions.

And we remember that the most important thing to bring is ourselves. No matter if we feel frazzled and far from spiritually "together." We go on retreat knowing that wherever we are *right now* can become a starting place. While we trust we will be made deeper, quieter, more relaxed, we need not feel we must achieve it all in order to go. What we want to become need not keep us from setting out as we are.

An essential of preparation, then, will be prayer-ful dependence on God. We begin, well before we bump out the door of our home, packed bags in hand, to ask God for his favor. We seek guidance even in the where and when and how we go. And we let God know once our decision is set that we are willing to be led, even through our anxieties.

Some find it helpful to begin biting off small bits of quiet, too, as a kind of conditioning for a retreat's longer stretches. Catherine de Hueck Doherty wrote of the Eastern Orthodox idea of *Poustinia*, desert soli-tude, as a discipline for daily life. Even before we make our departure for a retreat, she wrote, we pay attention to the "little departures," the small oases of quiet, that fill our ordinary days. "These 'little solitudes' are often right behind a door which we can open, or in a little corner where we can stop to look at a tree that somehow survived the snow and dust of a city street. There is the solitude of a car in which we return from work, riding bumper to bumper on a crowded highway. This too can be a 'point of departure' to a desert, silence, solitude."[1] Such little experiences can tone us up to the longer stretches of quiet and aloneness.

And we go remembering the priority of grace. Retreat is not about our heroic accomplishments, about spiritual notches of self-satisfaction to add to our belt. It grows rather out of trust in God. It is Christ's mercy, not our imagined righteousness, that best serves us. "I need thee every hour," as the old hymn has it, makes an appropriate refrain for one about to go. Only a sense of grace will help us settle more deeply into a relaxed, expectant frame of mind for leaving.

Travel Light

The most frequent temptation is to take too much.

I don't mean clothes and toiletries, though there is every reason to keep these to an uncluttered minimum. Certainly the normal common sense applies here: Anticipate a cooler (or warmer) climate if you are traveling any distance. Confirm that the retreat center will provide bed linens (most do but some don't). And plan to dress casually and comfortably (though, given the cloistered nature of some centers, one should also think modestly). In light of the pilgrim nature of such a trip (to say nothing of the preponderance of hiking paths at most centers), walking shoes make more sense than dress shoes. You need not feel like you are decking out for church or a funeral.

But to speak of traveling lightly has an even more significant context. We may think we need things that will keep us occupied. A weekend without television may, on the one hand, seem like a blessed relief; it may also provoke anxiety.

As innocuous as taking them along may seem, a radio or CD player or TV only places in our path the temptation to avoid being alone with our thoughts. Beepers and cell phones and laptop computers may feed our sense of indispensability, and even make a certain pragmatic sense, but ultimately they will create distractions that hinder the inner work needing to be done.

Especially seductive may be books. How tempting to pile up a stack, thinking here will be the perfect time to catch up on reading! But most books will only interfere and shield us from solitude and quiet encounter. "Books have voices," writes Philip Zaleski, "as surely as do people: When we ask what books to bring, in effect we ask which voices will break the silence of our weekend."[2]

Of course, a critical exception to my cautioning about books comes in the form of the Bible. Nothing can better inform and shape our silence. Christianity is a revealed faith; not an unguided wandering after nebulous truth. As religions of the Book,

Christianity and Judaism affirm the Bible as divinely inspired communication from God. Few prayers better guide praying than biblical standbys like the Bible's Psalms or the Lord's Prayer (found in Matthew 7). And the Gospels abound with inspiring stories about One who performed miracles and proclaimed that his appearing ushered in the dawning rule of God. The biblical accounts of Jesus' crucifixion and resurrection have created for countless believers nothing less than entry into eternal life. The Bible, far from distracting our retreat from the world's cares, will often make it possible. "The Bible is alive, it speaks to me," church reformer Martin Luther said. "It has feet, it runs after me; it has hands, it lays hold of me." No dull fare here, not when we can meet personally the God unveiled in its pages.

Prayer books, such as historical anthologies or Catholic missals or the Episcopal *Book of Common Prayer,* also can help our praying strike rich veins of life and power. We limit ourselves if we think prayer must always be a spontaneous affair. Sometimes our words need to fall into rhythm with the great prayers and pray-ers of the centuries. Sometimes the seeming woodenness of a printed prayer can limber up our soul and send our praying in directions we might otherwise never take. And if such prayer happens in the context of a wooded glade or a monastery church or quiet chapel, new worlds can open up.

The caution about books also deserves one more qualifier. Some will find value in some of the great spiritual writings of the church. Julian's *Showings,* Oswald Chambers's *My Utmost for His Highest*, Thomas Merton's *The Seven-Storey Mountain*, or Thomas à Kempis's *The Imitation of Christ* have a depth not common to much of what currently passes for devotional literature. They may feed your time apart.

That very quality of depth requires a certain approach to the reading we do on retreat, whatever book we might have: We practice what the ancients called *lectio divina*, usually translated as "spiritual reading." This practice means taking a text of Scripture or other writing (usually a short passage) and reading gently, reverently. Paramount is not hurrying through. The idea is to practice what my friend Tom Mockabee calls creative brooding. With *lectio divina* we are not after information as much as transformation. We patiently absorb, not scan. We worry less about getting through a long chunk of text and more about listening to the quiet truth that may be locked in one page, a solitary sentence, even a single word. Traditionally, *lectio divina* can be summarized in four basic movements:

- Read. This means selecting a text of reasonable length, such as a story, or a chapter, or a paragraph. This is not like reading for entertainment as much as for soul-searching. So it takes a meditative, unhurried approach. And we read looking for a word or phrase that especially seems to speak to us, that seems perhaps to be God's very own word for us.
- Reflect. We take the word or phrase that leapt out of our reading and spend time with it, ruminating, allowing its insight to search us or claim

us. We are like Mary, the mother of Jesus, who when the shepherds appeared to her with news of what the angels said about Jesus' birth, "pondered them in her heart."

☙ Respond. Here we take what we have heard and reflected on and turn it into loving, prayerful conversation with God. We pray about what we think God has been saying. We lift up both our pain and our joy. We present ourselves, ready to be touched and changed by God's presence.

☙ Rest. Gently, without hurrying, we allow our prayer to lead us into rest in One who has been with us through the process. We may even leave words˙ behind, content to simply *be* in God's presence. We receive whatever gifts of faith or joy or love God may want to bestow.

Bathe Your Travel in Prayer

No need to wait for arrival to begin praying. The spiritual work proceeds even as you travel to your destination. Allow the journeying to symbolize your pilgrimage to a time and place set apart for God. Let the moments in the plane or on the road become quiet invitations: opportunities to set fears to rest, to commit to God the projects and persons you leave behind, and most of all to wait expectantly for the good things God waits to reveal.

❧

What Do I _Do_ There?

Once I attended an evening banquet of a local arts
group with my then eighteen-year-old son. Abram
had returned that summer afternoon from a five-
day retreat at the Abbey of Gethsemani in Kentucky. As we ate, conversation at our table shifted
naturally to him. He told us where he had been and
how much he had enjoyed the leisurely hikes in the
woods, the quiet reverence of the abbey church, the
spiritual refreshment he felt from his time away.
There was a brief lull in the conversation.

I will never forget what happened next. A mid-
dle-aged woman stared at Abram in virtual disbelief
and blurted, "Why in the world would a healthy
teenage boy want to spend a week at a monastery?"
She could picture only a dreary, life-dampening reg-
imen. Surely it would stunt a young man's development. Our table soon became host to lively discussion of what longings lie behind much of our
culture's revival of interest in things spiritual—and
why so many people are rediscovering the joys of

retreat. Abram, with a twinkle in his eye, rose to the occasion.

A picture of ways a retreat can help us has been emerging in the previous chapters—it lets us get in touch with what's important, make room for God, listen for his voice in Scripture, replenish our tired spirits. But once you have arrived, how do you order your hours and days? Unless you are going on an organized retreat (and even if you are) questions about how to use the time, and how *best* to use it immediately arise. What do silence and solitude look like fleshed out? How can you meet God in the stillness?

You will already answer such questions in part in a very practical way: through your choice of where to go. A few days in an isolated hermitage will give a different flavor than will a stay at a bustling retreat center filled with motion and commotion. Staying at a monastery guest house where the Liturgy of the Hours (formal prayers offered periodically throughout the day and night, as often as seven times daily) will feel different than a Quaker service where liturgical prayer may be unknown. Some of the retreat centers listed in this book have a decidedly Eastern Orthodox flavor, others offer charismatic fervor, many a gentle interdenominational diversity. And certainly a retreat offered for a group and characterized by formal presentations and small group discussions will have fewer silent spaces than a quiet day with no agenda. To some degree you roll with the tide in which you find yourself. You imbibe the ambience of where you land. Some of your decisions about what the time will look like are made by the time you turn off the highway to enter the grounds.

In another sense, however, you don't sit passively by. So many options allow you creative choice. You should think through prayerfully and practically what a retreat can be (or needs to be) given your situation. To name some possibilities, consider:

❧ A prayer retreat—with no agenda but to rest in the presence of God or intercede in prayer for others. Usually this is done on what is called a private retreat, and such retreats may benefit from the guidance of a spiritual director at a retreat house. The prayers of a retreat house that offers community prayers will help shape your own praying, keeping it from becoming off kilter or bogged down in personal eccentricity. We don't pray only by feelings but also with guidance by the truth of revealed Scripture and the wise counsel of others more experienced than we are. A rhythm of private prayer while we wander the woods and corporate prayer and conversation with a spiritual guide may fit the bill.

On the other hand, perhaps you should launch out alone into the presence of God. That you don't feel like an expert at prayer need not stop you. We learn to pray by praying, and there may indeed be value in trying to pray for the day with the barest of plans. You may feel at times that you flounder in your praying, but in the trying and failing, the reaching out and discovering God reaching down, you learn much—and encounter what you still must learn.

Whether you put the accent on praying alone or with others, the sheer delight (and sometimes healthy terror) of conversing with the loving, awesome God can easily fill up the days.

꙳ A vocational discernment retreat—focused on gaining clarity about calling, job options, or general life direction. You seek guidance through prayer. Perhaps you take blank pads and write impressions, pros and cons about the options ahead. You rummage through the Bible with an ear to hear how God might guide you through it. You reflect on your gifts. Perhaps you consult a resource on vocational discernment. You meander through open spaces on the grounds or kneel in a chapel and lay your feelings out before God.

Philip Zaleski told of this kind of retreat: "A major decision loomed, one whose consequences would shake every pillar of my life. I fretted over my possibilities, I fiddled and fussed. Try as I might, I couldn't make a final choice. . . . To break the stalemate, I went on retreat. I borrowed a friend's cabin up in the New Hampshire woods, a rustic affair at the end of an unmarked dirt road, with night crawlers in the basement and bats in the attic. The nearest neighbors ran a small dairy farm a half mile to the south. . . . For five days I was cut off, cut loose, I was *away*. . . . I had little in the way of theology or metaphysics to guide me; I only knew that I needed a helpmeet infinitely more wise and ancient than myself. How to act? Where to turn? I did the only thing I could do: I fell to my knees and prayed. . . . [S]lowly the fog of my confusion began to lift. In time an answer came."[1]

A friend of mine faced a key job decision, and found a retreat a way to test his desires. "Should I stay in Toledo and take up the pastor-ate in which I was serving as interim?" John asked. "Or go to Gisborne, back to New Zealand, my home country? Toledo had been home for five years already. And while I was a New Zea-lander, I had never lived in Gisborne; it might as well have been Timbuktu. I was scared stiff. This was my life I was deciding about, and both places were light-years apart. Either way seemed to open up wonderful possibilities and great uncer-tainty. What was I called to do?

"I went to Gethsemani Abbey in Kentucky to make a retreat. Surely, God would tell me there! As I entered the guest house I was struck by the words chiseled in the lintel over an en-trance: 'God Alone.' The words stayed with me as I prayed. I put two photographs of the two churches on the desk in my room to help focus my praying. Somehow though, my attraction was drawn to God. Then, walking in the monas-tery garden, I came across a statue of Jesus in the Garden of Gethsemane. I realized that my issue didn't have the same 'sweat value' as Jesus' at all! When all was said and done, it seemed that the call was to draw closer to God. God seemed to be saying about my great, life-shaping decision, 'Choose me, then choose what you will. Do what seems best to you.' And I understood that the question was not, shall I go to Toledo or Gisborne, but do I desire God for God's own sake? The decision I eventually made was a hard one, but it was blessed with a great fruitfulness. I believe that God did guide me, and allowed me in the process to stop obsessing about particulars."

❧ A special-need retreat—for when you need inner healing, direction about personal trials, or light shed on a troubling relationship. Here also we may go with the goal of listening for guidance about a particular area. Perhaps it is to do the hard work of forgiving someone who has wronged or hurt us. Perhaps healing for some grief or hurt seems to need a longer frame and quieter space than provided by ordinary circumstances. "Some of life's experiences seem to fall beyond understanding," notes material from Retreats International. "Death and suffering, loss of friendship, hurt and pain all take their toll on our resources of faith. Jesus was no stranger to such as these. Edge of life experience drove Him to the desert, to the garden, to His friends, just as they do us! Memories that hurt need healing. Memories of joy need to be shared and celebrated." When it comes to healing memories or celebrating a milestone (such as turning fifty, for example) a retreat can be a wonderful way consciously to bring God into the picture. When dealing with particularly painful issues, a trusted counselor or spiritual director may provide indispensable guidance.

❧ A working retreat. Here the focus is a specific task that needs the prayerful setting of a retreat center or quiet place. Writing music, creating paintings, editing a book, setting down experiences in a journal all lend themselves to the kind of atmosphere a retreat setting provides. The idea is to invite God to sanctify the work, to allow divine impulses to enrich and expand creativity. Even rolling up your sleeves for physical labor might provide needed soul respite. Many monastic guest houses allow or invite guests to help with physical chores at designated times of day in the Benedictine tradition of establishing a rhythm of prayer and work. While generally we do well to leave our work behind when retreating, work and prayer sometimes belong together.

❧ A retreat spent with classical spiritual-life writings. Books abound that help the reader dive into a particular writer's insights. Several titles begin with the phrase, "A Retreat with . . ." and then name some spiritual authority whose writings are explored and often excerpted. Alternatively, you may simply adopt a writer or teacher and devote the retreat to learning about that person's life and key insights. You take books, depend on a retreat house's library (many centers stock them), and perhaps confer with a retreat director about your adopted spiritual mentor. Augustine's *Confessions,* for example, or Julian of Norwich's *Showings,* Thomas Merton's

New Seeds of Contemplation, or Oswald Chambers's *My Utmost for His Highest* all have a meatiness that could well support a retreat.

☞ A group retreat. This may be the most accessible place for many to begin. Many retreat houses hold these regularly and many combine lecture presentations (on the spirituality of Thomas Merton or contemplative prayer, to give two examples) with time for personal reflection. Some also employ a workshop format that allows informal interaction with others.

☞ A holy vacation—where travel is given a specifically spiritual accent. Your model is not that of a recreational sightseeing junket, but a pilgrimage. One could vacation in the Holy Land, for example, visiting reverentially the holy sites of the great figures of the Bible and Western religious tradition. Or one might tour the cathedrals of Europe. Or spend a week going through the glories of the Vatican. Or combine a visit to the glories of Yellowstone National Park with a retreat stay at Thomas the Apostle Center, an Episcopal retreat house in Wyoming that perches near the eastern gate of the great park.

☞ A retreat spent with a spouse or friend. Sometimes the anxious unknowns of going on a trip can be tamed by bringing along a friend. You can still guard times for prayerful silence and solitude, still seek God's presence in some quiet. But you will also be sharing the experience with someone else. You will have someone to debrief with once you have returned to the scenes of ordinary life.

Retreat Is a Many-Splendored Thing

Beyond those varied formats, you may want to think
in terms of these kinds of traditional retreats:

Preached or conference-style retreat: Those who have gone
to church-related camps as young people will
already know the flavor of a preached, or
taught, retreat. Here the weekend or day centers around content given by a leader or team. A
theme almost always dominates: prayer, the Bible, the life of Jesus, women's or men's spirituality, spiritual resources for twelve-step recovery.
A presenter alternates spoken material with periods of reflection or of optional personal sharing. It typically allows for discussion and reflection with a group. These often are held over
weekends, but some will last for a week or
more. Many of the retreat centers depicted here
offer this kind of format in addition to private
retreats.

Married or engaged couples' retreats: The format is similar
to the preached or guided retreat, but the experience allows the couple to reflect on their married life, see models of communication, learn
how prayer can enrich the family. Often couples have opportunities to talk about their relationship and process communication issues in a
spiritual context. Similar weekends are sometimes offered for engaged couples.

Guided retreats: In this form, smaller groups (five to
ten or more persons) gather for a daily conference with a monk or spiritual director or

teacher, and then are on their own the remainder of the day. Usually they can also meet privately with the leader for individual direction. Opportunity for spiritual direction (one-on-one guidance with a retreat guide) often accompanies this type of retreat.

Directed retreats: For those seeking a more extended retreat experience there is the option of a retreat period as long as thirty days. The retreatant meets daily with a director who facilitates the experience of prayer and personal growth. Modern-day spiritual direction, as such guidance is often called, emphasizes a climate of listening and a commitment to helping the retreatant discover how God can be discerned amid events of daily life.

The Shape of Your Days

Generalizations have limited value, but here, in broad strokes, is a map for ordering your time:

First day: Upon arrival, settle in. Catch up on rest, if needed. Begin praying. Don't expect much to "happen." If you are meeting with a spiritual director for a directed retreat, you will likely have your first meeting now, or perhaps beginning tomorrow. If prayer or chapel services are offered, they provide a good way to leave behind the work world and engage with the new setting. If anger or stress seems to bubble to the surface, don't be concerned; you are still in a time of transition. Unfinished hostilities from the week past and anxieties for the time ahead need time to expend themselves. Feel free to allow yourself time simply to adjust.

Second day: Begin your prayer (or *lectio divina* or vocational discernment or quiet listening) in greater earnest. Be sure to still allow time for walks in the woods, if possible, or spending time praying in your room or a chapel. Dive into any prayer homework assigned by the retreat director. If on your own, try not to turn your day into an agenda to be gotten through as much as an opportunity for open spaces and gentle growth. Feel free to nap, remembering that God restores the soul spiritually in concert with the body's physical rest. If you have a goal for this retreat, such as clarity for a decision, allow yourself to begin to consider it.

Third day (and following, if applicable): Listen for God more intently about issues that may be troubling you or pointing you in new directions. Allow space for God to speak, but feel free to more actively approach disciplines such as intercessory prayer, fasting, or Bible reading. Allow yourself the soul luxury of simply delighting in God's presence.

Final day: Allow yourself the same gentle pace in leaving that you tried to cultivate in coming. Be sure to thank God for any insights you gained. Begin thinking prayerfully about your "reentry" into your daily arenas of work and home.

Retreat Centers:

A DIRECTORY

Directory of Retreat Centers and Guest Houses

A Few Observations

Where to go? What can I expect? Will I find handicapped access? Can I come with my spouse? What will the spiritual climate be like? These are a few of the questions I answer in what follows. These listings, numbering more than two hundred and fifty and representing every American state and most Canadian provinces, will point you to the place that seems right for you.

I have included only those houses and centers that take individual retreatants, in keeping with the focus of this book. A number serve groups as well, but all welcome persons wanting a time apart in solitude and silence.

As Catholics have a long tradition of hosting guest retreatants at monasteries, Catholic centers predominate. But you will also find a wide range of denominational affiliations and theological traditions. As far as essentials, to the best of my knowledge the centers listed here can be said to be within the mainstream of traditional Christian teaching. Whatever the retreatant's spiritual orientation, these centers will offer a warm welcome to guests. Note that official Catholic teaching discourages non-Catholics from receiving the Eucharist. However, most Catholic retreat houses offer a warmly embracing stance toward non-Catholics and are glad for retreatants to participate in other aspects of their worship and daily life.

In almost all cases a prior reservation is required, so you will need to make contact in advance of your stay. Be prepared for some to be booked months in advance. A few places ask for mail-only reservations, but for most a phone call will make a good initial contact and give an opportunity to ask any unanswered questions related to your needs or preferences.

When contacted for this book, a number of directors stressed that they do not see their guest houses as cheap alternatives to motels for travelers wanting only room and board. The accent on this book has been on *spiritual* retreats. Some will verify that you are coming wanting a spiritual focus. Nevertheless, some quiet places listed here will host guests who come for any reason.

Most centers will accommodate both men and women (I have tried to note exceptions) and many can accommodate couples. Some require an advance deposit. Most that mention pets stress that they are not prepared to accommodate animals. Many maintain a smoke-free environment. Some charge nonnegotiable fees while most suggest a donation.

While the data is not exhaustive, enough facts are included to let you make at least preliminary decisions. Do not hesitate to call to ask questions or to request a brochure!

Using the Directory

Note that after address information (including E-mail addresses and Web sites where available) many entries contain symbols with the following meanings:

🧎 Spiritual direction is usually available for retreatants wanting guidance in spiritual growth or in the retreat experience. Almost always this must be arranged in advance of your arrival.

♿ The facility, to varying degrees, is handicapped accessible. Occasionally the symbol appears when the facility is only partly accessible (not all buildings, for example).

🏠 A hermitage; that is, a self-contained cabin, cottage, or detached apartment is available for retreatants wanting the utmost in privacy and solitude. These are typically spartan affairs though most have private baths. Many hermitages have kitchen facilities and do not require attendance at dining room mealtimes.

The main body of each entry contains the following information:

❧ *Description.* Here I convey something of the personality of each center and highlight aspects of the location and environs. I also try to note where spiritual direction is offered. Mention is usually made when faith communities attached to the centers offer group prayer or worship experiences.

❧ *Accommodations and Reservations.* This covers specifics about the facility's lodging, meals, and reservation policies.

❧ *Points of Interest.* Features of the facility, such as a chapel with striking architecture or a gift shop, as well as interesting sites in the surrounding communities.

❧ *Location.* While most of the entries give you enough directions to find your way, it never hurts to supplement with a map or with more detailed instructions from the retreat center's brochures.

United States

East and Northeast

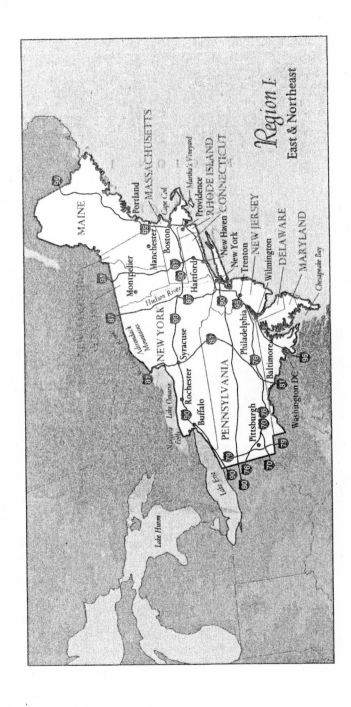

Region I:
East & Northeast

1. Mercy Center at Madison

A Center for Renewal and Human Development
167 Neck Road
P.O. Box 191
Madison, CT 06443-0191
203/245-0401
mercymad@aol.com
http://www.mercyctrmadison.com/index.html
Catholic/Sisters of Mercy

DESCRIPTION

Located on the Connecticut shore of the Long Island Sound with nearly forty acres of wooded walks,
lovely gardens, and 110 feet of private beach, this
center rests amid a setting of striking coastal beauty.

Directed retreats are adaptable to the needs and
desires of each retreatant. "As an experience of personal prayer based on Scripture," note the staff,
"this kind of retreat calls for receptivity to the
movement of the Spirit and the capacity to discuss
one's prayer with the director. Except for daily
meeting with the director, the day is spent in prayer
and quiet."

Some retreats have a special theme, such as a
Holy Week Guided Retreat, which includes guided
prayer on the themes of Jesus' death and communal
participation in the special worship services of Holy
Week. Spiritual direction is available; when registering, please indicate if direction is desired.

Also available: Thirty-day Ignatian retreat and
unscheduled directed retreats. Private retreats (no

director) may be arranged by contacting the Registrar. Directed retreats usually begin at 7 P.M. on the opening date and end at 10 A.M. on the closing date.

ACCOMMODATIONS AND RESERVATIONS
Beds for men and women in single and double rooms. Buffet-style meals.

POINTS OF INTEREST
Chapel, reading rooms, porches. The center rests along Connecticut's spectacular River Valley and Shoreline area, which includes numerous historic sites, state parks, and picturesque coastal New England scenery.

LOCATION
Not quite fifteen miles west of New Haven. From Interstate 95 North take Exit 59. Turn right off the exit, then left at the traffic light onto Route 1. Travel two miles and turn right at Neck Road. Mercy Center is about a half mile on the left.

2. My Father's House Spiritual Retreat Center
39 N. Moodus Road, Box 22
Moodus, CT 06469
203/873-1581
Fax 203/873-2357
Catholic

DESCRIPTION
Sixty-three acres of beautiful New England countryside provide the setting for this retreat and renewal center. "The spirituality," notes its founders, "centers on a personal relationship with Jesus Christ; the

formation of open, loving, sensitive, and forgiving relationships; and the enabling of everyone to realize and fulfill the personal call of God upon their lives. . . . The center's thrust is Catholic and ecumenical, charismatic and mainstream, individual and family." While its lifestyle is "simple, loving, and prayerful," with its expansive grounds it also has the feel of a resort setting.

ACCOMMODATIONS AND RESERVATIONS
An array of buildings provide varied possibilities for housing. The staff prepares and serves meals and some buildings have small kitchens.

POINTS OF INTEREST
Grounds have facilities for sport and play, picnic areas, and a large wooded hiking area. There are outdoor Stations of the Cross and a prayer area. Near Connecticut's River Valley, several lakes, and picturesque state parks.

LOCATION
From New York; Massachusetts; and Bridgeport and New Haven, Connecticut, take Connecticut Turnpike to Route 9, take Exit 7 to end of ramp. Take left on Route 154 and first right onto Route 82 across the bridge. Take first left onto 149 and follow to Moodus Center. Take left at blinker onto North Moodus Road.

3. Oratory of the Little Way

P.O. Box 221, 8 Oratory Lane
Gaylordsville, CT 06755
860/354-8294
Fax 860/354-0574
heal2@aol.com
http://www.cysol.com/oratory
Episcopal

DESCRIPTION

Nestled on four acres of land in a peaceful rural setting, the oratory is an eight-bed retreat house, with a chapel, where guests may come for an hour, a day, overnight, or longer. The oratory envisions itself as a setting for healing, "a place where the walking wounded and the spiritually dying may come for prayer, rest, and retreat." The model grows out of a spiritual house of healing in England called Crowhurst. The Oratory of the Little Way was established in 1965 by Episcopal priest Benjamin Priest and is now staffed by Nigel Mumford. The oratory welcomes people from all denominations.

Retreats are available for individuals, groups, healing ministry teams, and primary caregivers.

ACCOMMODATIONS AND RESERVATIONS

Generally if an individual desires a retreat centered on healing prayer, a spouse or a prayer partner accompanies the individual requesting prayers to learn how to pray for them as an ongoing ministry. If this is not possible, the oratory staff can make arrangements for a prayer partner to be present for the visit. Suggested donation for an overnight stay without meals is $50, $70 with three meals. Guided retreats have a negotiated fee.

Retreatants stay at the modest but comfortable country house that includes four bedrooms, a dining room, kitchen, and chapel.

POINTS OF INTEREST

Lovely grounds and country roads for walking. Weekly public healing services held at 10:00 A.M. on Tuesday mornings.

Fifty miles north of Bridgeport, not far from the New York State border. Twenty-two miles north of Danbury, seven miles north of New Milford. Take US 7 to Gaylordsville; cross the bridge and turn right immediately onto River Road. Take the first left onto South Kent Road and go a half mile to Oratory Lane on right.

4. Saint Edmund's Retreat
Enders Island
P.O. Box 399
Mystic, CT 06355
860/536-0565
Fax 860/572-7655
http://www.sse.org/enders
Catholic/Society of Saint Edmund

DESCRIPTION
Located on Enders Island in Fishers Island Sound, Saint Edmund's Retreat strives to be a place for spiritual retreat and renewal. It sits on a ruggedly beautiful twelve-acre island near the quaint seaport of Mystic, Connecticut. The monks offer private, guided, and directed retreats for laypersons, other members of religious orders, and priests. The entire complex is marked by stunning views of the Atlantic Ocean on all sides.

Central to the order's mission is proclaiming the Gospel of Jesus Christ and reminding people that the church is for them.

ACCOMMODATIONS AND RESERVATIONS
Facilities include modern, dormitory-style sleeping quarters, a separate conference center with three meeting rooms, a

full-service dining room, a handsome chapel, and a number of outdoor prayer gardens.

POINTS OF INTEREST
Saint Edmund's Retreat is home to The Saint Michael Institute of Sacred Art. The Institute hosts weeklong classes in the sacred arts of iconography, painting, sculpture, fresco, stained glass, and manuscript illumination. Instructors are world-class modern masters in these disciplines and classes are available to artists at every skill level. The Saint Michael Institute can be reached on the Web at www.artcatholic. com. The town of Mystic hosts a Marine Life Aquarium (with 3,500 types of sea life, including Beluga whales and Atlantic bottle-nosed dolphins) and a historic seaport (a re-created nineteenth-century New England whaling village with spectacular tall ships).

LOCATION
Take Interstate 95 North or South, to Exit 90. Take Route 27 South to US Route 1. Left on US Route 1 North and right at first light onto Mason's Island Road. Bear left at all forks and follow signs onto Enders Island. Mystic offers many seaport attractions.

 5. Villa Maria Retreat Center
159 Sky Meadow Drive
Stamford, CT 06903
203/322-0107
Fax 203/595-0647
Catholic/Franciscan

DESCRIPTION
A Georgian-style mansion, once owned by a Broadway producer and rented as a writing retreat by Clare Booth Luce, purchased by Bernadine Sisters in

1947, this retreat center also features eighteen acres of landscaped grounds. Dogwoods and pines abound.

There are regular liturgical prayers and Mass. While most frequently used for hosting weekend group retreats, it is also available for private directed and guided retreats and days of prayer. Spiritual direction is available by prior arrangement.

ACCOMMODATIONS AND RESERVATIONS
Ample rooms for singles and doubles for men and women. The estate garage behind the main house has been turned into a prayer house. It has a living room, kitchenette, and three bedrooms. Buffet-style meals.

POINTS OF INTEREST
Outdoor Stations of the Cross. Southern Connecticut attractions nearby, including the Stamford Museum and Nature Center and other cultural attractions of Stamford.

LOCATION
Off the Merritt Parkway (Route 15) via Exit 35. Turn left onto High Ridge Road (Route 137 North) and drive about two miles. Watch for a small sign on the right reading Villa Maria—Next Left.

6. Wisdom House

Retreat and Conference Center
229 East Litchfield Road
Litchfield, CT 06759-3002
860/567-3163
Fax 860/567-3166
info@wisdomhouse.org
http://www.litchfieldct.com/clt/wh/whindex.html
Catholic/Daughters of Wisdom

DESCRIPTION

On fifty-four acres of meadows, woods, and brooks off a quiet country road in the beautiful Northwest Hills of Connecticut, Wisdom House Retreat and Conference Center offers indoor and outdoor sanctuaries for meditation and prayer. A former center for the community of Catholic sisters, the Daughters of Wisdom, it is now an interfaith center for women and men who value seeking and learning in a contemplative environment. The *New York Times* called it "a resort for the spirit."

ACCOMMODATIONS AND RESERVATIONS

Buildings include a colonial-style brick building that houses 115 persons in semiprivate, private, or individual cubicle rooms and a roomy eighteenth-century New England farmhouse with fireplace. Wholesome meals, breads, and desserts are baked on premises by the staff chef.

POINTS OF INTEREST

Formal and informal meeting areas for individuals and groups. Marie Louise Trichet Art Gallery. Outdoor swimming pool during summer months. Outdoor labyrinth.

LOCATION

Approximately forty miles west of Hartford. From Boston (130 miles) take Route 90 West (Massachusetts Pike) to exit for Sturbridge. Route 84 West to Exit 39, Farmington. Take Route 4 West to Harwinton. Then Route 118 West, four and a half miles to Clark Road on left.

From Bridgeport (forty-five miles): Route 8 North to Exit 42. Take a left onto Route 118 West, two miles to Clark Road on left.

From Hartford (thirty miles) take Route 84 West to Exit 39, Farmington. Take Route 4 West to Harwinton. Take 118 West, four and a half miles to Clark Road on left.

From Long Island take Port Jefferson Ferry to Bridgeport. Take Route 8 North to Exit 42. Turn left onto Route 118 West, go two miles to Clark Road on left.

$\mathcal{D}$ e l a w a r e

7. Saint Francis Renewal Center
1901 Prior Road
Wilmington, DE 19809
302/798-1454
Catholic/Capuchin Franciscan Friars

DESCRIPTION
Just as centuries ago Francis of Assisi would take time out to retreat to the mountains above the city, "here, too," notes the brochure, "on the edge of the bustling city of Wilmington, Delaware, in a calm atmosphere and surrounded by nature, we would like to mirror Francis's attitude toward the need to be alone with the Sacred." The friars at the center strive to offer Franciscan simplicity and hospitality.

Liturgy is celebrated daily and retreatants may also join the friars for other hours of prayer. Private and directed retreats are available.

ACCOMMODATIONS AND RESERVATIONS
The retreat house is a refurbished century-old mansion. Home-cooked meals, taken with the friars, are provided or meals can be taken privately. Advance reservations required.

POINTS OF INTEREST
A lovely chapel. Several parks are nearby (Bellevue Park and Longwood Gardens).

Maine

 ## 8. Marie Joseph Spiritual Center
RFD #2
Biddeford, ME 04005-9561
207/284-5671
Catholic/Sisters of the Presentation of Mary

DESCRIPTION

Located on the southern coast of Maine and set above the dunes, the center, according to its vision statement, accommodates persons "seeking to encounter God in solitude and in stillness, in the beauty of nature, in the healing rhythm of the ocean, in the presence of a praying community." It is open to members of varied faith backgrounds. Daily Eucharist, morning prayer, and evening prayer allow retreatants to participate in community prayer. The staff also offers programs for retreatants on such themes as spiritual growth, forgiveness, solitude and silence, Advent spirituality, and the single life. The center also provides pastoral counseling and grief counseling.

ACCOMMODATIONS AND RESERVATIONS

Two dining rooms: one for private and silent meals and one where conversation is permitted. Weekend programs ($100 per resident; $60 for a commuter, with meals; $50 for a commuter, without meals) start at 7:00 P.M. on Friday eve-

ning and finish after lunch on Sunday. Private retreats are
$40 per day, including three meals. Directed retreats, $45
per day, including three meals.

The center requires nonrefundable registration deposits
as follows: $30 per weekend, $60 per week, $5 per person for
groups. Scholarships available.

POINTS OF INTEREST
Bookstore with books, videos, cards, and articles.

LOCATION
Take Maine Turnpike to Biddeford/Exit 4. After the toll
booth, turn left at the light onto Route 111 East. Follow 111
through four lights, staying between Sunoco Gas and
Burger King until the fifth set of lights. Turn right onto
Route 9/208 (Pool Street); continue for seven and a half
miles to Route 208. Turn left on 208 onto Bridge Road and
proceed six tenths of a mile on Bridge Road to a stop sign.
At stop sign, turn left onto Mile Stretch Road, following 208
South, bearing right at the fork. Three tenths of a mile
down, turn right at the Marie Joseph sign, staying left of the
large white building to come to the parking area.

9. Notre Dame Spiritual Center
Shaker Hill Road
P.O. Box 159
Alfred, ME 04002-0159
207/324-6160
Fax 207/324-5044
Catholic/Brothers of Christian Instruction

DESCRIPTION
A New England atmosphere abounds in the charming area that this monastery calls home. It is situated on 520 acres of woods. The twenty brothers

harvest three hundred apple trees to sell with fresh-baked goods in the fall. After harvesting and processing the sap from the numerous maples on the grounds, they host an annual Maple Syrup Sunday on the last Sunday of March. The center also has a strong historical flavor. From 1793 to 1931 the campus was home to the Society of Shakers, a millenarian communal Christian group known for its simple artwork, furniture making, and simple, celibate lifestyle. As the Shakers declined in numbers they vacated the premises and sold the property in 1931 to the Brothers of Christian Instruction, the Catholic teaching order that also runs Walsh College in Ohio. The brothers used the property as a school until 1980, when they opened the current retreat and conference center programs. Now they host up to three thousand guests annually for a host of seminars and retreats.

Private and guided retreats are offered. Mass is said every morning along with a daily Liturgy of the Hours service at 5 P.M.

ACCOMMODATIONS AND RESERVATIONS
Over thirty bedrooms, each with private lavatory and shared bath. Well-balanced meals, including vegetarian fare.

POINTS OF INTEREST
Southern Maine seacoast attractions. The grounds include miles of wooded trails, a fish pond, and a duck area. A half dozen special-purpose structures serve as repair shops, greenhouses, a store, and a maple sugar house.

From Interstate 95 take Exit 4 (Biddeford-Alfred). Turn right
on Route 111 West. Proceed about twelve miles to Highway
202; turn right (east). After the Alfred village square, continue for about one mile and watch for signs.

10. Saint Joseph Christian Life Center
93 Halifax Street
Winslow, ME 04901-6995
207/872-2370
Fax 207/873-1976
sjclc@mint.net
Catholic/Sisters of Saint Joseph

DESCRIPTION

The small town of Winslow hosts this retreat set on
twenty-eight acres bordering the Sebasticook River.
Trails through woods and along riverbanks offer opportunities for walks and reflective moments.

"We use the word 'retreat,' " notes the brochure
the center provides, "to describe a time set aside in a
place away from one's ordinary activities. It provides
the solitude to listen to the voice of God in our
hearts."

Directed, guided, and private retreats are all
available for the individual, along with thematic retreats for individuals and groups. Silence is culti-
vated at these experiences. "Series of Solitude" retreats allow individuals to participate in three
retreats, each longer than the first, to grow gradually more accustomed to silence and solitude.

Twenty-eight single rooms, two double rooms (all with sinks) have shared tub/shower facilities. Overnight fees vary depending on number of meals taken (an overnight stay with all three meals, for example, runs $35).

POINTS OF INTEREST
Small chapel, prayer room. Library. Activity room with fitness equipment. Scenic New England countryside.

LOCATION
Vermont Lines operates three buses daily to and from Boston's South Station via Portland, Waterville, and Bangor. Retreatants can be picked up at the bus station in Waterville by prior arrangement.

Maryland

 11. All Saints Episcopal Convent
P.O. Box 3127
Catonsville, MD 21228
410/747-4104
For men: Annunciation Monastery
P.O. Box 21238
Catonsville, MD 21228
410/747-6140
Episcopal/All Saints Sisters of the Poor

DESCRIPTION
Eighty-eight acres host this Episcopal center for monastic life and retreats, flanked by hiking trails and woodland of the Patapsco Valley State Park. The

complex includes a convent, monastery (part of the ministry of the convent), and a retreat center for group retreats. Prayers are offered seven times a day with attendance at Eucharist and vespers required.

The convent traces its roots to nineteenth-century London, where an Anglican church, All Saints, Margaret Street, provided the name of the order. In 1872, a group came to Baltimore to work with the city's poor, and in 1917 the order was given the Catonsville property. The sisters have carried out a number of charitable projects, including schools, a day camp for inner-city children, and care for terminally ill. Literature published by the sisters notes, "Life goes on frenetically around [the convent], yet the convent establishes a new meaning and perspective for those who visit. The sisters have answered the call to give instruction in the spiritual life and in prayer; they carry daily the great needs of the world to God in prayer. This cannot be explained—it must be experienced to be really felt."

ACCOMMODATIONS AND RESERVATIONS
Nine women in the convent in single rooms, three men in the monastery, with buffet meals at the convent dining room. Meals include homemade breads and excellent food. Freewill offering; average donation is $75 per night including three meals.

POINTS OF INTEREST
Gothic Revival stone chapel and other buildings. Woods, paths, gardens, and abundant bird life at the accessible state park grounds provide many opportunities for enjoying creation. Greeting cards are sold at the convent gift shop and by mail order.

Seven miles from Baltimore and forty miles from Washington, D.C. Take Interstate 95 to Catonsville Exit 47 to Rolling Road (Route 166). When Rolling Road intersects Hilton Avenue, take a sharp left. The convent lies at the end of Hilton Avenue.

12. Bon Secours Spiritual Center

1525 Marriottsville Road
Marriottsville, MD 21104
410/442-1320
Fax 410/442-8219
bssc@erols.com
http://www.erols.com/bssc
Catholic/Sisters of Bon Secours

DESCRIPTION

Located in south central Maryland, Bon Secours Spiritual Center sits at the highest point of 331 acres of farm and woodland. Surrounded by horse farms, the center commands spectacular views of some of Maryland's most beautiful countryside. Guests enjoy hiking trails that wind throughout the property or find a quiet spot to relax and enjoy the beauty of the landscape, including an island garden and footbridge.

Committed to the mission "to provide a Retreat and Conference Center within an atmosphere of hospitality where people can grow toward wholeness through enrichment of mind, body, and spirit," the staff is available for spiritual direction.

ACCOMMODATIONS AND RESERVATIONS

Bon Secours Spiritual Center is fully air-conditioned, with spacious and well-appointed rooms. Original oil paintings and antiques grace many of the rooms and corridors. Meals are served. Individuals and groups (including couples) are invited to come for private retreat day(s) whenever space is available.

POINTS OF INTEREST

A library is available for guests as well as an extensive bookstore with an assortment of contemporary books, tapes, CDs, cards, and other items. Guests may use the large, outdoor pool with attending lifeguards during the summer months.

LOCATION

Located between Baltimore and Washington, D.C. (twenty-five minutes from Baltimore's Inner Harbor, one hour from Capitol Hill, and two hours south of Philadelphia). Bon Secours is twenty minutes from Baltimore-Washington International Airport. A direct airport shuttle is available.

From Baltimore and points north take Beltway (Route 695 West) to Exit 16 to Route 70 West. Proceed eight miles to Marriottsville Road, turn right, continue north two miles to the center on right.

From Washington and points south take Baltimore-Washington Parkway or Route 95 North to Baltimore Beltway (Route 695), use exit marked "Towson West" and proceed as above, or take Route 29 to Route 70 West and proceed as above.

From Pittsburgh and points west take Pennsylvania Turnpike east to Route 70, proceed east to Route 40 (right fork) to Marriottsville Road. Turn left and proceed two miles to the center on right.

13. Christian Brothers Spiritual Center

2535 Buckeystown Pike
P.O. Box 29
Adamstown, MD 21710-0029
301/874-5180
Fax 301/874-3757
cbsc@fwp.net
http://www.fwp.net/cbsc
Catholic/Christian Brothers

DESCRIPTION

The center is set on a four-hundred-acre dairy farm in the Monocacy Valley, surrounded by the Catoctin mountain range, with Sugarloaf Mountain on the eastern vista and South Mountain on the western vista.

A variety of programs in spiritual growth for both youths and adults is available. Private and directed retreats are offered. A directed retreat is spent in silence. The retreat time is unscheduled except for Eucharist, meals, and a daily meeting with the retreat director. A private retreat is spent in silence, prayer, and reflection, without the assistance of a retreat director. The retreat day is unscheduled except for meals.

ACCOMMODATIONS AND RESERVATIONS

A ski-lodge design with four living areas provides comfortable accommodations for thirty-nine people with private rooms that include a sink, desk, and large picture window. There are common bathroom facilities. Two suites at extra cost have private baths. The retreat house is fully air-conditioned, with individual controls for heating and air-conditioning in each room.

The offering for a directed retreat is $55 per night (spiritual direction, overnight and three meals). A private retreat is $45 per night.

The Monocacy River and a wooded area for hiking and walking are within property boundaries. Outdoor basketball and volleyball courts and playing fields are available for guests' use.

LOCATION
Located on Route 85, the center is seven miles south of Frederick, Maryland, just off Interstates 70 and 270. Driving time from Washington, D.C., or Baltimore, Maryland, is about one hour on major highways. From Washington/ Northern Virginia: Take Interstate I-270 North to Exit 26, turn right on Route 80 and left on Route 85. The center is located one and a half miles on the left side.

14. Dayspring Retreat Center
11301 Neelsville Road
Germantown, MD 20876
301/428-9348
Fax 301/428-9348
Interdenominational/Church of the Savior

DESCRIPTION
Acres of woods and fields, the quiet of Merton's Pond (named after the contemplative monk and writer Thomas Merton), and a lodge nestled amid trails and forest, all are intended to provide a serene getaway for retreatants. This retreat center, located on more than one hundred acres of Maryland's hill country, was begun in the 1950s by the innovative Protestant Church of the Savior in Washington, D.C.

With all the intense demands of ministry and service and reaching out to others, writes one of the church's well-known members, the late writer Elizabeth O'Connor, "we needed to learn from a quiet center. We needed to learn the attitude of leisure when there is no leisure. We needed to learn how to let a friend know that we cared when we were pressured by the weight of unfinished work. We needed to learn to give a task wholly to God. And we needed to learn to forgive one another." All that, the church realized, would require times away and apart, for them to have opportunities to "get our lives more deeply grounded in the life of God."[1]

A variety of group retreats are offered to small groups of people. Individual retreatants are welcome.

ACCOMMODATIONS AND RESERVATIONS
Individuals or couples bring their own food. There are ample facilities for meal preparation and single rooms. The facility is handicapped accessible. Fee for overnight personal retreat is $35 per overnight (meals not included).

POINTS OF INTEREST
Hiking trails. A quiet atmosphere.

LOCATION
Transportation between Washington, D.C., and Dayspring can be arranged for $5 per person. Call the office for more details or for detailed directions.

15. DeSales Centre
1120 Blue Ball Road
Childs, MD 21916
410/398-3383

410/398-0116

Catholic/Oblates of Saint Francis de Sales

DESCRIPTION

Acres of quiet fields, hills, and wooded land allow retreatants a place to, as the directors of the center write, "encounter the God who loves you with an everlasting love." The nineteenth-century founder of the order, Francis de Sales, described a retreat as a time to "restore your strength, which has been impaired by time; warm up your heart; bring new life to your good resolutions; and make your soul's virtues flourish with fresh vigor" *(Introduction to the Devout Life)*.

The center staff provide a host of day programs, weekend theme retreats, and private or directed individual retreats.

ACCOMMODATIONS AND RESERVATIONS

Twenty-nine double-occupancy bedrooms and bathrooms are conveniently accessible on each of the building's two floors. Buffet-style meals served. Sheets and towels provided. Call for rates.

POINTS OF INTEREST

Nearby historical houses, gardens, zoos.

LOCATION

Between the Elkton and North East exits off Interstate 95.

16. Drayton Retreat Center

(of the United Methodist Church)
12651 Cooper's Lane
Worton, MD 21678-9180

410/778-2869
Fax 410/778-9180
drayton@juno.com
http://www.chestertown.com/drayton/index.html
United Methodist Church/Peninsula-Delaware Conference
♿ (limited)

DESCRIPTION

This center represents serenity and elegance on Maryland's eastern shore. The main building is a Georgian-style brick structure. Located on an inlet of the Chesapeake Bay near historic Chestertown, it is still only one and a half hour's drive from the urban centers of Philadelphia, Baltimore, and Washington, D.C. The area is steeped in the rich heritage of the early colonial period. Indeed, Drayton Retreat Center began its history as Drayton Manor, a land grant bestowed in 1667 by the King of England. The grounds retain the vistas of the fields and forests of a rural past. The facilities include wooded areas and gardens. The location is remote enough, say its staff, to give a sense of getting away from everyday demands, but close enough to be accessible. Its purpose is to "provide a facility for strengthening spiritual and intellectual lives of Christians of all denominations."

ACCOMMODATIONS AND RESERVATIONS

Both groups and individuals are welcome. Bed and bath linens are provided. Three meals served, either buffet or plate style. Some rooms have private baths. A deposit of 25 percent of the anticipated final bill is asked for. Sodas, snacks, copies, and gifts are available for purchase. Coffee, tea, water, and light snacks are available to guests without charge.

Grounds have thirty-three acres of rolling lawns and wooded areas, a formal garden, a large outdoor swimming pool with bath houses, a tennis court, and a trellised gazebo. It lies on a small peninsula of land formed by the eastern shore of the Chesapeake Bay, Churn Creek, and Still Pond Creek.

LOCATION

From north near Wilmington, Delaware, via Interstate 95 or Route 40, take MD 213 S; right on MD 298 S; right on Cooper's Lane for three and a half miles. From southwest near Annapolis, Maryland: Route 50/301 E across Bay Bridge; 301 N; left on MD 213 N; left on MD 297 N; right on MD 298 N for half mile; left on Cooper's Lane for three and a half miles. From southeast, Ocean City or Easton, Maryland: Route 50 N (or Route 404 N to Route 50 N); right on MD 213 N; left on MD 297 N; right on MD 298 N for half mile; left on Cooper's Lane for three and a half miles.

Massachusetts

17. Adelynrood

Byfield, MA 01922
978/462-6721 (May through September)
47 Keely Street
Haverhill, MA 01830
978/373-6354 (October through April)
Episcopal/Society of the Companions of the Holy Cross

DESCRIPTION

Thirty miles north of Boston in the Cape Ann/ North Shore area (which has spectacular New England coastline scenery), Adelynrood offers a full summer schedule of formal retreats and welcomes individuals who want to make a private retreat or just come away and rest in a caring atmosphere. Trails wind around the grounds. The center is operated by an international "companionship" of eight hundred Episcopal women.

Retreatants may worship in the chapel three times a day, with morning prayer or Eucharist before breakfast, intercessions at noon, and compline in the evening.

ACCOMMODATIONS AND RESERVATIONS

Simple but comfortable rooms, mostly single, with shared baths, with a few double rooms for those who come with a spouse or friend. Delicious, healthful meals are served at regular hours. Towels and bed linens provided.

POINTS OF INTEREST

Library with selection of classics and contemporary religious writings, as well as lighter fare. Exploration of salt marshes of Byfield. Near Plum Island beach and historic Newburyport. A large chapel for community worship and a small chapel for private prayer or small group meditation.

LOCATION

North of Boston and ten miles south of the New Hampshire state line. It may be reached by car from either Interstate 95 or US 1. From Interstate 95 take Exit 55 (Central Street) for three miles. Travel east following signs to Governor Dummer Academy. Look for the Adelynrood sign on the left just before reaching the academy. From US 1, turn west at Governor Dummer Academy sign and proceed beyond the academy to the Adelynrood driveway on the right.

18. Center for Christian Living

La Salette of Attleboro
947 Park Street
P.O. Box 2965
Attleboro, MA 02703-0965
508/222-8530
Fax 508/222-8558
lasalett@ma.ultranet.com
http://www.ultranet.com/~lasalett
Catholic/La Salette Missionaries

DESCRIPTION

This retreat center in scenic southeastern Massachusetts is set on spacious and well-landscaped grounds with peaceful nature trails conducive to prayerful walks and exercise. The center offers individual spiritual direction with prior arrangements. For those who desire a personal retreat without a director, a limited number of rooms are available for overnight use.

ACCOMMODATIONS AND RESERVATIONS

The Center for Christian Living is a modern retreat house with fifty-four single rooms. Each two rooms are joined by a semiprivate bath. The retreat house has two meeting rooms, a prayer room and chapel, sitting rooms, audiovisual capabilities, and elevators. The "Castle" (Provincial House) also offers single rooms with dormitory-style bath facilities, a large meeting room, and a chapel. The "Castle" has an elevator.

Retreatants are invited to make an offering in compensation for their retreat. The suggested offering is $95 for a weekend. Meals are included for private retreats, which cost $55 per night.

La Salette is within walking distance to the La Salette Shrine, including the People's Chapel, Rosary Walk, Stations of the Cross, cafeteria, and gift shop/bookstore.

LOCATION
The center is located on Route 118 in Attleboro. From Interstate 95 (North or South) take Exit 3 (Route 123 East). Follow Route 123 East and take a left after the second traffic light (follow about two and a half miles). Follow Route 118 South about two and a half miles. On the right, there is a blue and white sign for the center. Take a right down the driveway. The center is on the left and the parking lot is on the right.

 ### 19. Campion Renewal Center
319 Concord Road
Weston, MA 02493-3199
781/894-3199
Fax 781/788-4704
Catholic/Jesuit

DESCRIPTION
An expansive building twenty miles west of Boston houses this center of Ignatian prayer and spirituality. "The quiet and prayerful atmosphere of the house and extensive grounds," notes the brochure produced by the center, along with "daily liturgy, spiritual directors, and a skilled staff all contribute" to the center's goals to "help people find God, communicate with God, and most importantly, listen to God." While operating from a Catholic and Jesuit tradition, people from all faiths are welcome, as well as those who have become alienated from church.

Private directed, thematic group, and guided retreats are available. Liturgy is celebrated daily.

ACCOMMODATIONS AND RESERVATIONS
Extensive single and double rooms with shared baths are available.

POINTS OF INTEREST
Near Boston and other New England scenic and cultural sites.

LOCATION
Take Route 128 to the Route 20 exit. Head west for a mile or so. Just before reaching Saint Peter's Episcopal Church on the right, bear right at the fork onto Boston Post Road. Go through the commercial section of Weston Center and look for Concord Road on the right. Follow Concord over a railroad pass, fork left from Merriam Street, wind up the hill, and look for the parking lot on the left.

20. The Community of Jesus
P.O. Box 1094
Orleans, MA 02653
508/255-1094
Fax 508/255-9490
clergy@cofj.net
http://www.cofj.net
Protestant/Ecumenical

DESCRIPTION
Located in Orleans, Massachusetts, on the shores of Cape Cod Bay, the Community of Jesus is an ecumenical Christian community whose prayer, work, and fellowship are dedicated to transforming indi-

vidual lives through a way of life centered on Christ.

Members of the Community come from many walks of life and different denominational backgrounds, including Presbyterian, Episcopalian, Congregational, Baptist, Roman Catholic, Lutheran, Pentecostal, and Methodist. They have discovered both enrichment and strength in their diversity, as well as a common bond of Christian faith. Each member maintains a personal devotional life of prayer and Scripture study, and offers his or her work to the glory of God. Worship and prayer services are planned by Protestant clergy who come from a variety of denominational backgrounds.

The Community of Jesus has over three hundred members, including more than seventy-five families and single adults, more than twenty-five brothers and novices, and more than sixty sisters and novices (the latter two groups profess monastic vows of poverty, chastity, and stability).

Daily worship includes Holy Eucharist and the Liturgy of the Hours, sung in Gregorian chant. Together with the praises of God, daily intercessions are offered for reconciliation and healing, for other Christian communities, and for world leaders. Worship services are open to the public and visitors are welcome.

ACCOMMODATIONS AND RESERVATIONS
Bethany, the retreat house, consists of six bedrooms, some of which have private baths and air-conditioning. Sisters of the community prepare and serve exceptional meals. Fees by donation.

POINTS OF INTEREST

A lovely view of Rock Harbor. A shop, Priory Gifts, sells handcrafted items, gifts for all ages, books, and recordings of Gregorian chant and other sacred music. The community hosts a number of personal and group retreats as well as several events of cultural and artistic interest, including the "Star-Spangled Spectacular Festival" on or near the Fourth of July and the "Christmas Village Festival" in early December. They also offer dinner concerts and Advent and other seasonal musical events.

LOCATION

On the Mid-Cape Highway of Cape Cod, take Exit 12 (Orleans and Brewster). At the end of the exit ramp turn right onto Route 6A. Go straight through the first traffic light. At the next traffic light, which is in the center of Orleans, turn left. This puts you onto Rock Harbor Road. Drive for approximately one mile to a T-junction. Rock Harbor will be to your left. Turn left. The first driveway on the left is the Zion Friary Driveway. Park your car in the lot there, and follow signs to the Bethany retreat house, located to the right of Zion Friary and the Pastorium.

21. Emery House

Emery Lane
West Newbury, MA 01985
978/462-7940
Fax 978/462-0285
http://www.cowley.org/home/ssjinfo.htm
Episcopal/Society of Saint John the Evangelist

**See listing under Society of
Saint John the Evangelist**

22. Franciscan Center

459 River Road
Andover, MA 01810

978/851-3391
Fax 978/858-0675
FranRCent@aol.com
http://www.franrcent.org
Catholic/Franciscan

DESCRIPTION

The center offers Franciscan spirituality and hospitality on one hundred beautiful acres between two rivers—the Merrimack River and River Road—yet is conveniently located near Interstates 495 and 93. The town of Andover dates to 1646. Envisioned as an oasis of tranquillity and solitude or a place to find community, Franciscan Center can accommodate both groups and individuals.

ACCOMMODATIONS AND RESERVATIONS

Sleeping capacity is 103 persons, double occupancy, or 62 single rooms. Bed linen and towels are provided. Bathrooms are shared. An overnight stay for two nights, including five meals, costs $105.

Facilities include air-conditioned conference rooms, two dining areas, a chapel, a prayer room, and a coffee room.

The center is handicapped accessible and equipped with an elevator, access ramp, and bathrooms designed for persons with disabilities.

POINTS OF INTEREST

A lovely replica of the Lourdes Grotto, a Saint Clare Meditation Garden, outdoor Stations of the Cross adorn the property. Also, the center has a ballfield and a gift and bookshop.

LOCATION

From the north, take Interstate 495 South. Take Exit 39, Route 133, turn right. Take the first right after light, onto

Fiske Street. Follow to the end. The center is directly ahead. From Boston and points south, take Interstate 93 North to Exit 45. Bear right. Travel on River Road three and a half miles. Center is on the right.

23. Genesis Center at Westfield
Carriage House Conference
and Retreat Center
53 Mill Street
Westfield, MA 01085-4253
413/562-3627
Fax 413/572-1060
genretc@exit3.com
http://www.seeourtown.com/genesis.htm
Catholic/Sisters of Saint Joseph

DESCRIPTION

Nineteen acres of wooded property in the foothills of the Berkshires, within two hours of Boston, New England seashores, and within three hours of New York City, provide the setting for this center designed to nourish and nurture persons' growth into "the likeness of God."

"We have special concern," read the center's mission statement, "for persons in the health and healing professions, artists and craftspersons, all of whom are often in need of welcome, rest, and support."

Directed, thematic, and seasonal retreats, along with programs on journaling, ecospirituality, and creative arts round out the center's offerings. Private retreatants are welcome as space allows.

Genesis also welcomes guests for sabbaticals as short as one month and as long as a year. Those attracted to sabbaticals typically are looking for solitude and the opportunity to select programs from among the center's ongoing and varied offerings.

ACCOMMODATIONS AND RESERVATIONS
An original structure built in 1889, the Carriage House was renovated in 1991, retaining a distinctive style and charm. The center has thirty spacious single- and double-occupancy rooms, each individually decorated. An attractive common living area provides a comfortable space where guests may commune and relax.

Dining at Genesis is an experience in homestyle cooking and hospitality. Meals are wholesome and delicious. Some of the food served comes from the center's own garden.

POINTS OF INTEREST
Guests also take advantage of many cultural and educational opportunities in the beautiful Pioneer Valley and Berkshire Hills section of Western Massachusetts. It is also close to other regional attractions such as the Berkshires and the restaurants and art galleries in Northampton and Amherst.

LOCATION
Located ten minutes from the Massachusetts Turnpike and twenty-five minutes from Bradley International Airport, Genesis Center is easily accessible from Massachusetts, Connecticut, New York, and Rhode Island.

24. Glastonbury Abbey
16 Hull Street
Hingham, MA 02043
781/749-2155
Fax 617/749-6236

office@glastonburyabbey.org
http://www.glastonburyabbey.org/index.htm
Catholic/Benedictine

DESCRIPTION

Located less than two miles from the ocean (Boston Bay), Glastonbury is a small community of Benedictine monks striving to embrace the challenges of contemporary living within the time-tested values of a vital monastic spirit. Materials from the monastery quote Benedictine historian David Knowles as saying the Benedictine monks live neither at "a penitentiary nor a school of ascetic mountaineering, but [as] a family, a home of those seeking God." The core of monastic life at Glastonbury is envisioned as prayer, both communal and private. The monks strive for a healthy balance of prayer, holy reading, silence, and work.

Flowing from their ministry of prayer, the monks of Glastonbury engage in a diversity of services, both in the monastery and in the local area, offering retreats being one. Individual and group retreatants are welcome at Glastonbury throughout the year. "Guests," the monks write, "share in the monastic atmosphere of prayer and silence, and community are welcome to join the monks in their common prayer and daily Eucharist."

ACCOMMODATIONS AND RESERVATIONS

Two comfortable guest houses, informal and noninstitutional in character, provide housing for Glastonbury retreatants. Stonecrest, the large house, can accommodate up to twenty-one people; Whiting House, a maximum of eight. Private rooms are assured individual retreatants, a few rooms can accommodate couples. The Abbey provides all meals. However, in a spirit of community, retreatants are asked to help set tables and do some light cleanup after meals. The suggested offering for individuals is $45 per night for two or more nights, $50 for one night. A deposit of one night's offering is requested to confirm a reservation.

POINTS OF INTEREST
A bookstore that retains the monastic atmosphere by incorporating stained glass windows and a stone foundation. One side of the store is made of glass overlooking a meditative garden. The store sells over 2,500 titles, including theology texts, large-print books, audio books, music tapes, greeting cards, calendars, and a large selection of icons from all over the world.

Hingham is a historic town sixteen miles south of Boston. The town's Old Ship Church, established in 1681, is the last remaining Puritan meeting house in America.

LOCATION
By car from Boston, take Interstate 93 South to Route 3 South (Cape Cod) to Exit 14, which opens onto Route 228. Go north (Main Street, Hingham) about seven miles to the abbey. From Rhode Island, Connecticut, New York, take Interstate 95 to Interstate 93 North (toward Boston). Get off at Route 3 South (to Cape Cod) at Exit 14. Follow directions to Route 228 above.

 25. Miramar Retreat Center
P.O. Box M
Duxbury, MA 02331-0614
781/585-2460
Fax 781/585-3770
Catholic/Society of the Divine Word

DESCRIPTION

In a scenic area rich in American history, this retreat center is located on the South Shore of Massachusetts. The center, with its picturesque water tower, overlooks Duxbury and Cape Cod Bays from fields where the Wampanoag Indians once lived and where the Pilgrims settled.

Many topical retreats are scheduled for groups, as well as directed and preached/guided retreats. Also, individual guests may make unscheduled private retreats. Spiritual direction can be arranged.

ACCOMMODATIONS AND RESERVATIONS

The center has thirty rooms with twin beds and private bathrooms (linens and towels included). An overnight stay plus meals on a weekend is $110.

The dining room, chapel, and conference rooms are air-conditioned. The building has one handicapped-accessible bedroom.

POINTS OF INTEREST

Formerly part of an estate, Miramar has a lovely chapel that overlooks the ocean. The chapel has a tile floor, huge ceiling beams, and stained glass windows. The center also has a prayer room and a small library. The center is five miles from Plymouth, where the *Mayflower* landed.

LOCATION

Miramar is thirty-five miles south of Boston and five miles north of Plymouth. Via Route Interstate 495 follow 44 East to Route 3 North to Exit 10.

26. Saint Joseph Villa Retreat Center
339 Jerusalem Road
Cohasset, MA 02025

781/383-6024 or 781/383-6029
csjretrctr@juno.com
Catholic/Sisters of Saint Joseph

DESCRIPTION

Situated on the rocky coast of the Atlantic Ocean, this center offers what it calls "an ideal place for growth in the realization of the power of God in the beauty of nature and in the inner depths of the individual." A full program of thematic retreats and opportunities for private and directed retreats operate in a facility that overlooks panoramas of ocean and seacoast.

ACCOMMODATIONS AND RESERVATIONS

Twelve private rooms with shared baths in a well-kept one-hundred-year-old converted family house provides a homey atmosphere. Three meals a day are provided (continental breakfast). A large circular porch and lookout provide unhindered views.

POINTS OF INTEREST

Located within a half hour drive is historic Plymouth and the Kennedy Library. The Hingham commuter ferry to Boston waterfront markets lies within easy driving distance. Picturesque lighthouses dot the surrounding coastline.

LOCATION

Take Route 93 South to Route 3 South to Exit 14 (Route 228 Nantasket/Rockland). Continue on 228 for approximately eight miles. One mile after passing Glastonbury Abbey take right onto Jerusalem Road. Proceed through intersection with stop sign and go eight tenths of a mile.

27. Saint Joseph's Abbey

167 North Spencer Road
Spencer, MA 01562
508/885-8710
spenabby@spencerabbey.org
http://www.spencerabbey.org
Catholic/Cistercian (Trappist)

DESCRIPTION

Saint Joseph's Abbey is set among nearly two thousand acres of central New England hills blanketed in oak, maple, and pine. Pasture lands and meadows surround the immediate grounds, which rest atop a hillcrest. As a cloistered monastery, the monks want to "follow our contemplative way of life in a way that is faithful to tradition and open to our times. . . . Each day we praise God and intercede for the whole world in the Divine Office and the Eucharist and give ourselves to private prayer, work, and study."

ACCOMMODATIONS AND RESERVATIONS

The Abbey sponsors three types of accommodations at or near the monastery.

First, adjoining the monastery is a small retreat house, with eleven private rooms each with private bath. Retreats (men only) for clergy and laymen are offered midweek, Monday afternoon to Friday morning, and on weekends, from Friday afternoon to Sunday afternoon. While retreatants are not in direct contact with the monks, the retreat house closely conforms to the atmosphere of the monastery. The celebration of Mass and the Liturgy of the Hours provides the structure for each day, which includes ample time for prayer, reading, and contemplative quiet. Conferences are given by one of the monks who is also available for private talks and confession. Breakfast, lunch, and supper are provided. The Abbey Retreat House is usually filled six months in advance and reservations are accepted only for six months ahead. No fee is set for a retreat, though the average donation received ranges from about $60 to $150 for a weekend and from $100 to $300 for a midweek retreat.

Mary House also provides a retreat option. Located a quarter of a mile up the road from the entrance to the monastery on Route 31, "Mary House is a place of true retreat where adult men and women, clergy and lay, married or single, alone or in groups, stay in a gracious and relaxed atmosphere of prayer and silence." Guests at Mary House are welcomed in the visitors' chapels for daily Eucharist and Divine Office. Laypersons own and operate the house and all running expenses are derived from the generosity of guests. Requested offerings for stays at Mary House are from $20 to $60 per person per night according to one's means. (For reservations send requested dates and hours of arrival and departure to: Mary House, P.O. Box 20, Spencer, MA 01562, or call 508/885-5450.)

Finally, Brunelle House IV is an informal lodge just under a mile up the road from the abbey on Route 31 and is owned and cared for by abbey neighbors. This is a country lodge for individual men and women, couples, families with children, and groups of clergy and laypeople who wish to stay near the abbey in a family-style atmosphere. Guests may either prepare their own meals in the kitchen, dine out at a nearby restaurant, or take food with them to the house. While not a retreat house, individuals and groups may arrange times of silence, conferences, or prayer and study groups independently of the abbey.

POINTS OF INTEREST

The abbey produces a selection of jams, jellies, marmalades, and conserves known as Trappist preserves. Monks also design, create, and sell liturgical vestments to be used for officiants at worship services.

Approximately fifty miles west of Boston, northeast of Sturbridge, accessible by roads intersecting Interstate 90 (Massachusetts Turnpike). Nearest airport in Worcester.

28. Saint Scholastica Priory and Saint Mary's Monastery

The Benedictines of Petersham, Massachusetts
Petersham, MA 01366-0345
508/724-3227
http://www.petershamosb.org
Catholic/Benedictine

DESCRIPTION

Petersham, Massachusetts, is the home of twin Benedictine monasteries—Saint Scholastica Priory and Saint Mary's Monastery—which jointly run a guest house. Set on two hundred rural acres in the northeast corner of the Quabbin Reservoir, the wooded property is surrounded by conservation land and forests, hindering the possibility of urban development.

Retreatants can find quiet, privacy, time for reading or reflection, and a place apart with God. Ordinarily, the Benedictines of Petersham do not provide directed retreats. Confession is available on request. Guests are encouraged to join the monks and nuns in the daily celebration of Mass, vespers, and compline.

ACCOMMODATIONS AND RESERVATIONS

Write or call for reservations at least two weeks in advance. Linens, towels, and soap are provided, and bathrooms are shared. Women guests take all meals in the guest house kitchen. Men have breakfast in the guest house kitchen, but lunch and dinner are taken with the monks in their monastic refectory. There is a small library of books and tapes available in the guest house for the use of guests.

No charge is made for the use of the guest house, although donations are gratefully accepted.

Retreatants are free to walk in places not considered private by the monks and nuns. A map of the property is provided in the guest house kitchen. There are also walking trails in the Harvard Forest, a short walk from the entrance to the property. Guests may visit the new monastic church, which has beautiful stained glass windows.

Other features of the Benedictine community are a small book and gift shop, the monastery's cottage industries (including manufacturing natural beeswax skin balm and furniture polish), and Saint Bede's Publications, a religious publishing company staffed by the nuns of Saint Scholastica Priory.

The closest major airport is in Boston, with a smaller one in Worcester, Massachusetts. Car rentals are available at both airports. There is a bus shuttle from Logan Airport in Boston to Gardner, the nearest bus stop to Petersham, and arrangements can be made to pick retreatants up. Detailed directions to the monasteries are available upon request.

29. Monastery of Saint Mary and Saint John
Society of Saint John the Evangelist
980 Memorial Drive
Cambridge, MA 02138
617/876-3037
Fax 617/876-5210
http://www.cowley.org/home/ssjinfo.htm
Episcopal/Society of Saint John the Evangelist

The Society of Saint John the Evangelist, founded in England in 1866, is the oldest Anglican religious order for men. The brothers of the North American Congregation (including men from Canada and Great Britain) live at the monastery in Cambridge, Massachusetts, and at Emery House, a rural retreat center in West Newbury, Massachusetts, housed in a building that dates from 1745. The brothers make vows of poverty, celibacy, and obedience. The monastery is located on the Charles River, a short walk from Harvard University.

In addition to their prayer alone each morning, the brothers gather to pray the Divine Office throughout the day, and to share in the celebration of the Holy Eucharist, to which retreatants are invited. Guest houses in Cambridge and West Newbury offer hospitality to retreatants. Guests may come individually or attend a group retreat focused on a topic of prayer and spirituality.

The Society also sustains the publishing ministry of Cowley Publications, operates the Cowley and Cathedral Bookstore in downtown Boston, serves inner-city children and their families through Saint Augustine Ministries, and ministers to the homeless and to persons with AIDS.

The brothers offer directed retreats (to "open a silent space in life for receiving the gift of renewed intimacy with God in Christ") and private retreats, as well as a variety of theme retreats for groups.

In addition to those at the monastery, retreats are offered at Emery House, the rural retreat center of the society located on Emery Lane, West Newbury, Massachusetts, about one hour's drive from Boston, set on 120 acres of field and woodland bounded by the Merrimack and Artichoke Rivers.

ACCOMMODATIONS AND RESERVATIONS
For the Monastery Guest House: meeting rooms; large and small chapels; single bedrooms, each with its own sink; toilets and showers nearby. Bed and bath linens are provided. Three meals are served in silence daily, with reading at the midday and evening meals. Parking spaces are extremely limited and guests are encouraged to use public transportation or call for parking space availability.

For Emery House: similar accommodations as above, as well as the Coburn Hermitages, a cluster of six self-sufficient houses designed for solitary and group use. A modern chapel provides space for prayer four times per day. Address:

The Guestmaster
Emery House
Emery Lane
West Newbury, MA 01985
978/462-7940
Fax 978/462-0285

Suggested donation per night's stay at both houses is $50; when daily direction is sought it is suggested that another $15 be added. A smaller donation may be negotiated in cases of financial need.

POINTS OF INTEREST
The monastery is site of the Chapel of Saint Mary and Saint John, which achieves the architectural essence of the early Christian basilicas on a small scale. The walls are of selected local granite, with Indiana limestone for the pillars and arches. The floor in the back is slate while the marble in the choir and sanctuary comes from Belgium, France, and Italy. Rose windows front and back and clerestory windows portray in stained glass biblical and church history figures.

Emery House rests adjacent to a four-hundred-acre state park. Its chapel windows overlook fields and rivers beyond.

LOCATION

For directions to the monastery, take Route 128 to Route 2 East. Make a left onto Memorial Drive. Watch for the monastery on the left.

Emery House: an hour's drive from downtown Boston. Take Interstate 95 North to Exit 57 (Route 113, Newburyport/West Newbury). Go west on Route 113 for one mile. Watch for a sign on the right side of the road.

New Hampshire

30. Oblate Retreat House

200 Lowell Road
Hudson, NH 03051
603/882-8141
Fax 603/882-1052
http://www.oblateretreathouse.org/
Catholic/Missionary Oblates of Mary Immaculate

DESCRIPTION

Envisioned as a center for spiritual renewal, Christian formation and group, private, or directed retreats, the retreat house rests on over forty acres in southern New Hampshire. The wooded grounds have paths for walking and a beautiful reflection pond.

The retreat house is staffed by laypersons. Oblate comes from a Latin word, meaning "offering." The Missionary Oblates offer themselves to the service of the church as they live vowed lives as Roman Catholic brothers and priests.

Much of the oblates' mission surrounds evangelizing the poor, which can take place through rehabilitation of drug addicts, in the care of those suffering from AIDS, in planning for economic housing, and in reevangelization those who have become estranged from the faith. The oblates host a Taize prayer group twice each month.

ACCOMMODATIONS AND RESERVATIONS
Kitchen and dining room serve meals.

POINTS OF INTEREST
Bookstore and gift shop with art works. The Merrimack Valley Region hosts three major cities—Concord, the state's capital; Manchester; and Nashua. Nature centers, state parks, places to hike, fish, swim, and bike are not far.

LOCATION
Between Route 3 and Interstate 93 near Route 111.

31. Saint Anselm Abbey
100 Saint Anselm Drive
Manchester, NH 03102-1310
603/641-7115
webmaster@anselm.edu
http://www.anselm.edu/abbey/abbey.html
Catholic/Benedictine

DESCRIPTION
Now a community of approximately thirty-five monks composed of priests and brothers, Saint Anselm Abbey is one of the twenty-two houses of

the American-Cassinese Congregation of Benedictines. The namesake of this abbey was an eleventh-century theologian and Benedictine abbot at the monastery of Bec in France and later Archbishop of Canterbury in England. The abbey shares three hundred acres with Saint Anselm College and overlooks Manchester.

The monks' life, as described by the monks themselves, centers around three elements: "the Conventual Mass, a communal celebration of the Eucharist; the Liturgy of the Hours, the church's singing of Psalms to consecrate the morning, midday, and evening; and *lectio divina,* the ancient monastic practice of meditative reading of Sacred Scripture and other writings from a rich spiritual tradition." That pattern creates a reverent, quiet atmosphere in the abbey, felt even by guests. Most of the monks have some type of involvement with the work of Catholic higher education, especially at the adjacent college.

ACCOMMODATIONS AND RESERVATIONS
Men stay in the monastery where they are expected to follow the routine of the monks. Women are housed with the Sisters of Saint Benedict in Manchester Priory, a separate building a few hundred yards from the abbey, where family-style meals are served. At the monastery noon meal sacred writings are read for reflection. Freewill donations received.

POINTS OF INTEREST
New England picturesque sites. The grounds have woods and trails. The college has an extensive library.

Fifty miles north of Boston. Take Interstate 93 North to
Route 293 North, exit to Route 101 West. At the junction of
Routes 101 and 114, take 114 North. Proceed through traffic
lights to Saint Anselm's Drive. Turn right and proceed one
mile.

New Jersey

 32. Carmel Retreat

1070 Ramapo Valley Road (Route 202)
Mahwah, NJ 07430
201/327-7090
Fax 201/327-9133
Catholic/Carmelite

DESCRIPTION

Set in the Ramapo River Valley, some thirty minutes from New York City, Carmel Retreat boasts
twenty-eight acres of property surrounded by large
tracts of forest. It was formerly the summer home
of a well-to-do New York financier, built near the
turn of the twentieth century. The grounds abound
in native stone fences and old trees. The Carmelites
offer a spirituality rich with tradition, including the
likes of the sixteenth-century mystics Teresa of Ávila
and John of the Cross and nineteenth-century spiritual-life writer Thérèse of Lisieux. Private retreatants
are welcome for short stays and the center provides
a variety of weeklong retreats, weekend retreats, directed retreats, youth retreats, and seminars that

address specific themes or issues. Each day morning and evening prayer and Mass is celebrated in the chapel.

ACCOMMODATIONS AND RESERVATIONS
Three buildings, made from stone and timber, contain thirty rooms with fifty-five beds. Overnight stays with meals are $50, $120 for a weekend stay. A five-day individual retreat is $220. For each a nonrefundable deposit is required.

POINTS OF INTEREST
The landscape includes a sunken garden and the Rosary Garden. The center adjoins a state park, Campgaw Reservation.

LOCATION
Take the Garden State Parkway North to Exit 160; left to Route 208 North, then follow directions below.

Or take the George Washington Bridge to Route 4 West to Route 208 North; 208 North to Route 287 South to Exit 58 (Oakland) to Route 202 North. Right to Carmel (about three miles).

Or New Jersey Turnpike North to Exit 16W to Route 3 West to Route 17 North to Route 202 South. Left at end of ramp to Carmel (four miles).

Or New York Thruway (Interstate 87) to Exit 15 (Suffern) to Interstate 287 South; Interstate 287 to Route 17 South to Route 202 South. Left at end of ramp to Carmel (four miles).

From Morristown/Interstate 80, take Interstate 287 North to Exit 58 (Oakland). Take left at end of ramp, left on Route 202 North to Carmel (three miles).

Or Interstate 287 West (Tappan Zee Bridge) to Exit 15 (Suffern) to Interstate 287 South to Route 17 South to Route 202 South. Left at end of ramp to Carmel (four miles).

33. Saint Pius X Spiritual Life Center

Diocese of Camden
1846 Peter Cheeseman Road
P.O. Box 216
Blackwood, NJ 08012
609/227-1436
Fax 609/227-2907
Catholic

DESCRIPTION

Part of the center's mission is "to provide opportunities for personal and spiritual growth and lifelong learning for the people of God." A wooded South Jersey setting allows Saint Pius X to offer both private and group retreats, days of prayer, and other programs designed for specific groups of people, including law enforcement officers, firefighters, lawyers, nurses, and physicians.

ACCOMMODATIONS AND RESERVATIONS

Forty-five double-occupancy bedrooms, all with air-conditioning. Facilities to accommodate both large and small groups. In addition, special dietary needs can be met.

POINTS OF INTEREST

Located adjacent to diocesan youth center with up-to-date recreational facilities.

LOCATION

Across from Camden County College. Twenty minutes from Philadelphia bridges. Five miles from New Jersey Turnpike (Exit 3). Two miles from Atlantic City Expressway.

34. San Alfonso Retreat House

P.O. Box 3098
755 Ocean Avenue
Long Branch, NJ 07740
732/222-2731
Fax 732/870-8892
Redemptorist Fathers and Brothers

DESCRIPTION

Seated on eight acres along the shores of the Atlantic Ocean, San Alfonso draws some thirteen thousand visitors per year. The house offers group retreats focusing on various themes, including a married couples' retreat, a retreat for recovering alcoholics, a retreat focusing on charismatic renewal, and more. Retreatants may schedule a directed retreat. Individuals may participate in prayers and Eucharist with the Redemptorist community.

ACCOMMODATIONS AND RESERVATIONS

Most rooms are single occupancy (two rooms share a bathroom). All rooms are air-conditioned. Meals included. The house requires a nonrefundable $25 deposit per person to confirm reservations. Visitors pay the balance on arrival.

POINTS OF INTEREST

Gift shop, video and audio cassettes, small gymnasium, reading room.

LOCATION

By train from New York City: From Penn Station get off at Long Branch. Take a taxi to San Alfonso (five minutes). By bus from New York City: Buy tickets for West End at Port Authority Bus Terminal—Academy Bus Line (Asbury Park–

Point Pleasant Line). The driver will take you to the Retreat House. By train from Newark Airport: Take the bus at the airport (Airlink) to Penn Station in Newark. Take the train to Long Branch. Take a taxi to San Alfonso (five minutes).

Traveling south on the New Jersey Turnpike, get off at Exit 11 (Woodbridge and Shore Points). Follow signs for Garden State Parkway (South). Stay on Garden State Parkway to Exit 105. After exit, go straight through five traffic lights. Look for sign on right that says 71. Follow 71 South until it curves left (street is now Cedar Avenue). Ignore future 71 signs and follow Cedar to its end. Turn right on Ocean Avenue. San Alfonso is on the left.

From points south and west, take the New Jersey Turnpike to Exit 7A. Take Interstate 195 East to the Garden State Parkway North to Exit 105. Follow above directions to Retreat House.

35. The Upper Room Spiritual Center

P.O. Box 1104
West Bangs Avenue and Route 33
Neptune, NJ 07754
732/922-0550
Fax 732/922-3904
Catholic/Diocese of Trenton

DESCRIPTION

On the spacious grounds of Holy Innocents parish in a beautiful suburban area of Monmouth County, the center is near a state park and the ocean. A convent at one time, Upper Room is primarily a training center for spiritual directors. However, once a month, weekend retreats are open to the general public.

ACCOMMODATIONS AND RESERVATIONS

The center has fourteen bedrooms and two large teaching areas. The larger rooms, but not the bedrooms, are air-conditioned. Some bedrooms have private baths. Linens are provided. Although the center has a large kitchen facility, it provides no cook for its weekend retreats.

The chapel provides a warm atmosphere for prayer; all are welcome to celebrate the Eucharist at 11:30 A.M.

POINTS OF INTEREST
The center is close to Shark River State Park and a ten-minute drive from the Jersey Shore.

LOCATION
The Upper Room is on the corner of Route 33 and West Bangs Avenue in Neptune, New Jersey, one and two tenths miles from Exit 100 off the Garden State Parkway.

36. The Vincentian Renewal Center
P.O. Box 757
Plainsboro, NJ 08536-0757
609/520-9626
Fax 609/452-2851
Catholic/Saint Vincent de Paul

DESCRIPTION
This center is found on the campus of Saint Joseph's Preparatory Seminary. Days of retreat are available for many, from university students to social workers to the seriously ill to parish organizations. The center welcomes both individual and group retreats while also offering spiritual direction. The brochure describes the center's mission in the following way: "We recognize our ministry to be one of faith sharing, healing, and accompaniment for all who come seeking the Lord, especially the poor, clergy and

religious, and all who expend their energy in service
of the least among us."

ACCOMMODATIONS AND RESERVATIONS
Air-conditioned rooms, private baths, laundry room. For
further information write or call the director.

POINTS OF INTEREST
Chapel, indoor gymnasium. Surrounded by Lake Carnegie
and the Delaware Raritan Canal State Park.

LOCATION
In Plainsboro Township near Princeton. Exit US Route 1 at
College Road West. Follow signs to Saint Joseph's Preparatory Seminary. The Vincentian Renewal Center is next to
the Princeton Forrestal Village and Marriott Hotel.

New York

 ## 37. Abbey of the Genesee
P.O. Box 900
Piffard, NY 14533
716/243-2220
guestrsv@frontiernet.net
http://maple.lemoyne.edu/~bucko/genesee.htm
Catholic/Trappist

DESCRIPTION
Located in the picturesque and historic Genesee
River Valley, the monks say they live close to the
rhythms of nature. The enclosure encompasses a
thousand acres of forest, ravines, rolling hills, and a
meandering creek. Wildlife indigenous to Upstate
New York abounds. Another 1,300 acres of woods

and farmlands also help maintain a rural solitude. They describe their life as "a balanced daily round of prayer, *lectio* [sacred reading], and manual work in an atmosphere of simplicity, silence, and fraternal support." Of the forty or so monks, nearly everyone has a share in the work of baking Monks' Bread, which helps support the monastery. The monks also share in farming, cooking, cleaning, hospitality, formation, teaching, and caring for the infirm. The community celebrates liturgical prayer seven times a day beginning with vigils in the middle of the night and compline in evening. Retreatants are welcome to attend.

The late priest and author Henri Nouwen published a well-regarded book in the seventies called *The Genesee Diary,* which chronicled his seven-month sojourn among the monks.

ACCOMMODATIONS AND RESERVATIONS
Several retreat options exist. Bethlehem House offers space for sixteen guests in single rooms, most with shared baths, plus three meals a day. Bethany House and Cana House accommodate more, all with shared bath, but require guests to prepare own food.

Those capable of doing so are asked to give $30 a day donation.

POINTS OF INTEREST
A well-stocked library of over thirty thousand select volumes and numerous journals. Letchworth State Park, not far from the abbey.

LOCATION
Approximately five miles west of Genesco, New York, and about one mile north of Highway 63 on River Road, just

west of Piffard, New York. New York City is approximately 350 miles; Rochester, New York, 35; Syracuse, 90; Toronto, Canada, 170.

38. Beaver Farm Retreat and Conference Center

Underhill Avenue
Yorktown Heights, NY 10598
914/962-6033

DESCRIPTION

A gracious, rambling Victorian house on thirteen natural and landscaped acres (including a pond) provide a rustic setting for this interfaith retreat center. The center began in 1926 when Gilbert and Jean Beaver sold their 150 Ayrshire cows, closed down their thriving dairy business, and hosted their first retreat group: twenty young men who came to discuss war, peace, and Christian Scripture. In 1951, the Beavers incorporated the house and farm as a nonprofit retreat center, welcoming individuals and groups of any (or no) religious orientation.

ACCOMMODATIONS AND RESERVATIONS

Antique furniture and wood floors give a sense of the venerable heritage of this facility. Towels, sheets, and blankets are provided, but shampoo and other toilet articles are not. Rates vary.

POINTS OF INTEREST

Yorktown Museum has exhibits of Early American and Algonquin Indian life. The surrounding Hudson River Valley is considered one of the most picturesque in the country. Numerous historical sites in driving range.

Thirty-five miles north of Manhattan in upper Westchester
County. Take the Saw Mill Parkway to Taconic Parkway
North to the Underhill Avenue/Yorktown Heights exit.
Turn right onto Underhill. The farm is one and a half miles
on the left, just before the traffic light.

39. Bethany Retreat House

202 County Route 105
Highland Mills, NY 10930-1003
914/928-2213
Fax 914/928-9437
thevenet@frontiernet.net
http://www.rc.net/newyork/bethany
Catholic/Jesuit

DESCRIPTION

Located at the foot of the Catskills fifty miles northwest of New York City, the property of Bethany
Retreat House borders on Lake Cromwell. Its beautiful, quiet setting is conducive to a retreat.

Arrangements can be made for private and directed retreats. Sabbaticals or prolonged periods of
renewal can also be designed to meet individual
needs. The community has daily Eucharistic liturgy
as well as morning and evening prayer. All guests
are welcome to participate.

ACCOMMODATIONS AND RESERVATIONS

Bethany can accommodate up to sixty people for day retreats. Thirty bedrooms are available for overnight retreats,
with bed linens and towels provided. The retreat house
serves excellent meals and recently has expanded and air-
conditioned the retreatants' dining room. A weekend at

Bethany (Friday night to Sunday after dinner) is $95. An overnight on weekends is $50.

For those who desire solitude, Bethany has a small cottage and a hermitage overlooking Lake Cromwell.

POINTS OF INTEREST

Bethany has an up-to-date spiritual-life library, an earth-care library, and a card and book shop. Outdoor activities include taking long walks in the partly wooded terrain and boating and swimming in Lake Cromwell at certain times of the year. A new screened-in gazebo has been installed on the shore of the lake.

LOCATION

From New York Throughway: Traveling North or South, take Exit 16, Harriman. Turn right (North) onto Route 32 past Woodbury Common and go two and a half miles into Highland Mills. After the fire station, turn left onto County Route 105. Bethany is one mile on the right.

 ## 40. Cenacle Retreat Center

310 Cenacle Road
Ronkonkoma, NY 11779
516/588-8366
Fax 516/588-1729
Catholic/Cenacle

DESCRIPTION

The retreat house is approximately fifty miles from Manhattan in the center of Long Island, yet it provides solitude, space, and beauty. At the Cenacle, the sisters work in collaboration with laypeople to provide an atmosphere of peace and simplicity. Cenacle sisters offer individual spiritual direction. The flow of each day is up to the individual, but guests can expect regular mealtimes, a daily meeting with the retreat director, and for Catholics, an opportunity to share in the Eucharist.

ACCOMMODATIONS AND RESERVATIONS

The Cenacle accommodates forty-three persons overnight in single rooms. Each room has a sink and a fan. Bathrooms are centralized. Three rooms have private baths. Bed linen is provided, and guests bring their own towels. Simple and nutritious meals are prepared on the premises and served buffet style.

A weekend retreat is $125, with a nonrefundable deposit of $25, which is applied to the overall cost of the retreat. A day/evening program is $10. Reservations must be made well in advance for weekends, which fill quickly.

POINTS OF INTEREST

The retreat center has forty-five acres for guests to explore and enjoy. The property originally belonged to Broadway actress Maude Adams. In 1922, she donated her "farm" to the sisters at the Cenacle. The sisters built the current facility in 1926.

LOCATION

Driving east on Long Island Expressway: Take Exit 61 (CR19 Patchogue Holbrook Road). Go north (left) to end of road, turn right onto Portion Road and proceed three traffic lights to Cenacle Road. Turn left—the entrance driveway is on the left.

41. Christll the King Retreat and Conference Center

500 Brookford Road
Syracuse, NY 13224
315/446-2680

Fax 315/446-2689
Catholic

DESCRIPTION

Originally a private home built in the grand style of the 1930s, Christ the King Retreat and Conference Center invites guests into its quiet, private atmosphere. The secluded mansion with its high ceilings, sprawling spiral staircase, and abundant natural light with stained glass windows is located in the Bradford Hills section of Syracuse.

Guests may come for group or private retreats during a day or evening, or overnight.

ACCOMMODATIONS AND RESERVATIONS

Some rooms have private bathrooms. An overnight retreat including three meals is $50 per person. A full dining facility serves family-style meals.

The center is handicapped accessible. Also, there is ample free parking on site.

POINTS OF INTEREST

Christ the King Retreat and Conference Center has spacious grounds with an Olympic-size pool.

LOCATION

The center is conveniently located less than ten minutes from downtown Syracuse.

42. Community of the Holy Spirit

Saint Hilda's House
621 West 113th Street
New York, NY 10025
212/666-8249, ext. 304

chs@interport.net
http://www.users.interport.net/~chs/
Episcopal/Community of the Holy Spirit

DESCRIPTION

The sisters at this retreat house seek to "provide a place where people can come to find quiet and respite in the midst of a crowded and intense external environment—at least as quiet as any place in the heart of New York City can be!" Located on Manhattan's Upper West Side, the Community of the Holy Spirit, says the group, "is an Episcopal monastic community for women called by God to witness to the Holy Spirit in the church and the world, and to foster and express unity in diversity in its life and work." Since its foundation in 1952, the sisters have lived in community by making lifetime vows, by participating in daily liturgical and personal prayer, and through giving service to others. The celebration of the Eucharist (Communion) and daily prayer are central to their life.

"Outpourings," the name of the program of retreats, workshops, and cultural events at Saint Hilda's House, provides overnight guest accommodations for individuals and groups who seek rest, prayer, and quiet. Guests are invited to join the sisters at mealtimes and for chapel services. Individual self-directed retreats and *Poustinia* (a special experience of fasting and prayer) may be made with prior arrangement.

ACCOMMODATIONS AND RESERVATIONS

Can accommodate twenty guests in fourteen single rooms (with shared hallway baths); two rooms, each with double

bed and private bath; and one room with two twin beds
(shared hallway bath). The Community also has a convent
in the country. There Saint Cuthbert's Retreat House provides a more rural experience on twenty acres of fields and
woods (120 Federal Hill Road, Brewster, NY 10509-5307; 914/
278-2610; E-mail: chsmelrs@interport.net).

POINTS OF INTEREST
The many cultural and religious attractions of Manhattan.

LOCATION
Accessible by public transportation on Manhattan's Upper
West Side.

 43. Dominican Spiritual Life Center
1945 Union Street
Niskayuna, NY 12309
518/393-4169
Fax 518/393-4525
Catholic/Dominican Sisters of Saint Catherine de'Ricci

DESCRIPTION
The ten beautifully landscaped acres and converted
farm house of this center have been the site of spiritual retreats for fifty years. A larger retreat house
was added in 1958 with accommodations for fifty
people. The center is designed to be "a place of
peace and safety, rooted in Gospel values, open to
all people who seek to grow in relationship to
themselves, others, and their God." A wide range of
group and private retreat options are offered.

ACCOMMODATIONS AND RESERVATIONS
In addition to facilities for a wide range of group retreats,
the center offers a hermitage, a stone-faced onetime wind-

mill tower converted into a retreat bungalow with a kitchenette and living room on the first floor, a prayer room and
full bath on the second, and a spacious bedroom with two
single beds on the third. Rates for stays at "The Windmill"
are $20 for day use and $30 for an overnight stay.

POINTS OF INTEREST
A chapel with a large mural painted by renowned children's
book illustrator Tomie de Paola highlights five important
women in the history of the church.

LOCATION
Located off Route 7 on the corner of Rosendale and Troy
Roads. From Syracuse and west, take the Thruway to Exit 25
(890 West) to Route 7 East. From New York City and south,
take the Thruway to Exit 24 (Northway) to Exit 6. Take
Route 7 West approximately seven miles.

44. The Graymoor Spiritual Life Center
P.O. Box 300
Garrison, NY 10524
914/424-3671, ext. 3515
Catholic/Franciscan Friars of the Atonement/Graymoor

DESCRIPTION
The mission of this center set in scenic Hudson Valley, as its brochure notes, is to "invite the church
and the unchurched to renew themselves by relaxing, reflecting, and being revitalized in mind,
spirit, and body in order to awaken or deepen a faith
commitment in everyday living." A year-round
schedule of group retreats are offered on aspects of
twelve-step programs, dealing with stress, using a
journal for spiritual growth, arts and spirituality,

and other topics. Days of grace, scheduled during the week, can last one, two, or more nights and give individuals the opportunity to explore silence and solitude, though individual retreatants are welcome to join the friars for prayer.

ACCOMMODATIONS AND RESERVATIONS
Days of grace retreats generally begin on a Tuesday late afternoon and end with the noon meal the next day. Cost is $55 per person.

POINTS OF INTEREST
Christian bookstore. Serene setting on four hundred acres. Near West Point and other historic sites.

LOCATION
Accessible by Metro North train from Grand Central Station to Peekskill. Accessible by car by traveling four miles north of Peekskill (or thirteen miles south of Fishkill) on Route 9. (From the Bronx River Parkway, take Route 202 West to Bear Mountain Parkway to Route 9.)

45. Holy Cross Monastery
P.O. Box 99
West Park, NY 12493
914/384-6660, ext. 302
Fax 914/384-6031
guesthouse@idsi.net   http://www.idsi.net/holycross
Episcopal/Order of the Holy Cross

DESCRIPTION
The monastery and guest house sit on the banks of the Hudson River in the Mid-Hudson Valley. It is a

152

contemporary Benedictine community of men within the Anglican (Episcopal) communion.

The buildings are historic and sites of the National Historic Register. The monks live a monastic life following a Benedictine rule. Daily life includes monastic offices and a daily Eucharist and attempts to provide stability through a balance of work, recreation, prayer, and study.

The monks' primary work is a guest ministry through scheduled retreats for guests throughout the year, as well as providing space for individual and group retreats. Direction is provided.

ACCOMMODATIONS AND RESERVATIONS

Single rooms with shared baths. Three meals are served daily. The grounds consist of two guest houses, a refectory, the monastic enclosure, and the monastery Church of Saint Augustine. A suggested fee of $60 per day covers meals and a room.

POINTS OF INTEREST

The monastery operates several enterprises, including Holy Cross Incense, Holy Cross Publications, and the Monk's Cell gift and book shop.

Across the Hudson lies Hyde Park, where visitors can tour the Vanderbilt Mansion and the Franklin D. Roosevelt home, library, and museum. Also nearby are West Point and historic Newburgh, where George Washington set up headquarters.

LOCATION

Eight miles north of the Mid-Hudson Bridge on US 9W. Take Exit 18 from the New York State Thruway (Interstate 87) and turn right onto Route 299 East. Go about five miles to the end of the road where it meets US 9W. Turn left (north) and drive about five more miles into the village of West Park. The entrance to the guest house is on the right side of the road in the center of the village.

By Interstate 84, exit on 9W and drive toward Kingston, New York.

Service from Grand Central Terminal is available to Poughkeepsie via the Metro North commuter railroad. A taxi service is available to the monastery for a reasonable fee.

The nearest and most convenient airport to West Park is Stewart International Airport in Newburgh, New York. From New York City airports the Cary bus service runs service to Grand Central Terminal.

 46. Linwood Spiritual Center
139 South Mill Road
Rhinebeck, NY 12572
914/876-4178, ext. 301
Fax 914/876-1920
Catholic/Society of Saint Ursula

DESCRIPTION

Linwood is made up of fifty-five acres on a hill with a magnificent view of the Hudson River, two hours north of New York City. A range of programs, including private retreats, seek to provide "personal development in which our spiritual and human dimensions are integrated so that we may be people fully alive for the glory of God." Directed retreats, at certain weeks in the summer months, help people discern how to listen to what God is saying. Scripture and life experience provide the primary material for prayer.

ACCOMMODATIONS AND RESERVATIONS

Air-conditioned rooms with shared baths, along with a hermitage, provide ample space for a variety of retreat experiences. A weeklong directed retreat typically carries a suggested fee of $275. A nonrefundable deposit is required.

POINTS OF INTEREST
Chapel, tennis court, and swimming pool. Hudson River Valley scenery and other attractions.

LOCATION
Three-plus miles off Route 9. From the north or the south via NYS Thruway take Exit 19 for Kingston. At traffic circle follow signs for Route 209/Kingston-Rhinecliff Bridge. After bridge proceed to second intersection; turn right to Route 9G South. At next light turn right to Route 9 South. In Rhinebeck, take first right after Beekman Arms Hotel (Mill Road). Proceed three and a third miles. Amtrak trains stop in nearby Rhinecliff. Shortline buses stop in Rhinebeck.

47. Mount Saint Alphonsus
Redemptorist Retreat Center
P.O. Box 219
Esopus, NY 12429-0219
914/384-8022
Fax 914/384-6522
Catholic/Redemptorist

DESCRIPTION
The castlelike Mount Saint Alphonsus was built along the banks of the beautiful Hudson River in 1905. In all seasons, the granite retreat center is an imposing, grand sight.

The facility is open year-round and caters to large groups. The entire retreat house is also available for religious meetings and retreats. If space permits, the center welcomes persons who wish to make a private retreat. Retreatants set their own schedule and are provided with a room and meals.

The retreat center has 106 rooms with 161 beds. Each room has a fourteen-foot ceiling with a ceiling fan and a large window. Rooms have the use of common sinks, showers, and toilets.

The center provides meals, coffee breaks, and meeting rooms. There is an elevator, and one shower is handicapped accessible.

A nonrefundable deposit of $25 per person must be paid fourteen days prior to arrival and confirms registration. The balance of the $55 fee for private retreats is paid on arrival.

POINTS OF INTEREST
The property features one mile of riverfront, with roads and trails.

LOCATION
Located on Route 9W, eight miles south of Kingston and twelve miles north of Poughkeepsie. Take New York State Throughway to Exit 18—New Paltz. Take a right on 299 East, which dead-ends into Route 9W. Take a left onto Route 9W North. The center is seven miles north on the right.

48. Mount Saviour Monastery
231 Monastery Road
Pine City, NY 14871
607/734-1688
Fax 607/734-1689
Msaviour@Juno.com
http://www.servtech.com/public/msaviour
Catholic/Benedictine

DESCRIPTION

The monastery has aimed, since 1951, to be "a community of monks striving to live a simple, genuine, and full monastic life" according to the Bible and the Rule of Saint Benedict. The monks use 250 acres of the land for raising sheep and producing market lambs, yarn, and pelt products while many other acres serve as a woodlot. Concern that the door appears clearly open to those who wish to visit has largely determined the physical development of the hilltop. The chapel, for example, is an octagon with the altar placed in the middle.

The monks do not ordinarily provide direction or conferences. Guests are invited to structure their own day according to the monastic schedule of the Divine Office, silence, and reflection. At times guests are invited to join the monks in some aspects of the daily work.

ACCOMMODATIONS AND RESERVATIONS

Saint Joseph's Men's Guest House contains fifteen small private rooms. Male guests take meals with the monks in the monastery. Saint Gertrude's Guest House for women and couples has two double rooms (twin beds), three single rooms, and is a fifteen-minute walk (uphill) from the chapel. Women take meals at Saint Gertrude's. If reservations are made at Saint Gertrude's for two women coming together, they can assume they will share a room unless specifically requested otherwise. There are three separate facilities equipped with private kitchens, open to men, women, and married couples desiring a more private retreat: Saint Peter's farm house, the West Casa, and the East Casa. In these facilities, guests may bring and prepare their own meals if they wish.

Normal length of stay is two nights to one week. The

monks suggest $40 per night per person. "We are grateful," they note, "to those who can give more and welcome those whose means allow for less. The generosity of our guests permits us to run the guest houses and we are grateful for [such] support." Linens and towels are provided. Private baths in some rooms.

Note: Informal clothing and sturdy seasonable footwear are in order. Evenings and early mornings can be chilly even in summer. Winters are cold and springs are wet.

POINTS OF INTEREST

Book and gift shop. The monastery is located in the scenic Finger Lakes region. Within easy driving distance are Cornell University, the Corning Glass Museum, and Mark Twain's home.

LOCATION

From the east take Route 17 to the second Elmira exit, marked Church Street/Route 352. Follow Church Street through the city to Route 225. Turn left, continue four miles to Monastery Road on the right. From the west take Route 17 to Exit 45/Route 352 through Corning. At the last traffic light, turn right on Route 225 (be prepared to bear left just after you enter this road). There are two turns but they are well marked. Continue on 225 until you come to Monastery Road on the left. From north or south, Route 14 crosses Church Street (Route 352) in Elmira. Continue on Church Street to Route 225, turn left, and continue to Monastery Road on the right.

The Elmira/Corning Airport is about ten miles away. Southern Tier Express (a shuttle service) will take you from the airport to the monastery for $15. Call them ahead at 607/739-5499. The same bus terminal in Elmira serves inter-city and local buses. A local bus marked Golden Glow stops at Elon Place, the end of the line, one block short of Hendy Creek Market on Route 225 four miles from the monastery. (Do not take the bus marked "Pine City.") Arrivals before

5:00 P.M. may make prior arrangements with the Guest
Brother to be picked up at Hendy Creek Market.

49. New Skete Communities
P.O. Box 128
New Skete Lane
Cambridge, NY 12816
518/677-3928
Fax 518/677-2373
Orthodox Church in America

DESCRIPTION
North of Albany, New York, the communities of
New Skete are members of the Orthodox Church in
America. The monks' monastery is located on a
mountaintop in Upstate New York; the nuns'
monastery is set on a hillside not far away, and the
companions' community (which includes married
couples) is halfway between the two. The complex
of buildings sits amid five hundred rural acres. The
three houses gather twice daily for services, chanting the Orthodox liturgy a capella in multipart harmony.

The New Skete communities breed, raise, and
train German shepherd dogs, as well as train all
breeds at their kennels. They have also written two
definitive, popular books on dog care: *How to Be Your
Dog's Best Friend* and *The Art of Raising a Puppy*. The
communities also offer hospitality to visitors and
pilgrims.

ACCOMMODATIONS AND RESERVATIONS
A guest house contains a lounge and rooms for retreatants.
Retreats are private and informal; meals are taken with the

monks; guests attend the services and spend time in reading, prayer, and relaxation as well as working with the community.

Advance reservations are necessary, and stays are limited to two or three days because of the many people who wish to visit.

POINTS OF INTEREST
All three communities produce gourmet food products (under the New Skete Farms label), in addition to selling music and translations for church services. Gift shop.

LOCATION
Go east on Route 29 (off New York State Adirondack Northway, Interstate 87, Exit 7) then north on Route 22 (Route 684 out of New York City); at light in Cambridge, head east out of the village on East Main (Ash Grove Road, County Route 68); nuns are a half mile on left, monks and companions are about three miles to Chestnut Hill Road, right for half mile to New Skete Lane on left, then a quarter mile up the mountain dirt road.

50. Our Lady of the Resurrection Monastery
Barmore Road
La Grangeville, NY 12540
Catholic/Benedictine

DESCRIPTION
The monastery and its small Saint Scholastica Guest House inhabit a secluded rural hilltop of Duchess County in Upstate New York. Founded by Brother Victor-Antoine d'Avila-Latourette to foster a Benedictine vision of simplicity, beauty, and prayer, the monastery has a charming rustic flavor. The chapel

is built from fieldstones. An herb and flower garden supply delectable food, many recipes of which can be found in Brother Victor-Antoine's widely praised cookbooks, including *From a Monastery Kitchen* and *From a Monastery Garden.*

The goal is to provide "a space of silence, a place of quiet and repose, an atmosphere of simplicity, [and] a house of prayer where one can participate in the liturgical life of the monastery and find time to listen to the Word of God in the solitude of one's heart."

ACCOMMODATIONS AND RESERVATIONS

The monastery has six single rooms, and the guest house has four bedrooms (two with twin beds) and a kitchen for breakfast and snacks.

Reservations are taken only by mail and because the number of rooms is limited and in demand, a waiting period of six to eight weeks is typical. Please send a self-addressed, stamped envelope for a prompt reply.

Stipend for stays by donation.

POINTS OF INTEREST

Gift shop with icons, cards, cookbooks, and other books. Well-stocked library. Scenic Upstate New York attractions.

LOCATION

From the north go six miles south of the village of Millbrook to Barmore Road and turn left. Watch for the monastery entrance on the right. From the south take the Taconic Parkway North to Route 82. Continue north to Barmore Road and turn right. Watch for the monastery entrance on the right. A daily train service runs from Grand Central Station in New York City and from Albany, New York. The two stations nearest the monastery are the Poughkeepsie

Station and the Dover Plains Station, each of which will take you to within about fifteen miles of the monastery, and from which you will need to take a cab.

51. Saint Columban Center

6892 Lake Shore Road
P.O. Box 816
Derby, NY 14047
716/947-4708
Fax 716/947-5759
columban@buffnet.net
Catholic

DESCRIPTION

A Georgian mansion on fifteen acres of grassy, wooded land overlooking Lake Erie allows this "Christ-centered facility" to afford "all people an opportunity for renewing and discovering ways of living in harmony with God, self, and others." It was founded by lay Catholics and offers a wide range of programs, including private and directed retreats at designated times. A staff of clergy, nuns, and laypersons provide a welcoming atmosphere.

ACCOMMODATIONS AND RESERVATIONS

Sixty-one bedrooms. Home-cooked, buffet-style meals served in an elegant dining room. Contact the center for reservation information.

POINTS OF INTEREST

Wooded prayer path with Stations of the Cross. Bookstore and gift shop. Two chapels for prayer and adoration. A small prayer room overlooking the lake. Beaches nearby for walk-

ing and swimming, along with a spectacular view of the
Canadian shoreline and downtown Buffalo.

LOCATION
West of Interstate 90 Thruway. From Route 5 traveling from
the south, turn west (left) on Sweetland Road, then right
on Lakeshore Road. From Route 5 traveling from the north,
turn west (right) on Nettlecreek Road and left on Lakeshore
Road.

52. Saint Cuthbert's Retreat House
Route 5
118 Federal Hill Road
Brewster, NY 10509
914/278-4854
Fax 914/278-2610
Episcopal

**See listing under Community of the
Holy Spirit/Saint Hilda's House above.**

53. Saint Ignatius Retreat House
P.O. Box 756, Searingtown Road
Manhasset, NY 11030
516/621-8300
Catholic/Jesuit

DESCRIPTION
A majestic Long Island mansion on thirty-three
acres of beautiful lawns and woodlands houses the
retreat house. A former private estate, the property
was given to the New York Province of the Society
of Jesus in 1937. Now the retreat house is used three
hundred days a year for spiritual purposes.

Retreatants are invited to participate in weekend

retreats, directed retreats (the retreatant and director meet daily to discuss the retreatant's prayer experience and mutually discern the movements of the Spirit), guided retreats (a presentation each day is offered to help facilitate the retreatant's prayer; the rest of the day is free for private prayer and quiet reflection), and private retreats. Retreatants gather daily to celebrate the Eucharist.

ACCOMMODATIONS AND RESERVATIONS

All forty-five rooms except one have shared bathrooms. Most single rooms have queen beds; nine rooms have two twin beds. The rate is $45 per twenty-four hours, $150 for a weekend. Breakfast is $5, lunch $8, and dinner $14.

The dining room, library, and two main rooms have air-conditioning. The retreat house is handicapped accessible, but bathrooms are not.

POINTS OF INTEREST

The former estate of Nicholas and Genevieve Brady holds many treasures for retreatants' enjoyment. Elaborate plaster ceilings, grand carved staircases, handwrought copper doors, a retreatants' library, a solarium, the exquisite Saint Genevieve's Chapel, framed leaves from original Bibles from 1121 to 1935, a shrine of Our Lady, a sunken garden, and the outdoor Stations of the Cross make Saint Ignatius Retreat House an exceptional retreat destination.

LOCATION

Take the Long Island Expressway to Exit 36 (Searingtown Road). The house is a quarter mile north of the expressway on the west side of Searingtown Road.

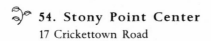

54. Stony Point Center

17 Crickettown Road

Stony Point, NY 10980
800/253-4285
914/786-5674
Fax 914/786-5919
stony_point_center@pcusa.org
Presbyterian Church (USA)

DESCRIPTION

Stony Point Conference Center occupies a thirty-acre campus in the town of Stony Point, located amid the rolling hills of the Hudson Valley. On the west side of the Hudson River, it sits midway between the Bear Mountain ridge and the Tappan Zee Bridge. New York City is thirty-five miles away. The beauty of the center grounds and the surrounding hills provides a relaxed and informal setting for discussions, personal reflection, and retreat. The center owes its existence to four women. Early in the twentieth century, they opened their home and later bequeathed it and twenty-six acres of farmland to the Presbyterian Church (USA) to give overseas missionaries a place to come on furlough for training and renewal. That program came to a close in 1972. In 1977, the Presbyterian Church reclaimed the center and opened its doors as a center for education, mission, and retreat.

Resident staff often includes political and economic refugees, scholars in residence, world church leaders, and mission workers from various denominations. Individual retreatants (called sojourners) are welcome to come for time to read and write, take a pastoral or educational study leave, enjoy creation in a serene setting, or simply be spiritually renewed. People simply en route to another destination are also welcome.

ACCOMMODATIONS AND RESERVATIONS

Comfortable, double-occupancy rooms in the lodges, Stone House and Leber Lodge, and the Victorian Gilmor Sloane House. Each room has a desk/study area. Rates for weekends (deduct 15 percent for other nights) range from $25 per night at the lodges to $55 to $90 per night at the Gilmor Sloane House. Rates include continental breakfast; other meals are extra.

POINTS OF INTEREST

Retreatants can browse books of the Readers' Service (which provides books to churches, schools, hospitals, and mission stations in eighty countries around the world). The Booktique offers for purchase books on theology, spirituality, Christian education, and other topics, as well as Third World crafts and greeting cards. Stony Point Battlefield State Historic Site is nearby, as are other Hudson River Valley historical sites and museums.

LOCATION

Thirty-five miles northwest of New York City. Extensive information on options for bus transportation and the center's own van service is available from the Conference Service Office. From the Palisades Parkway, take Exit 15. At the end of the exit, follow the arrow toward Stony Point and continue two miles on RC 106 East to the traffic light at the intersection of 9W. Turn left, go a quarter mile over the bridge to the first traffic light. Turn left at the light onto West Main Street (RC 108). Go a half mile to Crickettown Road and turn right. The center is less than a quarter mile on the left.

55. Community of Celebration

P.O. Box 309
809 Franklin Avenue
Aliquippa, PA 15001
724/375-1510
Fax 724/375-1138
mail@communityofcelebration.com
http://communityofcelebration.com
Episcopal

DESCRIPTION

Near Pittsburgh, Celebration is a religious order established in the Anglican (Episcopal) Church in England and Scotland. "Our roots," write the leaders,
"stretch back over thirty years to Houston's inner-
city Church of the Redeemer," a parish well known
in earlier years for leadership in congregation renewal. The members are quick to say that they are
different from traditional religious orders: "we don't
wear habits, for instance, and our membership includes men and women, married and single, adults
and children, clergy and laity." At the heart of the
community is worship, the source of identity, ministry, and a special brand of folk-influenced and recorded hymnody.

With a mission to "proclaim the Gospel of Jesus
Christ by living in community and offering our-
selves in service to the Church and to the world,"
Celebration has an active ministry of hospitality.
"Our self-catering guest house has served both as a
place of refreshment for our many friends and fami-

lies who visit and as a home away from home for weary travelers from around the world." Corporate prayer is offered morning, midday, and evening. Private and directed retreats are available, as are thematic retreats.

ACCOMMODATIONS AND RESERVATIONS
A fully self-contained guest house has a living room, kitchen, and two bedrooms, each with two single beds. The guest house is part of a series of three-story brick row houses that face a busy street on one side and a common yard and wooded hillside on the other. All linens are supplied. The community provides breakfast foods to prepare and hosts guests in households for lunch and dinner. The schedule includes regular directed retreats during Advent, Epiphany, and Lent. Private retreats may be made at any time. Suggested donation is $20 per night's stay.

POINTS OF INTEREST
Library, small chapel. The community is very involved in creating and leading workshops on liturgy and worship music and produces varied recordings.

LOCATION
Accessible from Pittsburgh via the Pennsylvania Turnpike, from Interstate 80, from Washington, D.C. via 270 North or from Interstate 79. Call or write for detailed directions.

56. Dominican Retreat House
750 Ashbourne Road
Elkins Park, PA 19027-2596
215/782-8520
Fax 215/782-1744
Catholic/Dominican

DESCRIPTION
Passing through the wrought-iron gates and up the picturesque drive of the Dominican Retreat House,

retreatants find an environment of tranquillity and refreshment. The forty-two acres of rolling lawns, trees, ponds, and nearly 400 rose bushes, formerly the estate of the Elkins family, have become a suburban oasis for those who need a time apart. Numerous shrines and grottoes are placed in special spots around the grounds to give retreatants places to meditate and pray. The center welcomes private retreatants as well as groups who understand and respect the mission of the Dominican Sisters. Professional chefs prepare the meals, and special dietary needs can be accommodated. As their mission statement proclaims, the Dominican Sisters look to Jesus as their model and "offer hospitality, compassion, peace and spiritual renewal to those who spend time here."

ACCOMMODATIONS AND RESERVATIONS
There are two retreat houses at the center. Some single rooms are available. Suggested contribution for a private retreat is $35 per day. Suggested contribution for group retreats overnight plus three meals is $35 per person.

POINTS OF INTEREST
A greenhouse is open weekends and sells plants and flowers. Hundreds of attractions of historical significance in nearby Philadelphia.

LOCATION
From the Pennsylvania Turnpike take the Willow Grove exit. Follow Route 611 South through Willow Grove, Abington, and Jenkintown to Elkins Park. Ashbourne Road (white picket fence at corner) is located at the fourth traffic light after crossing Church Road. Turn right on Ashbourne. Re-

treat house is at first intersection (Juniper Avenue) on the left.

From Northeast Philadelphia follow Route 73 West, Cottman Avenue, which becomes Township Line Road. Follow 73, cross Roosevelt Boulevard and proceed just over three miles to Church Road. Turn left on Church Road to Route 611 (Old York Road). Turn left on 611 South; go four traffic lights to Ashbourne Road (picket fence at the corner on your right). Turn right on Ashbourne Road. Retreat house is at first intersection on your left.

From New Jersey take the Tacony-Palmyra Bridge. From the bridge follow Route 73 West. Follow directions above under Northeast Philadelphia.

57. IHM Spiritual Renewal Center
Box 568, RR 1
Cresco, PA 18326
717/595-7548
Catholic

DESCRIPTION
The Catholic sisters who operate this center do so, according to their brochure, to provide a place "to nourish the hungers of the human heart for peace, prayer and holy leisure—for God." Located in the Pocono Mountains, the center welcomes people who seek a deeper relationship with God. Tapes and books are made available for the use of private retreatants. Retreatants may request the guidance of a director during their retreat experience to help focus, reevaluate, and reflect.

ACCOMMODATIONS AND RESERVATIONS
Air-conditioning in some rooms; private baths in some. Suggested donation for overnight stay with meals is $35. Friday

to Sunday morning, $65. Make reservations by letter or phone.

The hermitages have bath and kitchenette (stove top, toaster oven, and refrigerator). Bed linens and towels are provided. Guests bring their own food and prepare their meals. Hermitages are available. Suggested offerings: $25 per day. For reservations at the hermitages write IHM Center, Marywood, Scranton, PA 18509; 717/346-5404.

POINTS OF INTEREST
Within easy driving range of state parks, Pocono Lake, and the Pocono Mountains.

LOCATION
From Scranton and vicinity take 380E to Exit 7 (Tobyhanna). Bear right off exit onto 611. Follow 611 for about seven miles to bottom of hill at Mount Pocono. At the second light at the Mount Pocono intersection make a left onto 940E. Go about three miles. Make a left onto 390N. At the top of the hill you will see Msgr. McHugh School. IHM Center is next building.

From New York and New Jersey take 80W to Exit 45 (Tannersville). At the end of the ramp, turn right. At traffic light turn left onto 611. Go about seven miles to Mount Pocono. At first traffic light in Mount Pocono turn right onto 940E. Follow directions above.

From Pittsburgh take 22E to 80E to 380W. Go about one and a half miles to Exit 8 (Mount Pocono). At end of exit ramp, make a right onto 940E. At the second light turn right, then an immediate left (still 940E). Follow directions above.

58. Jesuit Center for Spiritual Growth
Church Road
Wernersville, PA 19565-0223
610/670-3642

The center's beautiful grounds with its tree-lined groves and reflection pools allow retreatants to spend time seeking God and "healing from the frenzy and bruises of our contemporary world." Private retreatants as well as groups are welcome to enjoy the quiet intimacy of the center and its 250 acres. Retreats with a specific focus as well as seasonal days of prayer and seasons of liturgy are some of the programs hosted by the center, for which it has become famous.

ACCOMMODATIONS AND RESERVATIONS
Air-conditioning in some rooms; common baths. Private retreat: $45 per night. Costs of scheduled program vary. Request brochure from secretary by calling 610/670-3640 or 678-8085; press #1. For inquiries as to programs and retreats, call 610/670-3642, Monday to Friday, 9:00 to 11:00 A.M. and 1:15 to 3:30 P.M. No registrations are accepted by phone. Arrange for a retreat by writing to Jesuit Center for Spiritual Growth, Business Office, Box 223, Church Road, Wernersville, PA 19565-0223.

LOCATION
Nine miles west of Reading, Pennsylvania. Directions sent upon request.

59. Laurelville Mennonite Church Center
Route 5, Box 145
Mount Pleasant, PA 15666
724/423-2056 or 800/839-1021
Info@Laurelville.org
http://www.laurelville.org
Mennonite

DESCRIPTION

Laurelville Mennonite Church Center is a two-hundred-acre camp, conference and retreat center located at the foot of the Laurel Mountains of southwestern Pennsylvania. Services and facilities are available to churches, synagogues, schools, service clubs, families, and individuals. The center offers year-round retreats and conferences designed to enable individuals and congregations to integrate faith and daily living.

ACCOMMODATIONS AND RESERVATIONS

The center has dining, sleeping, and meeting space for individuals and groups of up to three hundred people. They offer three meals daily, served family style, as well as a variety of lodging facilities, from private, deluxe accommodations to comfortable dorm-style cottages and rustic cabins, with a choice of private or shared bath facilities. In addition to this indoor lodging, eight campsites are available for tents and travel homes, with water and electric hookups, a picnic area, and bathhouses. Per-night costs range from $12 for individuals to $102 for an entire cottage, with room rates of $25 to $55 per night regardless of number of occupants.

POINTS OF INTEREST

On-site recreational facilities include hiking trails, a swimming pool, miniature golf, volleyball, basketball, tennis courts, and a new recreation building. At the base of the Laurel Highlands, the center is also a short distance from state parks, numerous hiking and bike trails, white-water rafting, and ski slopes.

LOCATION

Laurelville Mennonite Church Center is located approximately forty miles southeast of Pittsburgh, at the foot of the

Laurel Mountains, accessible from the Pennsylvania Turnpike. For directions, call or check the center's website at
http://www.laurelville.org.

 60. Pendle Hill
338 Plush Mill Road
Wallingford, PA 19086
610/566-4507, ext. 142 or 800/742-3150
Quaker

DESCRIPTION

This Quaker center for study and contemplation
was founded in 1930. Twelve miles southwest of
Philadelphia, it is set on twenty-three acres of gardens and tree-studded land with sixteen buildings.
Staff lead a wide range of study programs, classes,
sabbaticals, daily quiet worship meetings, Bible studies, and retreats. "Sojourners," the term for those
who wish to join residential community for as little
as one day or as much as several weeks, are free to
join classes and participate in other community
functions (including the community's cooperative
work). "Those sojourners who seek retreat, solitude,
and quiet," notes the brochure, "will find their
wishes honored." In summer months and between
term breaks, sojourning is by nature a quieter, more
independent experience. Two hermitages allow for a
private retreat and the retreat coordinator or another staff member can be available at predeter-
mined times of the day for guidance, provided prior
arrangements are made.

ACCOMMODATIONS AND RESERVATIONS

A variety of room arrangements are available, including dorm-style housing (some rooms with private baths) and two hermitages, one of which is available only for daytime use. Hermitage retreatants may fast, prepare light meals using very modest kitchen facilities, or purchase meals at the dining room. Typical stay for sojourners is $62.50 per day for singles; $97 for couples' fees include meals. Fees for stays for longer than one week are reduced.

POINTS OF INTEREST

Library, craft studio, walking paths. Pendle Hill Books has published books and pamphlets for decades, which the bookstore sells along with other titles. The Pendle Hill campus is near more than forty colleges, including Swarthmore College, which is accessible through a hike through the woods. Nearby Philadelphia offers museums, parks, gardens, and theaters.

LOCATION

From Interstate 476 take Exit 2 (Swarthmore/Media) onto Baltimore Pike. Take the first left turn onto Turner Road. Proceed on Turner Road to the second left turn, Plush Mill Road. Look for Pendle Hill about 200 yards on the right. By train from Philadelphia's 30th Street Station take the SEPTA Media/Elwyn Local (R-3) to the Wallingford Station. Pickup from Wallingford by someone from Pendle Hill can be arranged.

61. Saint Paul of the Cross Retreat Center

148 Monastery Avenue
Pittsburgh, PA 15203
412/381-7676
Catholic/Passionist

Perched on a hill that provides a panoramic view of the Pittsburgh skyline, Saint Paul's provides visitors a place to retire for a time to renew spiritual ties. The fourteen acres of landscaped grounds invite retreatants to stroll along the pathways, which lead to quiet spots for prayer and reflection, or to explore the unique characteristics of the chapels and buildings. There is a spacious chapel for services and private meditation on the grounds.

The center's hospitality includes offering home-cooked meals three times a day, and if dietary restrictions are to be considered, arrangements can be made. Saint Paul's is fully accessible for handicapped persons with ramps, elevator, and specially adapted showers and bedrooms to provide ease of mobility. During retreats staff members are available for private conferences if individuals so desire.

ACCOMMODATIONS AND RESERVATIONS
For information on registering for a retreat and information on accommodations, call 412/381-7676.

POINTS OF INTEREST
Tours of Pittsburgh can be arranged.

LOCATION
Five minutes from downtown Pittsburgh. Easily accessible via East Carson Street and South 18th Street/Brownsville Road in the South Hills.

62. Mount Saint Joseph Spiritual Life Center

13 Monkey Wrench Lane
Bristol, RI 02809
401/253-4630
Fax 401/253-7835
Catholic/Sisters of Saint Dorothy

DESCRIPTION

Situated on Rhode Island's Narragansett Bay, the state's main natural feature, the center offers a hospitable environment in which to ponder, discern, and respond to God's desire for peace and justice for the poor, youth, and women.

Private and directed retreats, as well as day retreats for groups, are available. A maximum of three persons at a time are scheduled in the center's calendar for spiritual direction, so prospective retreatants should call first for the retreat schedule.

ACCOMMODATIONS AND RESERVATIONS

In addition to the main house, which can accommodate day groups, there is a smaller house available for private and directed retreats. Located on the bay, it has seven private bedrooms, a kitchen, and a lounge.

Private retreats are for six days ($240) or eight days ($320). Directed retreats are available for six days ($265) or eight days ($350). Meals are included. A $50 nonrefundable deposit must be received one week in advance. Dates are nontransferable.

The center's setting is full of history and natural beauty. The first of the thirteen colonies to declare independence from Great Britain, tiny Rhode Island is dominated by Narragansett Bay, an estuary home to many different bird species.

LOCATION
From Bristol: On Route 136 South, turn right on Low Lane (opposite Roger Williams College); take a left on Monkey Wrench Lane, follow signs for Sisters of Saint Dorothy.

63. Our Lady of Peace Spiritual Life Center

P.O. Box 507
333 Ocean Road
Narragansett, RI 02882
401/783-2871
Fax 401/884-7676
Catholic

DESCRIPTION
Situated on thirty-eight acres across from the ocean, the center grounds include a pond, bridges, gardens, pathways, and meadows, all of which contribute to the peaceful atmosphere. In this setting retreatants can "encounter the Word of God anew in their personal lives and to renew their commitment to the social dimensions of discipleship." The center, started by the Roman Catholic Diocese of Providence in 1952, is open year-round, offering such experiences as hermitage days, spiritual direction, guided and personally directed retreats, and extensive training programs that develop and offer re-

newal for Christian leadership. Weekend retreats at the center explore such themes as dreams in the Christian imagination, the spirituality of Saint Ignatius, the integration of human sexuality and spirituality, and the Trinity. Worship and prayer can both be communal. Further, Our Lady of Peace allows for seminars and group retreats.

ACCOMMODATIONS AND RESERVATIONS
Fifty-two private rooms with sink; most share community bathrooms. The dining room serves buffet-style meals. Meeting rooms. Four hermitage units, each offering a sleeping area, kitchenette, and private bath.

Hermitage stay, $55 per night (monthlong stays also available). Spiritual direction, $30 per session (flexible scheduling). Weeklong guided or directed retreats are in the $300 vicinity. Nonrefundable $50 registration fee.

POINTS OF INTEREST
Stations of the Cross. Recently added Contemplative Art Center.

LOCATION
From the north take Interstate 95 to RI Exit 9 (left) to Route 4 to Route 1. Exit at Pont Judith, Scarborough (right). Cross Route 1, proceed through traffic light to South Pier Road to end at Ocean Road. Turn right onto Ocean Road. The center is a half mile on the right.

From the south take Interstate 95 to Exit 92 (Stonington/Pawcatuck) right. Take Route 2 East for one and a half miles to Route 78 and turn right. Follow to end at Route 1. Left on Route 1. Travel twenty miles to Narragansett/Point Judith/Scarborough exit and take a right at top of ramp. Cross traffic light to South Pier Road. Continue with directions as listed above.

Public transportation to Narragansett: train, Amtrak to

Kingston. Bus, Greyhound or Bonanza to University of Rhode Island, Public Transit Authority from Providence to Narragansett. Plane, TF Green State Airport (near Providence) is forty-five minutes from center. It is possible to arrange for transportation to center from airport or train station.

64. Portsmouth Abbey (of Saint Gregory the Great)

Portsmouth, RI 02871
401/683-2000
Catholic/Benedictine

DESCRIPTION

This abbey, which has accommodations for men only, is situated on five hundred acres of land on the banks of Narragansett Bay. Since its inception in 1918 the monastery has had a mission to "seek God in community, guided by the Gospel and the Rule of Saint Benedict." The monks of the abbey maintain a coeducational college preparatory boarding school. Individual retreats to the abbey are self-directed; visitors attend the daily Divine Office with the monks and are permitted to share in the monks' daily life to the extent they desire. For example, retreatants may ask to assist the monks in manual labor. Spiritual direction and the sacrament of reconciliation may also be requested of the monks. Silence is observed in the dining hall, halls, and library. After compline, the Greater Silence (no speaking at all) is practiced.

ACCOMMODATIONS AND RESERVATIONS

Casual dress is welcomed. An offering of $15 to $20 per day is suggested, according to means.

The large property allows for many walks.

Seven miles north of Newport, Rhode Island.

Vermont

65. Monastery of the Immaculate Heart of Mary

HCR 13, Box 11
4103 Vermont Route 100
Westfield, VT 05874
802/744-6525
Catholic/Benedictine

DESCRIPTION

This beautiful red-brick monastery is surrounded by splendid New England countryside. It affords a view of Jay Peak. Woods behind the monastery host wildlife: deer, moose, porcupine. It was founded in 1981 by the Abbaye Sainte-Marie des Deux-Montagnes in Canada. It belongs to the Congregation of Solesmes.

The nuns gather seven times a day (from 6 A.M. to 8 P.M.) and once at night (8:45 P.M.) to sing and pray, using Latin and Gregorian chant.

ACCOMMODATIONS AND RESERVATIONS

The monastery has a small guest house (with four rooms, one with a private bath) for women who would like to share in the monastery's life of prayer, silence, and peace. The guest mistress provides welcome on behalf of the community to guests and visitors. Prices range from $30 to $35 per night, including meals.

Attractions abound in this corner of Vermont, known as the
Northeast Kingdom.

LOCATION
From Interstate 89 or 91 take Route 100 to Westfield. Airlines
fly to Burlington (two hours away) and buses serve Newport
(thirty minutes away). Taxis or car rentals are available from
either location.

$\mathcal{W}ashington,$ $\mathcal{D}.\mathcal{C}.$

 66. Saint Anselm's Abbey
4501 South Dakota Avenue, NE
Washington, DC 20017
202/269-2300
dcabbey@erols.com
http://www.ee.cua.edu/~stanselm/Pages/retreat.htm
Catholic/Benedictine

DESCRIPTION
The monks at this red-brick abbey just inside the
northeast boundary of D.C. strive to live by the
words of Benedict in his Rule: "All guests who present themselves are to be received as Christ." They
inhabit forty acres just inside the northeast boundary of the city. Realizing the opportunities inherent
in living in what some call "Powertown," the
monks host individuals from many walks of life.
Members of religious orders, for example, who have
business in Washington frequently stay at the abbey
and are able to share prayer. The greatest number of

visitors come simply for a retreat, a day or two or three or a week, getting away from a hectic schedule and absorbing the atmosphere of quiet, worship, and reverence. Many guests do come to celebrate the various hours of the Divine Office. The chapel is always open for guests.

The monks do not offer organized retreats for groups, but a small group might come with its own leader. There is always opportunity to consult with a monk. Individual directed Ignatian retreats can be arranged with a retreat master beforehand.

A large meeting room, the Fort Augustus Room, is used frequently by many groups. A Gregorian chant group comes weekly for practice. A charismatic group sponsored by the monks also meets here every week.

ACCOMMODATIONS AND RESERVATIONS

As the monks do not have a separate guest house, they are limited in their capacity to receive women overnight, since all guests share meals in the monastic refectory and the guest rooms are within the monastery enclosure, though that may change.

A modest suggested offering per day covers room and meals.

POINTS OF INTEREST

Washington, D.C., is host to gardens, historical monuments, museums, and of course, the buildings of government and various public service organizations. Tours of the abbey are available. D.C. sites are accessible by public transportation from the abbey.

LOCATION

Public transportation allows you to take the Metro to Brookland-CUA (red line), then an R bus to 14th Street and Michigan Avenue.

67. Washington Retreat House
400 Harewood Road, NE
Washington, DC 20017-1595
202/529-1111
Fax 202/529-2102
Catholic/Franciscan

DESCRIPTION

"Rooted in the spirit of Franciscan hospitality," reads part of the mission statement. This retreat house "offers an environment of peace and prayer to all who come here for personal and spiritual renewal. . . . We are dedicated to support and encourage each other and those who come to the Retreat House to live the fullest expression of faithful love." Directed and nondirected private retreatants are welcome. A number of days and evenings of prayer and weekend retreat are offered.

The house is situated in the northeast area of D.C., with access to the Brookland-CUA Metro Station.

ACCOMMODATIONS AND RESERVATIONS

Fifty-two air-conditioned rooms and home-cooked meals served with Franciscan hospitality are provided for guests. Offerings for days and evenings of prayer: $16. Call for suggested donations for overnight stays.

POINTS OF INTEREST

Well-stocked library. One block from the Basilica of the National Shrine. Access to Washington, D.C., sites via public transportation.

LOCATION

From north and west: Take the Capitol Beltway (Interstate 495) toward Baltimore/Silver Spring. Take New Hampshire Avenue (Exit 28) south about four and a half miles to North Capitol Street and turn left. Turn left onto Clement Street at the sign for Providence Hospital. Turn left again on Harewood Road/Taylor Street. Turn right on Harewood.

From Baltimore/Washington Parkway: Turn right on New York Avenue and then right on South Dakota Avenue. After several miles turn left on Michigan Avenue to the Basilica of the National Shrine of the Immaculate Conception. Turn right on Harewood Road.

South and Southeast

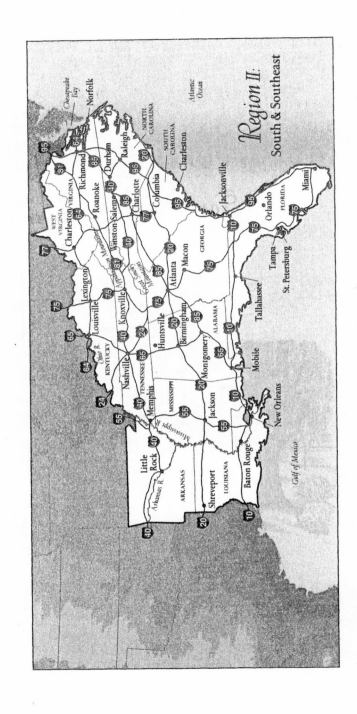

Region II:
South & Southeast

68. Benedictine Spirituality and Conference Center

Sacred Heart Monastery
P.O. Box 488
Cullman, AL 35056-0488
256/734-4622
shmon@hiwaay.net
http://fly.hiwaay.net/shmon/shm.html
Catholic/Benedictine

DESCRIPTION

Beautiful stone buildings grace the grounds that include stately trees and a lake. From the early 1900s, Sacred Heart Monastery (formerly Convent) has been a center of prayer and education, and the place from which sisters were sent to staff schools in Alabama and surrounding dioceses.

The Benedictine Spirituality and Conference Center is one of its newer ministries, responding to the needs of the church by providing space and services for a variety of retreats and diocesan programs. It also develops and implements special programs in prayer, spirituality, and human development.

The center sees much of its mission as "praying the Liturgy of the Hours, celebrating the Eucharistic liturgy in a monastic setting, and witnessing the value of community living."

Private and directed retreats are available, as well as on-site chair massage, a twenty-minute acupressure massage to help restore energy and bal-

ance, or full body massage, all designed to help the
retreatant leave behind worries and stresses during
the retreat.

ACCOMMODATIONS AND RESERVATIONS
$55 for first day, $40 each day thereafter. Add $15 per day
for direction.

POINTS OF INTEREST
Library. An impressive, seventy-five-foot neo-Gothic chapel
built of native sandstone and embellished with cast stone.

LOCATION
Sacred Heart is located in Cullman, approximately two and
a half miles east of Interstate 65 Exit 308, two blocks north of
Highway 278 East. Follow Highway 278 through Cullman; it
becomes Third Avenue. Turn left off 278 East at Convent
Road at the three-way traffic light. Go two blocks and enter
the second gate on the right.

69. Saint Bernard Conference and Hospitality Center
1600 Street Bernard Drive SE
Cullman, AL 35055-3057
205/734-3946
Fax 205/734-2925
Catholic/Benedictine

DESCRIPTION
Guests at the conference center have more than
eight hundred acres in the Mountain Lakes district
of North Alabama to enjoy. The many trails offer
the opportunity to experience quiet and peace in a
natural setting.
    Located on the grounds of Saint Bernard Abbey

(established in 1891), the conference center provides the space for individuals or groups to "come away" for prayer, meetings, seminars, retreats, sports training camps, celebrations, and reunions.

ACCOMMODATIONS AND RESERVATIONS

Fifty semiprivate rooms can sleep one hundred. Bathrooms are adjoining. Guests seeking peace, quiet, prayer, and meditation also may have accommodations in Saint Bernard Abbey.

There are complete meal and banquet facilities at the center. The stay for private retreatants is limited to three days and three nights. There is no fee for these private retreats, although donations are gratefully accepted.

Groups have two meeting rooms in the main building and additional rooms in the new athletic center and gymnasium.

POINTS OF INTEREST

The Ave Maria Grotto is on the campus of Saint Bernard Abbey. The grotto, a setting of 125 miniature buildings and shrines handcrafted by Benedictine monk Brother Joseph Zoettl over a period of fifty years, encompasses an area of more than three acres. The miniatures include detailed groupings of Jerusalem and Roman buildings, as well as Lourdes Basilica and the Hanging Gardens of Babylon.

The conference center has tennis courts, volleyball, baseball fields, and an air-conditioned basketball court.

LOCATION

Cullman is located near many of the Southeastern United States major metropolitan areas, including Birmingham, Huntsville, Nashville, and Atlanta. Traveling on Interstate 65 between Huntsville and Birmingham, take Exit 308-Cullman. Go east on Highway 278 for three and a third miles, following the signs to the Ave Maria Grotto.

70. Visitation Monastery
2300 Spring Hill Avenue
Mobile, AL 36607
344/474-2321
Catholic/Visitation Nuns

DESCRIPTION

This monastery and its grounds date to 1832, when five Benedictine sisters came to open a school at the request of the local bishop. The monastery's century-old buildings on seventeen acres exude a stately charm. An eight-foot-high wall surrounds a smaller compound of two acres with well-kept trees and lawn. The sisters offer a "desert experience" of from two to eight days of silence and solitude for women. Men and married couples are also welcome for retreats. The nuns are cloistered.

ACCOMMODATIONS AND RESERVATIONS

While the monastery dates back to 1832 and is one of the historic monuments of Old Mobile, the retreat house has been modernized with air-conditioned rooms and a restaurant-equipped kitchen that serves delicious meals. Fees by donation.

POINTS OF INTEREST

Chapel. Elegant Southern mansions in the area.

LOCATION

Take Springhill Avenue off Beltline Highway (Interstate 65) or Broad Street.

71. Coury House Retreat Center

Subiaco Abbey
340 North Subiaco Avenue
Subiaco, AR 72865
501/934-4411
Fax 501/934-4040
Catholic/Benedictine

DESCRIPTION

Coury House lies in the picturesque Arkansas River Valley, fifty miles east of Fort Smith. The retreat center, note the staff, "assists the church in its pastoral care by working together with all people to bring the love of God and the peace of Christ by personal concern and awareness." The grounds provide ample walking and hiking opportunities. Days and evenings of recollection offer opportunity to have conferences with a director, partake of the Eucharist (for Catholics), and receive the sacrament of reconciliation.

ACCOMMODATIONS AND RESERVATIONS

All rooms have private bathrooms. Payment by fee or donation. All linens supplied.

POINTS OF INTEREST

Chapel, library, coffee bar, tennis courts, basketball courts, all-weather track. Directed tours of the striking abbey church and grounds available.

Fifty miles east of Fort Smith on Highway 22, twenty miles south of Clarksville. From Interstate 40 take Exit 55 at Clarksville and follow the signs.

72. Hesychia House of Prayer
204 Saint Scholastica Road
New Blaine, AR 72851
501/938-7375
Catholic/Benedictine

DESCRIPTION
Located in a rural area amid cattle pastures and mountain ranges of exquisite beauty, the setting for this house facilitates communion with God, say the Catholic sisters who host the center, and this in turn relates to its purpose and name. *Hesychia* is a Greek word meaning "resting in God." The community has ties to Saint Scholastica Monastery in Fort Smith, Arkansas.

Retreatants may participate in the prayers of the small community of nuns (Eucharist most mornings and sung morning and evening prayers). Retreatants may have a Scripture-based retreat with guidance from the sisters or simply choose to stay alone.

ACCOMMODATIONS AND RESERVATIONS
Four air-conditioned hermitages provide accommodations for a day, several days, or even longer. Hermitages have limited cooking and refrigerator capabilities. Retreatants prepare their own morning and noon meals and are welcome to join the community of sisters for the evening meal or maintain solitude.

No set fee is required, but guests are asked to donate a stipend according to their means. Phone reservations preferred.

LOCATION
Between Midway and New Blaine off State Highway 22. Turn on gravel road at sign for House of Prayer (Old Military Road).

73. Little Portion Retreat and Training Center
171 Hummingbird Lane
Eureka Springs, AR 72632
501/253-7379 or 501/253-7710
Fax 501/253-2640
bscharity@aol.com
http://john-michael-talbot.org/retreats/rtrtcntr.htm
Brothers and Sisters of Charity

DESCRIPTION
In the late sixties and early seventies, John Michael Talbot helped lead the buckskin-shod band, Mason Proffit, in creating issues-oriented country-rock and folk-rock music for large and enthusiastic audiences. A conversion to Christianity changed his goals and musical direction, and soon Talbot became the internationally acclaimed pioneer of a mellow form of folk- and classical-influenced music.

Talbot also became a Catholic and a follower of Francis of Assisi. He eventually formed an international Catholic-based ecumenical community called the Brothers and Sisters of Charity. The Franciscan-influenced community resides at Little Portion Hermitage in the wooded Ozark Mountains of rural

Arkansas, not far from the retreat and training center. Its members follow a "Gospel-centered" way of life either in homes or in an integrated monastic community of families, celibates, and singles. Nearly all of John's music and books have been written at the secluded hermitage. The growing community lives simply and self-sufficiently.

The retreat and training center sits atop an Ozark Mountain with an expansive view and a caring staff that works to cultivate a feeling of "relaxed, family relationship in Christ's peace." In addition to private retreats, the center hosts group silent, contemplative, charismatic, and prayer and Scripture retreats. In addition to the Retreat and Training Center, the monastic motherhouse of the whole community, the Little Portion Hermitage, is located several miles away and is open to day visits.

ACCOMMODATIONS AND RESERVATIONS
Fifteen spacious bedrooms include twin beds and simple furnishings along with either a private or attached bathroom. A regular, home-size kitchen is available for private retreatants and small groups.

POINTS OF INTEREST
Chapel has one wall of mostly glass, giving a mountaintop view of Ozark sunrises.

LOCATION
East of Eureka Springs off Onyx Cave Road on More Mountain.

74. Saint Scholastica Center

1205 S. Albert Pike
P.O. Box 3489
Fort Smith, AR 72913
501/783-1135
scholast@ipa.net
Catholic/Benedictine

DESCRIPTION

The retreat center shares a sixty-seven-acre wooded site with Saint Scholastica Monastery, whose sisters sponsor and assist with the center's retreat programs. "We strive to nourish the whole person," the brochure states, assisting in guests' growth "by providing a sense of order and harmony and by sharing our resources, ourselves, and our way of life." A further goal is to help people "grow in the knowledge of the Good News that we have been redeemed and forgiven through Christ out of God's immeasurable generosity."

Sister Macrina Wiederkehr, known for popular spiritual-life books such as *Seasons of Your Heart* and *A Tree Full of Angels,* lives in the monastery and frequently leads group retreats on topics such as "The Gift of Surrender: A Lenten Retreat" and "The Poet Within: Contemplative Seeing."

ACCOMMODATIONS AND RESERVATIONS

The residence hall has accommodations for seventy-two in private and semiprivate rooms. Each floor has a kitchenette and lounge area. Meals are served cafeteria style. Rooms are air-conditioned; some have private baths.

Retreats and spiritual direction are offered year-round,

including group retreats, private retreats (with spiritual direction available on request), directed retreats, and quiet days. Four hermitages are available.

POINTS OF INTEREST
The sisters operate a bakery and gift shop.

LOCATION
Two miles east of downtown Fort Smith, north of Rogers Avenue on Albert Pike.

Florida

 75. Benedictine Sisters of Florida
Holy Name Monastery
33201 State Road 52
P.O. Box 2450
Saint Leo, FL 33574-2450
352/588-8320
mgelis@saintleo.edu
http://monet.saintleo.edu/holyname/retreats/retreats.html
Catholic/Benedictine

DESCRIPTION
Located on Lake Jovita amid hill country and orange groves, the extensive grounds provide opportunities to pray, exercise, and enjoy solitude. The sisters offer group and individual retreats and several are trained in spiritual direction. Mass is celebrated daily in the chapel and retreatants are welcome to share other times of prayers and meals with the sisters. Located adjacent to Saint Leo College.

ACCOMMODATIONS AND RESERVATIONS

Guest rooms are available for private and group retreats. Private rooms have common baths. There is an elevator and rooms are air-conditioned.

POINTS OF INTEREST

Nearby are Saint Leo College and Saint Leo Abbey.

LOCATION

Thirty-five miles northeast of Tampa off Interstate 75 on State Road 52, six miles west of Dade City.

76. The Cenacle

Spiritual Life Center
1400 South Dixie Highway
Lantana, FL 33462
561/582-2434
Fax 561/582-8070
cenacle2@ix.netcom.com

DESCRIPTION

The center is designed to be "an oasis" where people can "come away to reflect, ponder, be challenged, and seek a vision for their lives and a greater awareness of God." A directed retreat has retreatants meeting daily with one of the Cenacle sisters who help with discernment and guidance. The suggested stay is three to eight nights. Provisions also allow for a private retreat. A "Hosting the Soul" sabbatical leads participants on a twelve-week program for people in ministry and/or in transition.

ACCOMMODATIONS AND RESERVATIONS

Directed retreats include private room, meals, access to the center's resources, and a daily meeting with one of the

sisters at $55 per night. Private retreats provide private room
and meals at $45 per night. All bathrooms shared. Bed lin-
ens provided but not towels.

POINTS OF INTEREST
Bookstore. Massage. Wednesdays: Taize evensong (prayer
service of song and silence patterned after that of the Taize
Monastery in France).

LOCATION
Via Interstate 95 at Hypoluxo Road east to US 1 (Dixie
Highway). Turn left (north) at US 1.

 77. Dominican Retreat House
7275 Southwest 124th Street
Miami, FL 33156
305/238-2711
Fax 305/238-2717
Catholic/Dominican

DESCRIPTION
A quiet, residential area in a suburb of Miami hosts
this ten-acre property with air-conditioned facilities.
The mission is to "conduct religious retreats, to afford religious instruction, to foster and develop the
spiritual, cultural, moral, and social well-being of all
and to promote the recognition of the dignity of the
individual and the safekeeping of his or her spiritual
beliefs."

Two thousand people annually participate in a
variety of retreats, including weekend programs for
women, weekends for men, retreats on twelve steps,
the Bible, centering prayer, as well as programs for
married couples, Spanish-speaking people, and pro-

grams during Lent and Advent. Also offered: days of reflection.

Directed retreats are scheduled on an individual basis and can vary in length from one day to eight, depending on director and facility availability, as are private retreats.

ACCOMMODATIONS AND RESERVATIONS
Suggested donation for a directed retreat is $55 per day.

LOCATION
Kendall, a suburb of Miami.

78. Franciscan Center
3010 Perry Avenue
Tampa, FL 33603
813/229-2695
813/228-0748
Francntr@aol.com
Catholic/Order of Saint Francis

DESCRIPTION
Located on the Hillsborough River on eight acres of land characterized by natural beauty and waterfront vegetation. The sisters offer a wide array of group retreat and workshop offerings on topics such as "workplace spirituality" and "spirituality and gardening," even a "day for secretaries"—a "daylong coffee break" with spiritual presentations and time for renewing quiet and reflection.

ACCOMMODATIONS AND RESERVATIONS
Thirty-eight bedrooms with air-conditioning and private showers. Private retreat rate is $40 per day ($50 per day with spiritual direction). Eight days: $350.

Book Nook gift and book store, chapel.

LOCATION
Accessible from Orlando from Interstate 4 to Interstate 275; from Sarasota, Ocala, and Saint Petersburg via Interstate 275.

79. Mother of God House of Prayer
17880 Cypress Creek Road
Alva, FL 33920
941/728-3614
Fax 941/728-3760
moghop@horizon.net
http://www.moghop.com

DESCRIPTION
Fifteen miles east of Fort Meyers, this house of prayer nestles in the old tropical woodlands of Alva, a tiny city on the Caloosa River.

Spiritual direction and morning and evening prayers make up part of the community's retreat hospitality. Morning Eucharist is available at nearby Saint Vincent de Paul Catholic Church.

Here is what the house describes a retreat may look like: "Retreatants may choose to walk the grounds, bike to the river, or stroll nearby country roads. They may swim in the screened-in pool, spend time in their rooms, the Eucharistic chapel, or the library. Many retreatants spend hours at the three-tiered deck overlooking Cypress Creek, which meanders along the easterly border of the property. The new butterfly garden, too, is a multiple delight for the senses. Wooded Stations of the Cross also provide powerful times of reflection."

Saturdays of recollection are offered monthly, which include presentations, personal reflection time on the grounds and in the chapel, and group response.

ACCOMMODATIONS AND RESERVATIONS

There are four air-conditioned bedrooms; guests share two full baths. All linens provided. Daily suggested donation for Saturdays of recollection or a private day of prayer: $20. Overnight: $70 per day (includes meals and daily session with a spiritual director).

POINTS OF INTEREST

Wooded Stations of the Cross area.

LOCATION

From the north, take Interstate 75 to Exit 26 east (Route 78). After about three miles, Route 78 ends at Route 31; turn left. In a little more than one mile, turn right onto Route 78 again (North River Road). Proceed eight miles to Cypress Creek Road on the right and turn right. Watch for second driveway on the left. From the south, take Interstate 75 to Exit 25 east (Route 80). Travel about twelve miles to a flashing yellow light and Alva sign; turn left on Broadway. Cross the Caloosahatchee River. The road comes to a "T" at Alva Elementary School. Turn left (onto North River Road/ Route 78). Go one and a half miles to Cypress Creek Road on the left.

80. San Pedro Center

2400 Dike Road
Winter Park, FL 32792
407/671-6322
Fax 407/671-3992
Catholic/Franciscan

DESCRIPTION

Peacefully tucked away on lovely Lake Howell, the grounds of San Pedro Center are an Audubon-listed bird and wildlife sanctuary and a haven for majestic trees. Boardwalks winding through the forests create the perfect setting for relaxing and reflecting.

The Franciscan friars who live on the site intend to provide warm hospitality in a community environment to all who come. The center hosts retreats, Engaged Encounter, Marriage Encounter, Cursillo, and other workshops, along with individual retreats.

ACCOMMODATIONS AND RESERVATIONS

The center has pleasant, motel-style overnight accommodations and dining facilities. One building provides a comfortable setting for a group of eighty. Equipped with its own kitchenette and a piano, it can be divided into two rooms and has glass doors that open onto its woodland surroundings. Another building has a cozy fireplace, efficiency kitchen and a stunning view of the forest setting. There is also a more rustic area called Campside.

POINTS OF INTEREST

San Pedro Center's chapel is a stunning structure, with a high, wood-beamed ceiling and huge windows.

LOCATION

Just outside Orlando. From Interstate 4 go three miles south on SR 436 (Semoran Boulevard) to Howell Branch Road. Turn east and go one and a half miles to Dike Road. Turn north, go seven tenths of a mile. San Pedro Center is on the left.

81. Monastery of the Holy Spirit

2625 Highway 212 SW
Conyers, GA 30094-4044
770/760-0959
http://www.ga.monks.org
Catholic/Trappist

DESCRIPTION

Stately magnolias line the entranceway to the monastery. On an old cotton farm formerly called Honey Creek Plantation in northwest Georgia, the monastery offers its guests isolation and austere beauty. Situated about thirty miles from downtown Atlanta, the monastery is the first native-born Trappist foundation in the United States. The monks of the abbey have landscaped their grounds with ponds, hardwoods, cactus, and succulents. A creek and natural spring provide delicious drinking water. The abbey has become a natural preserve, with its 1,800 acres populated by deer, birds, and animals of many species.

Individuals and small groups of different religious backgrounds are welcome at the abbey. A retreat director is available for those wishing assistance.

ACCOMMODATIONS AND RESERVATIONS

The monastery invites retreatants to come and experience a few days of restful recollection and spiritual renewal in a prayerful and peaceful environment. Retreats are normally scheduled between Monday after 1:00 P.M. through Thursday at 1:00 P.M.; or Friday after 1:00 P.M. through Sunday at 1:00 P.M. Retreatants stay at the fifty-room guest house and follow a daily schedule for meals and times of prayer, to which they are invited. Guests are asked to schedule their arrival after 1:00 P.M. but before 9:00 P.M., since the monastery gate is locked at that time.

The nonrefundable registration fee is $15. Although there is no established retreat fee, a donation of $40 a day would help cover operating expenses.

POINTS OF INTEREST
Beautifully landscaped grounds with a handsome, centrally located abbey church and a greenhouse. The Abbey Store offers excellent books and unique religious articles as well as special sales. An unusual feature is the monastery's bonsai business, which offers bonsai trees, pottery, and tools.

LOCATION
Thirty miles from downtown Atlanta. From Atlanta, take Interstate 20 East to Exit 36. Turn right onto Wesley Chapel Road. Go to the first traffic light and turn left onto Snapfinger Road. Go two and a half miles and turn left onto Highway 212 (Browns Mill Road). Proceed about ten and a fifth miles. The monastery is set back on the left-hand side (watch for a brown wood sign on the right, just before the entrance).

 82. Saint Ignatius House
Jesuit Retreat Center
6700 Riverside Drive NW
Atlanta, GA 30328-2710
404/255-0503
Fax 404/256-0776
Catholic/Jesuit

DESCRIPTION

Set on a pristine, tree-lined stretch of the Chatta-hoochee River, this center offers weekend retreats for those seeking spiritual guidance in a tranquil atmosphere. "We welcome people of all denomina-tions," the brochure notes, "anyone who needs a break from daily pressures to rest and focus on one's relationship with God." Each day, a series of half-hour presentations by the retreat master provide the retreatant with material for reflection and prayer. Eucharist is celebrated each evening and Sunday morning, with communal prayers offered morning and evening.

ACCOMMODATIONS AND RESERVATIONS

Retreats begin on Thursday or Friday evening and end after lunch on Sundays. Except for opening and closing meals, silence is observed during the retreat. Private rooms and baths provided, along with linens, towels, and soap.

There is no set fee, though donations are expected, and a deposit when registering is appreciated. Suggested dona-tion (given or pledged) is $150.

POINTS OF INTEREST

Nearby Atlanta offers many big-city attractions.

LOCATION

From Interstate 285, take Exit 16 for Riverside Drive. From the west turn left, from the east turn right. The center is two miles north.

83. Abbey of Gethsemani Retreat House
Trappist, KY 40051
502/549-4129
Catholic/Cistercian (Trappist)

DESCRIPTION

The gently rolling hills and woodlands of Kentucky provide the graceful setting for this abbey's impressive grounds and buildings. "There is a wonderful peace in this place," one retreat goer explains of her attraction to Gethsemani. "The silence took some getting used to at first, but now it seems wonderfully rich and refreshing."

In the words of Gethsemani's most famous resident, Thomas Merton, this monastic setting offers a place apart "to entertain silence in the heart and listen to the voice of God—to pray for your own discovery." The Trappist Abbey of Gethsemani has opened its doors to receive guests since its founding in 1848. Trappists (a reform order of Benedictines) cherish silence, so a retreat here will be short on words and noise. "Silence fosters and preserves the climate of prayer," the abbey's brochure notes, "and is thus a fundamental part of the Gethsemani experience. Retreatants are asked to limit talking to the period after meals and the designated areas." The emphasis on silence is aided by the extensive spaces for reflection and prayer on the abbey's many acres of woodlands and fields.

Guests may join the monks at the serving of the

Eucharist (the Christian commemoration of Jesus' death through the use of bread and wine) and during the services of prayer (at seven designated times of day and night). Upon request, a monk is available for consultation. The sacrament of reconciliation is available regularly. For those interested, the retreat master conducts conferences on various topics.

ACCOMMODATIONS AND RESERVATIONS

Each guest room is private, with its own shower, and accommodations for the disabled are provided. Time frames for retreats are midweek (Monday afternoon to Friday afternoon) and weekend (Friday afternoon to Sunday afternoon). The first and third full weeks (Monday through Monday) of each month are set aside for women. The remainder of the month is for men. Many rooms are air-conditioned and have private baths. Reservations may be made by mail or phone, 502/549-4133. Payment is by voluntary donation.

POINTS OF INTEREST

The library has an ample selection of classic and contemporary religious books, periodicals, and tapes for use during retreat. Some two thousand acres of wooded grounds and farmland provide hiking trails. Nearby Bardstown, Kentucky, has a bookstore stocked with many Thomas Merton titles. Bardstown is the historic home of American composer Stephen Foster.

LOCATION

The abbey is southwest of Lexington and south of Bardstown, Kentucky. Take the Blue Grass Parkway to Exit 21. Make a right (south) onto Route 31 E. Go seven and a half miles to Culvertown and go one quarter mile farther to Route 247 and turn left. Go three and a half miles to monastery.

84. Knobs Haven
515 Nerinx Road
Nerinx, KY 40049-9999
502/865-2621
Catholic/Sisters of Loretto

DESCRIPTION

Spacious grounds in the heart of Kentucky's "knob country," about fifteen miles south of Bardstown, provide a quiet setting for retreat and renewal. Knobs Haven rests on the land of Loretto Motherhouse, one of the oldest religious communities of women in the United States.

Guests share the simple lifestyle of the community. Meals are shared in a dining room.

ACCOMMODATIONS AND RESERVATIONS

Private and double sleeping rooms, shared bath facilities. Requested donation is $25 per day for the first day and $20 on subsequent days. Further contributions are gratefully accepted.

POINTS OF INTEREST

The grounds include a farm with an organic vegetable garden, wooded areas, a lake, a fitness trail, and an art gallery.

LOCATION

Traveling from Lexington southeast on the Blue Grass Parkway take US Highway 150 to Springfield. Pick up State Highway 152 to Nerinx. Or take State Highway 49 South from Bardstown and turn left (east) on State Highway 152.

 85. Marydale Retreat Center
945 Donaldson Highway, Erlanger
Covington, KY 41018-1093

800/995-4863 or 606/371-4224
Catholic

DESCRIPTION

Situated above a large scenic lake and surrounded by acres of well-kept grounds, walkways, and trees, Marydale offers retreats for individuals and groups.

Private retreatants are welcome on a space-available basis. Retreats include time for reading and private and communal prayer, conferences by an experienced retreat director, an opportunity for private counseling and spiritual direction, and celebration of the Eucharist.

ACCOMMODATIONS AND RESERVATIONS

The main retreat house has private air-conditioned rooms. Fifteen rooms have double beds, and two rooms have two twin beds: These seventeen rooms have private baths. There are two central bathrooms and two central shower rooms. All rooms have their own wash stands. An absence of radios, televisions, and telephones in guest rooms minimizes distractions. Delicious meals are served family style. Retreatants are asked to submit a $10 registration fee in advance.

POINTS OF INTEREST

The main retreat house has a spacious and comfortable lounge with a full-length window that gives a picturesque view of many acres of lawn, trees, hills, fields, and a lake. The main chapel is convenient and inspirational. The beautiful sanctuary is joined to the multipurpose room by folding doors.

LOCATION

Marydale is located four miles from the Greater Cincinnati International Airport. It is nine miles south of Cincinnati, a

half mile from Interstates 75 and 71, and close to the Interstate 275 Circle Expressway. (Take Exit 184 off Interstate 75
and Interstate 71, and then onto Kentucky Route 236 West.)

 ## 86. Mount Saint Joseph Center

8001 Cummings Road
Maple Mount, KY 42356-9999
502/229-4103
Fax 502/229-4127
msjcenter@mindspring.com
http://www.owensborodio.org/msjcenter
Catholic/Ursiline Sisters

DESCRIPTION

A rural setting of trees and grassy knolls and
lakefront picnic areas provides the setting for this
center with roots in the late nineteenth century.
The large brick building was once an academy
school for girls run by Ursiline Sisters, a Catholic
order known for an emphasis on educational ministry. Now, says Sister Amelia Stenger, director of the
newly renovated retreat and conference center, the
education takes a different turn. It has become "a
place to rest and reflect," she says. "We still provide
people with an education, an education of mind,
body, and spirit." A wide range of programs and
retreats are now offered, including individual private
and directed retreats.

ACCOMMODATIONS AND RESERVATIONS

Air-conditioned bedrooms with twin or double beds with
private bathrooms. Home-cooked, buffet-style meals. Private
chapel. Private prayer house, available for a solitude experience or for a directed retreat.

Bookstore and gift shop. Heated indoor swimming pool.

LOCATION

Fifteen minutes west of Owensboro, Kentucky, in the northwest part of the state near the Ohio River. Mount Saint Joseph Center is accessible from Pennyrile Parkway, Interstates 431 or 231 via Kentucky Road 56.

Louisiana

87. Ave Maria Retreat House

HC 62 Box 368AB
Marrero, LA 70072
504/689-3838
Fax 504/689-2785
Catholic/Missionary Oblates of Mary Immaculate

DESCRIPTION

Twenty beautiful acres along the Barataria Intercoastal Canal planted with shrubs and many old trees surround the Ave Maria Retreat House. The wooded expanses include a gazebo for visiting or study, a grotto for prayer and meditation, and the Stations of the Cross nestled among hundreds of pine trees.

Ave Maria makes itself available for directed, private and group retreats, student days, monthly days of prayer, spiritual direction, spiritual conferences, and workshops. The large variety of retreats offered includes women's and men's retreats, Engaged Encounter, Marriage Encounter, Retrouvaille Weekends, drug-free programs, and AA retreats.

ACCOMMODATIONS AND RESERVATIONS

Fifty rooms provide private or semiprivate quarters. The rooms have bathrooms, and most rooms have twin beds. The dining room provides delicious meals. Prices vary. For current rates call the center.

POINTS OF INTEREST

The contemporary chapel, which is the scene of sacred liturgies and private prayer, can accommodate 120 persons. New Orleans attractions lie thirty minutes north.

LOCATION

From Greater New Orleans Bridge continue on West Bank Expressway over Harvey Canal. Turn left on Barataria Boulevard and turn left on LA 3134. Cross LA 45, go under bridge, and pass Saint Pius X Church. The next entrance is Ave Maria.

 88. Jesuit Spirituality Center

P.O. Drawer C
Saint Charles College
Grand Coteau, LA 70541-1003
318/662-5251 or 318/662-5252
Fax 318/662-3187
jespirtcen@aol.com
Catholic/Jesuit

DESCRIPTION

"A quiet and restful environment," is how the staff describe this center. Group retreats here cover a range of topics. A personally guided retreat with spiritual direction typically lasts three, five, eight, or thirty days, following the *Spiritual Exercises* of Ignatius of Loyola, the Spanish founder of the Jesuit order. Group retreats center on topics such as "Praying with the Poet," "Advent Day of Prayer," and "Judges and Lawyers Retreat."

ACCOMMODATIONS AND RESERVATIONS
Rates vary; a three-day (directed) retreat runs $135. A registration form with deposit is required for confirmation. A retreatant who cannot afford a retreat may apply to the director for a waiver, reduction, or extension of time of payment. Retreatants are asked to bring a Bible, notebook, alarm clock, and comfortable walking shoes.

POINTS OF INTEREST
The center shares the campus of Saint Charles College. There is walking, hiking, and swimming in warm weather. A historic district in Grand Coteau preserves the past. Grand Coteau also features two of the nation's oldest religious institutions and opportunities to experience Cajun cuisine and culture.

LOCATION
From Interstate 10 take the exit for Interstate 49 in Lafayette, exit north to the exit for Grand Coteau. Proceed east and turn left to the junction with Highway 93.

89. Lumen Christi Retreat Center
100 Lumen Christi Lane, Highway 311
Schriever, LA 70395-9352
504/868-1523
Catholic/Franciscan

DESCRIPTION
The name for this center comes from a Latin phrase, "The Light of Christ." A lakefront woodland setting of fifty acres surrounds this relatively new brick building. Classes and group retreats take place

throughout the year and private and directed retreats are available. Also provided are days of prayer and ongoing spiritual direction and counseling.

Mass is offered daily and a healing Mass every Monday at noon.

ACCOMMODATIONS AND RESERVATIONS
Air-conditioned rooms, some with private baths. Linens provided. Call for rates.

POINTS OF INTEREST
Bayous, lakes, and salt marshes nearby provide opportunities for outdoor recreation, including hunting, fishing, boating, and camping. Several annual festivals, historic sites, museums, and nature tours display the area's cultural heritage, including French, Cajun, and Spanish influences.

LOCATION
Southeast Louisiana on the Intracoastal Waterway and near the Gulf Coast. From New Orleans take Highway 90 to Highway 3052 to Morgan City. Exit right on Highway 311, toward Houma. Lumen Christi is about two and a half miles toward Houma, past the diocesan chancery office (three flag poles).

Mississippi

 90. The Dwelling Place
HC-01 Box 126
2824 Dwelling Place Road
Brooksville, MS 39739-9537
601/738-5348
Fax 601/738-5345
dwellpl@tilc.com

http://www.dwellingplace.com
Catholic/Franciscan

DESCRIPTION

Located on a seventeen-acre tract of rural, pine-covered land, The Dwelling Place welcomes retreat-ants from various religious, racial, and economic backgrounds. While the center emphasizes the her-mitage experience, it also offers individual retreats (private or directed) and group retreats designed to address specific issues. The staff invites retreatants to join in daily community worship and intercession. Since 1987, as the brochure notes, the house has sought to serve as "a place of hospitality and prayer for all who seek peace, joy and healing through God's loving presence."

ACCOMMODATIONS AND RESERVATIONS

Weekend retreats begin on Friday evening and end Sunday after lunch. The fee is $90, plus a $25 registration deposit required one week in advance. $42 per weekday for hermit-age stays (the center offers three cottages), directed retreats, and private retreats. Call for information on group fees.

Rooms are air-conditioned and have private baths. The Dwelling Place provides meals for its hermitage retreatants.

POINTS OF INTEREST

The physical plant contains the three hermitages, Our Lady of Portiuncula Chapel, and a library.

LOCATION

Two miles north of Brooksville. One mile north of the flashing red light on Highway 45, turn east at The Dwelling Place sign at the three-way intersection. Go precisely three miles. Look for the pine-lined lane and the silver mailbox on the left.

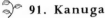 North Carolina

 91. Kanuga
Postal Drawer 250
Hendersonville, NC 28793
828/692-9136
Fax 828/696-3589
kanuga@ecunet.org
http://www.kanuga.org
Episcopal

DESCRIPTION
Situated within a peaceful valley and overlooking a large lake, Kanuga consists of 1,400 acres of pine-studded North Carolina mountains. The center enjoys a moderate climate with four beautiful seasons. The staff describe Kanuga as "a place for quick laughs among friends [and] a place where deep thoughts come easily." Founded in 1928, Kanuga's purpose, according to a brochure, is to "provide for God's people in this broken world a glimpse of the Kingdom." Although the center is mostly used for group retreats and large religious conferences, it also offers to private retreatants guest periods, which are generally taken during eight summer weeks, October, Thanksgiving, and Christmas. Guest periods allow visitors to come on individual retreat for anywhere from a few days to a month. Each guest period features a different chaplain, and offers Bible

studies, evening programs, arts and crafts, and opportunities for quiet reflection.

ACCOMMODATIONS AND RESERVATIONS

Some forty or more cottages available. Six large, well-equipped guest houses, each with a capacity for eight. Kanuga Lake Inn has sixty-two motel-style rooms with two beds. Family-style meals, buffet-style breakfasts. Linens provided. Private baths. Meeting rooms, reading rooms, fireplace lounge.

For guest periods, a deposit is required. Inn rates: single occupancy, $74–$84 per person per night, $510–$580 per person per week; double occupancy, $42–$44 daily, $285–$295 weekly. Two-bedroom cottage or guest house, $61 per person per night, $420 per week. Three bedrooms, $71 per night, $490 weekly. Does not include charge for meals, programs, or facilities. Some need-based scholarships offered. Call for further price information.

POINTS OF INTEREST

A Mountain Trail Outdoor School is offered. Four chapels, two of which are outdoors, for groups or individuals. The grounds have a gymnasium, four tennis courts, a climbing tower, canteen, bookstore, and library. Bird-watching, swimming, some boating, fishing, hiking trails are also available. Golf courses, historic attractions and the Blue Ridge Parkway are located nearby.

LOCATION

Reachable from Asheville, North Carolina, and Greenville-Spartanburg, South Carolina, airports. Accessible from Interstates 26, 40, and 85. From Interstate 26, Exit 18-B on US 64 West into Hendersonville. Left on US 25 South (Church Street); drive nine blocks. Right on Kanuga Street, four miles to Kanuga triangular sign. Turn right and proceed one and a half miles to Kanuga Entrance Park.

**92. Living Waters Catholic Reflection
Center**
103 Living Waters Lane
Maggie Valley, NC 28751
828/926-3833
Fax 828/926-1997
Catholic/Augustinian

DESCRIPTION

Four miles from the Blue Ridge Parkway, nestled amid the blue-green Smoky Mountains in North Carolina's far western tip, this retreat center accents group retreats on spiritual themes but also schedules guided and directed retreats. Because retreatants like to take advantage of exploring the beauty of the surrounding Smoky Mountains and the nearby Cherokee Indian Reservation, arrangements can be made to come a day early or stay a day beyond scheduled retreats. No meals are available for such days, but a do-it-yourself breakfast is offered.

Also available: sabbaticals, where a guest designs the program, takes advantage of material provided by the center, and attends the scheduled group retreats as desired. Craft lessons in carving, finger weaving, and pottery can be arranged with local Cherokee artisans for sabbatical guests.

ACCOMMODATIONS AND RESERVATIONS

Suggested donations for guided retreats in spring range from $100 to $200. Donations for directed retreats (May or August) range from $200 to $300.

POINTS OF INTEREST

Local Cherokee Indian Reservation with local Native American artisans. Hiking in the surrounding Great Smoky Mountains.

LOCATION

By car follow US 19 into Maggie Valley approximately forty miles west of Asheville; the center is next to Ghost Town. By bus take the Greyhound/Trailways buses to Waynesville. By plane use the Asheville Airport.

93. Stillpoint Ministries, Inc.

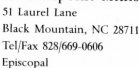

51 Laurel Lane
Black Mountain, NC 28711
Tel/Fax 828/669-0606
Episcopal

DESCRIPTION

Scenic western North Carolina forms the setting for this homestyle retreat center. While some retreats are offered at Stillpoint itself, the ministry holds many of its offerings at other facilities. Stillpoint features a twenty-one-month retreat leaders training program. In addition, various programs are offered covering such subjects as forgiving, yearning hearts, Benedictine experience, parenting, and the spirituality of Teresa of Ávila. The Eucharist is offered.

ACCOMMODATIONS AND RESERVATIONS

Stillpoint has two guest rooms (with shared bath) for those wishing to make personal retreats. Guests prepare their own breakfast and lunch; dinner is provided. A nonrefundable $15 deposit is required for all registrations. Nondirected retreat, $40 per day (includes meals). Directed retreat, $65 per day. Some scholarship assistance is available. Prices for work-shops vary.

POINTS OF INTEREST
A spiritual direction group meets on occasion. Black Mountain is a rustic town with antique shops. Historic Asheville is nearby.

LOCATION
A dozen miles east of Asheville via US 70 or Interstate 40. Call for further directions and a map.

South Carolina

 94. Mepkin Abbey
1098 Mepkin Abbey Road
Moncks Corner, SC 29461-4796
843/761-8509
Fax 843/761-6719
mepkin@infoave.net
http://www.mepkinabbey.org
Catholic/Trappist

DESCRIPTION
According to local legend, the word "Mepkin" originated with Native Americans and means "serene and lovely." Large moss-covered oaks and quiet terraced gardens grace the three-thousand-acre tract of land. Since 1681, when the land was first recorded, it has changed hands several times. In 1936, Henry and Clare Boothe Luce acquired the property and soon donated a large portion to Trappist monks from the Abbey of Gethsemani, who founded Mepkin in 1949.

The monks seek communion with God through *lectio divina*, the Liturgy of the Hours, and work. The abbey welcomes retreatants of all faiths. The monks welcome retreatants to all liturgical services. While the abbey does not offer conferences, a visitor can request spiritual counsel.

ACCOMMODATIONS AND RESERVATIONS

Facilities available for group or individual days of recollection. Individual retreats range in length from one to six days. Rooms in guest houses contain a bed, desk, and reading chair. Most rooms have a private bath (shower, toilet, and sink). The monastery provides bed linens, towels, and soap, and can accommodate married couples.

At meals retreatants follow the monks in their vegetarian diet and by eating in silence. At one of the meals, a monk may read aloud from a book for the edification of those present. Mepkin gratefully accepts any retreatant donations, but no fee is expected of its visitors. Call the guestmaster to see when space is available for reservations.

The church remains open at all times for prayer and reflection.

POINTS OF INTEREST

Award-winning Mepkin Abbey Church, Luce Gardens.

LOCATION

From Moncks Corner, South Carolina, go north on Interstate 52/17-A. Cross the Tail Race Canal Bridge. At the bridge's bottom, turn right at the traffic light and right again onto State Route 402. Immediately after the first bridge (Wadboo Bridge), turn right onto Doctor Evans Road. Mepkin Abbey is six miles down this road and on the right.

From Charleston, South Carolina, head west on Interstate 26. Take the Goose Creek/Moncks Corner/Interstate 52

Exit. Follow Interstate 52 to Moncks Corner. Follow the directions from Moncks Corner as above.

From Columbia, South Carolina, head east on Interstate 26. Take Exit 199B to Alternate 17 all the way to Moncks Corner. Follow the directions from Moncks Corner as above.

From Savannah, Georgia, head north on Interstate 95. Take Exit 53 to State Route 63 to Walterboro. Take Alternate 17 to Moncks Corner. Follow the directions from Moncks Corner as above.

From Fayetteville, North Carolina, head south on Interstate 95. Take Exit 122 to Interstate 521 toward Manning. Take State Route 375 at Greeleyville. Where State Route 375 intersects Interstate 52, turn right onto Interstate 52 East. Interstate 52 then joins Alternate 17 just before Moncks Corner. Turn left at the traffic light onto State Route 402. From 402 follow the Moncks Corner directions as above.

 ## 95. Saint Christopher Camp and Conference Center

2810 Seabrook Island Road
Johns Island, SC 29455
843/768-0429
Fax 843/768-0918
http://www.stchristopher.org
Episcopal

DESCRIPTION

The three-hundred-acre Saint Christopher Camp and Conference Center is found on the waterfront island of Seabrook. In addition to its regularly scheduled conferences and programs, the camp and center offers personal retreats several times each year. These retreats, amid the natural outdoor setting of oaks, palmettos, water, and a scenic shoreline, afford the individual opportunities for quiet prayer and reflection. On request, spiritual direction is available. The center is offered year-round to most groups for conferences and workshops.

ACCOMMODATIONS AND RESERVATIONS
Air-conditioned motel-style bedrooms, each with two double beds and private baths. Personal retreats begin Monday with dinner and finish Wednesday with lunch. Single occupancy, $90 per person. Double occupancy, $75 per person. Prices include lodging and three cafeteria-style meals per day. $30 deposit also required. Linens provided. Meeting rooms with comfortable chairs. Cabins for youth retreats.

POINTS OF INTEREST
Trails through the woods. Fishing, swimming, dolphin watching, shelling, athletic field. Bikes available for rent. Golf courses in the area. The kitchen is managed by Chef Stephen Boyle, who received Charleston's 1989 Chef of the Year Award.

LOCATION
Thirty miles from downtown Charleston.

96. Sea of Peace House of Prayer
802 Jungle Road
Edisto Island, SC 29438
843/869-0513
Catholic/Order of Friars Preach (Dom Friars)

DESCRIPTION
An ecumenical endeavor, Sea of Peace House of Prayer has as part of its mission "reflecting God's beauty and love with tranquillity near the ocean."

Visitors' stays may be long or short, and include private retreats, directed retreats, days of prayer away, and some day retreats for small groups. The group retreats deal with various themes, such as the art of aging, women mystics, sharing one's faith with others, and centering prayer.

ACCOMMODATIONS AND RESERVATIONS

Air-conditioning. Three single bedrooms, one room with double bed. Two rooms share a bath. Overnight accommodations are for individuals only.

A $20 nonrefundable registration deposit is requested; it can be applied to the offering. A private retreat is $40 per person. Directed, $45 per person. Price includes nutritious meals and lodging. Spiritual direction is accessible at the rate of $25 per hourlong session.

POINTS OF INTEREST

Videos, audio tapes, and books available. Lagoon fishing. Paths for walking and biking. Ocean view.

LOCATION

From Interstate 26 take Interstate 526 West to US 17 South toward Savannah to Highway 174 (shortly after junctions with 162 and 165). Continue on 174 toward Edisto Beach twenty minutes. One block before beach, turn right onto Jungle Road at the blue Fairfield sign. It is eight blocks to 802 Jungle Road; the retreat house is on the left.

For a small fee, transportation from the Charleston International Airport is available.

97. Iona House

4577 Billy Maher Road
Memphis, TN 38135-1119
Episcopal
901/377-9284

DESCRIPTION

One who wants to step away from the demands of ordinary living into a sanctuary of wild flowers, trees, and blossoming shrubs may do so at Iona House. The center is situated in Memphis on ten beautiful acres where retreatants find refreshment and renewal in the perpetual silence—no talking is permitted except in designated areas. They draw close to God in meditation by the still lake or in daily worship in the chapel; then leave empowered to return to their duties in the world.

ACCOMMODATIONS AND RESERVATIONS

The one-room hermitage is air-conditioned, has a shower, and is otherwise equipped for basic needs. There is no stated charge, but offerings are appreciated.

POINTS OF INTEREST

Chapel. Spiritual direction is available from Father Stevens, who resides at Iona House.

LOCATION

Ask for directions when scheduling a retreat.

98. Penuel Ridge Retreat Center
1440 Sams Creek Road (State Road 249)
Ashland City, TN 37015
615/792-3734
Ecumenical

DESCRIPTION
Retreatants are encouraged, in the words of Penuel Ridge's brochure, to "sit by the lake, write in a journal, walk the trails, browse through books, or simply 'be' in the presence of God." The center's 120 acres afford plenty of trails and wooded ridges.

Facilities support individual retreat (one day, overnight, or longer), small group facility use, regularly programmed group retreats (on weekends throughout the year), and Sabbath rest/quiet days offered once a month on a weekday (includes opening meditation, optional lunchtime gathering, and closing reflection time). A weekly worship is offered on Saturday afternoons.

ACCOMMODATIONS AND RESERVATIONS
Several rooms are available in the main house, along with two hermitages and a prayer building. A small shelter near the lake provides space for relaxation, picnics, or camping for one or two.

POINTS OF INTEREST
Adjoins Cheatham Wildlife Preserve. Nashville sites within easy driving distance.

LOCATION
Twenty miles west of Nashville. From Nashville take Interstate 40 to Exit 201, turn right on Charlotte and go a half

mile to River Road and turn right. Go about twelve and a half miles and turn left on State Route 249 (Sams Creek Road). Go one and a third miles on Route 249. The driveway, with a sign, is on the right.

From Memphis take Interstate 40 to the Ashland City exit (188). Follow Route 249 North to Highway 70. Turn right. Go one quarter mile to Route 249 North. Turn left and continue about eight and a half miles to Penuel Ridge.

99. Retreat Center

at Scarritt-Bennett Center
1008 19th Avenue South
Nashville, TN 37212-2166
615/340-7557
pilcher@ncs.infi.net
http://www.umc.org/scarritt
United Methodist

DESCRIPTION

With historic ties to the United Methodist Church, the center emphasizes cross-cultural understanding, education, creativity, and spiritual formation. It is located in the heart of Nashville on ten tree-filled acres that were formerly Scarritt College and Scarritt Graduate School.

Resources available to retreatants include two chapels and two quiet rooms for meditation, Laskey Library with books, magazines, audios, and videos, an international garden with peace pole, an organic garden, and a gift shop. A wide array of programs are offered through the year.

ACCOMMODATIONS AND RESERVATIONS

Most of the center's sleeping rooms have a single bed and share a full bath with one other person. For personal retreats every effort is made to put retreatants in a private room. Meals are usually available in the center's Gothic dining hall. Served cafeteria style, the meals always include vegetarian and low-salt options. Meals are served whenever there is a group on campus.

POINTS OF INTEREST
The center is located near many of Nashville's tourist sites, including, across the street, the Upper Room Chapel and Museum.

LOCATION
Near downtown Nashville's major thoroughfares and two blocks east of Vanderbilt University. (Consult a Nashville map for directions.)

 100. Saint Mary's Retreat and Conference Center
P.O. Box 188
Sewanee, TN 37375-0188
931/598-5342
Episcopal/Community of Saint Mary

DESCRIPTION
Set atop Tennessee's Cumberland Plateau in southern Tennessee, the center's miles of trails take guests to all parts of the two-hundred-acre facility—over rocky slopes and through forests and fields of wild flowers. Sisters worship and gather for morning and evening prayers in a lovely chapel on the property, at which retreatants are welcome. Spiritual direction available when arranged in advance.

ACCOMMODATIONS AND RESERVATIONS
Rooms allow for up to one hundred guests. Towels and linens are provided. A small lodge called the "Hermitage"

has a bedroom, kitchenette, and private bath for individual retreats (meals not provided). Rate for staying at the hermitage is approximately $35.

POINTS OF INTEREST
The nearby University of the South offers cultural and educational events. State parks (including Tims Ford), seven natural areas, and tourist attractions (such as Old Jail Museum and Hundred Oaks Castle) are within a short driving distance.

LOCATION
Ninety miles southeast of Nashville and forty-five miles northeast of Chattanooga in Sewanee. From Interstate 24 take the Monteagle/Sewanee exit onto Highway 64 to Sewanee. Travel through Sewanee until you reach State Highway 56. Turn left toward Sherwood. Travel one mile to the first bend in the road and turn right onto Saint Mary's Lane at the sign.

$\mathcal{V}irginia$

101. Holy Cross Abbey (Retreat House)
Rural Route 2, Box 3870
Berryville, VA 22611
540/955-3124
Fax 540/955-4006
Catholic/Cistercian (Trappist)

DESCRIPTION
Sixty miles from Washington, D.C., this monastery occupies over a thousand acres of farmland that once saw the Civil War battle of Cool Spring. The retreat house, which is open year-round, is for indi-

vidual, nondirected retreats, or meditative retreats, but is also available for groups of up to fifteen. A monk can be available for direction, counseling, or for the sacrament of reconciliation (a personalized conversation and prayer wherein a person confesses sin and hears words of forgiveness and absolution). The abbey church celebrates the daily Eucharist as well as five services of readings and Psalms. Retreatants can attend either type of service. Priests are welcome to concelebrate the Mass.

ACCOMMODATIONS AND RESERVATIONS
Suggested scale for donation: $100–$200 for weeklong retreat (Monday late afternoon through Friday morning); $75–$100 for weekend retreat (Friday late afternoon through Sunday afternoon). Cost includes lodging and three meals (continental breakfast, lunch, dinner). All rooms are single with private bath. It is advised that visitors take with them a flashlight, rainwear, and comfortable shoes.

Advance reservation and a deposit, which is applied to the offering, are required. Call for reservations Monday through Saturday between 9:00 A.M. and noon and between 1:15 P.M. and 5:00 P.M.

POINTS OF INTEREST
Chapel for prayer and meditation. Library with books and tapes.

LOCATION
Five miles east of Berryville. Seventeen miles from Winchester. From Route 7, going west, cross the Blue Ridge Mountains and Shenandoah River. Turn right immediately after crossing river (Route 603).

From Route 7, going east, turn left immediately before bridge over Shenandoah River (Route 603).

Pickup at Winchester Bus Depot may be arranged in advance.

102. Phoebe Needles Retreat and Conference Center

732 Turners Creek Road
Callaway, VA 24067
540/483-1518
Fax 540/483-2235
jheck@ferrum.edu
Episcopal

DESCRIPTION

Located on the former site of an Episcopal mission school an hour southeast of Roanoke, the retreat and conference center has been, as the staff describes, "a place apart for reflection, interaction, spiritual growth, and renewal" since the 1960s. Its forty acres set in the foothills of the Blue Ridge Mountains, along with its wooded trails, serve as a setting for reflective solitude. While the center offers programs dealing with various topics of Christian spirituality, it also welcomes private retreatants for directed or nondirected retreats. An Episcopal priest provides direction and administers the sacraments.

ACCOMMODATIONS AND RESERVATIONS

Day accommodations for as many as seventy. Overnight accommodations for twenty-eight (fourteen rooms with two single beds). Linens and towels provided. Country-style cooks prepare three meals a day. Special dietary needs can be met.

Call for information regarding rates and reservations.

Saint Peter's Episcopal Church is adjacent. Guests are invited for Sunday worship.

LOCATION
One hour southeast of Roanoke. Under two hours southwest of Lynchburg. Fifteen minutes north of Ferrum. Detailed map available upon reservation.

 103. Tabor Retreat Center
2125 Langhorne Road
Lynchburg, VA 24501
804/846-6475
Catholic/Diocese of Richmond

DESCRIPTION
Set in a wooded area in the beautiful historic city of Lynchburg, the retreat center is open to all who seek God's peace and quiet.

Tabor is appropriate for personal days of prayer and individual spiritual direction. It is also available for group meetings and retreats. Most Thursdays are set aside as days for individuals to make private retreats. A spiritual director is available.

ACCOMMODATIONS AND RESERVATIONS
The center can accommodate up to thirty-two persons overnight in sixteen rooms. Linens and towels are provided. Bathrooms are semiprivate. Full kitchen facilities are available for use by retreatants, though meals are provided for private retreatants. The center has a large dining area. Some of the building is handicapped accessible.

For overnight, the cost is $20 per person not including

meals or $36 including meals. Several meeting areas are available.

POINTS OF INTEREST
The retreat center has a lovely courtyard. Deep woods that border the beautiful Blackwater Creek Natural Area, featuring a six-mile creekside trail excellent for hiking, surround the property.

LOCATION
Historic Lynchburg's central Virginia location is easily accessible from all directions.

104. The Virginia Diocesan Center at Roslyn

8727 River Road
Richmond, VA 23229
804/288-6045 or 800/477-6296
Fax 804/285-3430
Episcopal

DESCRIPTION
This year-round conference and retreat center in Henrico County, encompassing some 150 scenic acres of fields, trees, and woodlands, is set on the James River on the outskirts of Richmond. Since 1934, it has served churches and nonprofit organizations through day meetings, residential conferences, seminars, retreats, and picnics. Individual retreatants are welcome when space allows. Roslyn's atmosphere, one of the center's brochures notes, allows for private retreatants to be "in the silence of God's presence or in animated conversation with our Creator."

All buildings have air-conditioning. The lodges have twenty-four hotel-style rooms with private bath. The dormitory building houses twenty rooms with shared baths. When space permits, some single rooms are available. Towels, bed linens supplied. Towels changed daily, bed linens every three days.

Visitors usually schedule their private retreats two weeks or less in advance. Personal retreat, $25 per night. Cost includes private room, full access to center grounds, but does not include meals. Meals are available only when there is a conference in residence. Meals: breakfast, $5.50; lunch, $8; dinner, $9.50. The center accepts cash or check.

POINTS OF INTEREST
Outdoor swimming pool, tennis courts, nature trails, horseshoe pits, volleyball. Sabbatical house for clergy.

LOCATION
Two miles west of Richmond. Accessible from Chippenham Parkway (150 North), Interstate 64, Interstate 95, and Parham Road. Call for more detailed directions.

105. Richmond Hill Retreat Center
2209 East Grace Street
Richmond, VA 23223
804/783-7903
Ecumenical

DESCRIPTION
Set atop Church Hill, just east of downtown Richmond, this retreat center was formerly a monastery. Now, according to one of the center's brochures, Richmond Hill is open to "all who are drawn by the

Spirit to seek God, to be still, to learn, to work, to minister, or to study." The staff at Richmond Hill takes very seriously its task to pray daily for the city of Richmond and the surrounding area. Among the center's program offerings are community worship, centering prayer, healing prayer, Celtic spirituality, and a two-year school of spiritual guidance. During most weeks the center is open for private retreat from Monday afternoon through Saturday or Sunday afternoon. The chapel and gardens add to the atmosphere of quiet prayer and personal reflection. All guests are invited to join in daily communal prayer, meal service, and housekeeping chores. Visitors may observe a rule of silence if they wish.

ACCOMMODATIONS AND RESERVATIONS

Requested donation of $35 for a twenty-four-hour personal retreat. Day retreat with lunch, $10. For guided personal retreat, add $25. However, the staff does not wish to deny spiritual direction for lack of money. Prices for program retreats vary.

POINTS OF INTEREST

Library. James River within view.

LOCATION

From downtown proceed east on Broad Street, right on 22nd Street to Grace Street. Watch for courtyard entrance; parking area is straight ahead.

From Interstate 95 North take Exit 74C (Broad Street East). Take left on Broad Street.

From Interstate 95 South take Exit 74B (East Franklin Street). Take right on Franklin, right on 14th Street, right on East Broad Street to right on 22nd Street.

106. The Well Retreat Center
18047 Quiet Way
Smithfield, VA 23430-6411
757/255-2366
Catholic/Diocese of Richmond

DESCRIPTION

A serene, wooded setting near a spring-fed lake makes The Well Retreat Center a place of peace and prayer for guests. Surrounded by nature and nestled in pine trees, the retreat center makes binoculars and bird and animal books available to guests.

The Well has grown since 1981 from a small house of prayer to a thirteen-acre complex. Opportunities for preached, directed or guided, personalized, and private retreats are provided. For individuals, spiritual direction and guidance for personal prayer life is available.

ACCOMMODATIONS AND RESERVATIONS

The retreat center includes a prayer chapel, assembly room, two private conference rooms, a library, kitchen, and dining room. Private rooms for individual retreatants are available. Private retreatants prepare all of their own meals, using food from the retreat center.

Accommodations are also available for the handicapped: The center and two bedrooms are specially equipped.

The overnight rate for a private retreat, including room, linens, and meals, is $40 per person. For directed/guided retreats, the rate is also $40 per person, plus a donation for spiritual direction, if possible. Reservations are made on a first come, first served basis.

A lending library offers a collection of more than three thousand inspirational books and tapes. The Well has a special membership at the Suffolk YMCA, which is only twelve miles away. Individuals making private or directed retreats may use the exercise room and pool for a nominal fee.

LOCATION
A forty-five-minute drive from most areas of Hampton Roads, The Well is located in a corner of Isle of Wight County near the Suffolk line on Cherry Grove Road (State Route 600).

West Virginia

107. Good Counsel Friary

493 Tyrone Road
Morgantown, WV 26505-9199
304/594-1714
Fax 304/594-9247
Catholic/Franciscan

DESCRIPTION
Located near Cheat Lake seven miles east of Morgantown, the staff of this friary wishes to "serve the whole Christian community in its area" through retreats and programs for parish groups, married couples, college and high school students, charismatic groups, and individual retreatants, among others. The friary is set on fifteen acres dominated by a twenty-three-room stone "castle" built in 1933. Programs address such themes as service, Bible study, self-awareness, music, marriage encounter, and charismatic renewal. The friary also offers days

or weekends of renewal and recollection for different groups of sisters. Further, the friary welcomes individual private retreats.

ACCOMMODATIONS AND RESERVATIONS
Call Monday through Friday, 9 A.M. to 4 P.M. for further information on rates and reservations.

POINTS OF INTEREST
Chapel, lounge, meeting rooms, library, picnic area.

LOCATION
Seven miles north of Morgantown. Accessible from Interstates 79, 68, 70, and Route 119. Call for more detailed directions.

108. Peterkin Camp and Conference Center

Box 823 River Road
Romney, WV 26757
304/822-4519
Episcopal

DESCRIPTION
Currently undergoing renovations for expansion, this center focuses on relationships and family renewal. The environment is rustic and simple. The staff describes this center as "a safe place, one where it is appropriate to test openness." Here, visitors can seek a greater awareness of God in their daily lives. Private retreatants welcome.

ACCOMMODATIONS AND RESERVATIONS
Several lodges are available. Lodging fees are currently in the price range of $20–$28 per night. Add $20 for three meals per day. Call for further rate information.

POINTS OF INTEREST

Softball field, soccer field, basketball court, swimming pool, tennis courts, camp store, chapel.

LOCATION

Northwest West Virginia, near the intersection of State Road 20 and US 50.

REGION III

Midwest

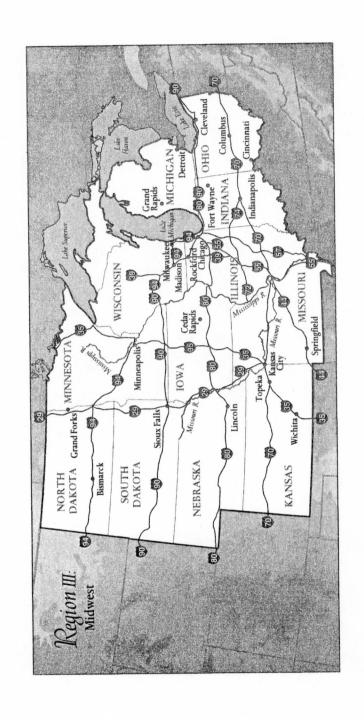

Region III: Midwest

109. Cenacle Retreat House

P.O. Box 797
Warrenville, IL 60555
630/393-1231 or 800/240-6702
cenaclemin@aol.com
http://www.cenacle.org
Catholic/Congregation of Our Lady in Retreat in Cenacle

DESCRIPTION

Twelve sisters live, work, and pray on the center grounds, set amid forty-two acres of woods along the tranquil banks of the DuPage River in the western suburbs of Chicago. An integral part of the sisters' mission is to pray and offer spiritual counsel to retreatants. A wide range of conferences with speakers complement the ongoing availability of individual retreats. A private retreat, says the Cenacle brochure, "allows you to get away from your daily busy life, to seek some quiet and solitude and to spend time with God in prayer, meditation, and reflection." No direction is provided. In a directed retreat, the retreatant plans with an assigned spiritual director the day (or days) of prayer. The latter may be as short as one day or as long as thirty. (Suggested daily donations for directed retreats are slightly higher.)

ACCOMMODATIONS AND RESERVATIONS

Ninety beds and six conference rooms. Call for rates.

POINTS OF INTEREST

An adjacent forest preserve and Prairie Path provide ample walking opportunities. Proximity to Chicago sites.

West of Chicago. From Interstate 88 take Winfield Road to
Butterfield Road to Batavia Road, where the Cenacle is located.

 110. Divine Word International
Techny Towers Conference Center
2001 Waukegan Road
P.O. Box 176
Techny, IL 60082
847/272-1100
Fax 847/272-9363
dwi_tech@one800.net
http://www.svd.org/Techny.html
Catholic/Society of the Divine Word

DESCRIPTION
Planned to be "an ecumenical place for spiritual
growth," this center offers spiritual direction for
group and private retreats, along with days of
prayer. Beautiful wooded grounds have picnic area
and pond. Sponsored by the Society of the Divine
Word, commonly known as Divine Word Missionaries in the United States, members of the Society of
the Divine Word arrived in Techny at the turn of
the century. Founded in Steyl, Holland, by Arnold
Janssen, SVD, in 1875, this Catholic missionary orga-
nization now has nearly six thousand members serving in nearly sixty countries worldwide.

ACCOMMODATIONS AND RESERVATIONS
Wide selection of rooms, including those with air-conditioning and private baths. Prepared meals available. Rates vary
depending on options chosen.

A bookstore sells a wide selection of eight hundred titles of
Christian literature from about forty publishers. A chapel,
completed in 1925, is an example of Old World architectural
beauty. Some ninety-nine stained glass windows designed in
Munich, Germany, adorn this ornate place of worship.
There are two other chapels available.

LOCATION
Nineteen miles from downtown Chicago. Seventeen miles
from O'Hare International Airport. Lake Michigan nearby.
Located on Highway 43 (Woken Road) one mile north of
Willow Road between Glenview and Northbrook. From the
north via Interstate 94 (Edens Expressway) take Exit 33A
(West). Go two miles west on Willow Road to Highway 43.
Take a right on Highway 43 to Techny Towers. From the
south via Interstate 294 (Tri-State Tollway) take exit for
Willow Road. Proceed three miles east on Willow Road to
Highway 43. Take left on Highway 43 to Techny Towers.

111. King's House

Retreat and Renewal Center
700 N 66th Street
Belleville, IL 62223-3949
618/397-0584
Fax 618/397-5123
Catholic/Missionary Oblates of Mary Immaculate

DESCRIPTION
Forty-five wooded acres surround this center a fifteen-minute drive from downtown Saint Louis, Missouri. The staff try to welcome people of faith "with
warm hospitality and many opportunities for spiritual and personal growth." The center strives for a
reflective atmosphere. "All loving relationships need

time, care, and some work," notes their brochure, "and so does your relationship with God. During a retreat you can learn some tools for prayer, find the support you desire, and relax in a quiet space for a while."

A variety of group and private retreats are offered, as are annual quiet retreats, days of prayer, and special interest retreats.

ACCOMMODATIONS AND RESERVATIONS
Air-conditioned rooms with private baths are available, with some limited handicapped access. Delicious meals served. Call for rates.

POINTS OF INTEREST
Inviting, modern chapel; grounds for hiking and walking. Near the attractions of Saint Louis, Missouri.

LOCATION
Take Interstate 64 going east to Route 157 South/West to West Main. Turn left and take West Main to 66th Street. Turn left.

112. Saint Noel Retreat and Conference Center
Route 1 Box 6
Ozark, IL 62972
618/695-3590
Fax 628/695-3593
Catholic/Diocese of Belleville

DESCRIPTION
In the peaceful Shawnee National Forest, Saint Noel Retreat and Conference Center gives guests modern

comforts without the distractions of modern life. The center offers a haven for meetings, conferences, spiritual retreats, and special events.

The entire facility is contained within one building and is located on a thousand spectacular acres. Abundant creeks, canyons, waterfalls, wildlife, and forests let retreatants be as active or as contemplative as they wish.

ACCOMMODATIONS AND RESERVATIONS

Guests stay in one of twelve individually decorated suites. Each suite includes two double beds, sitting area, private bath, telephone, and individually controlled heating and air-conditioning. Suites can accommodate one to four adults or families of five to six. Most suites are two rooms, and some offer balconies, fireplaces, or cathedral ceilings. Several are wheelchair accessible. Rates depend on the services chosen.

Other areas include a dining room, chapel, library/game room, reception room, front deck, and rear stone patio.

POINTS OF INTEREST

Activities at the conference center include a team-building course, guided nature hikes, horseback riding, boating and canoeing, fishing, and fresh-lake swimming.

Saint Noel is close to Garden of the Gods, Bell Smith Springs, Fort Massac, and Cave-in Rock.

LOCATION

Saint Noel is located at Camp Ondessonk, in southeastern Illinois. Approximate driving times: less than one hour from Carbondale, Illinois, and Paducah, Kentucky; three hours from Saint Louis, Missouri; and six hours from Chicago. Off Interstate 24 travel ten miles north on US Route 45. Turn right at the Camp Ondessonk/Ozark.

113. Benedict Inn Retreat & Conference Center

1402 Southern Avenue
Beech Grove, IN 46107-1197
317/788-7581
Fax 317/782-3142
http://www.benedictinn.org
Catholic/Benedictine

DESCRIPTION

The quiet, spacious grounds of this retreat center invite reflective strolls and relaxation. Flower gardens, benches, and bird feeders on forty landscaped acres with tree-lined walkways enhance the beauty of this large center, which facilitates programs hosted by other groups as well as private retreats.

Guests can design their own retreats or make a directed retreat and speak with a spiritual director once a day for thirty to sixty minutes. The monastery welcomes guests to its Liturgy of the Hours and the Eucharistic liturgy celebrated daily.

ACCOMMODATIONS AND RESERVATIONS

Forty-seven bedrooms with in-room sinks and mirrors accommodate single or double occupancy. Bathrooms are shared. Dining is cafeteria- or buffet-style, and special menu services are available. Guests may eat at picnic grounds, a private dining room, and a 150-seat hall.

Facilities include a chapel and a monastic library. The center is handicapped accessible, and conference rooms but not bedrooms are air-conditioned.

The center has a gift shop, an art room, and television rooms. The fitness center (with personal trainer) has an indoor heated swimming pool, a double-court gymnasium, and a workout room. Massage can be scheduled for an additional fee.

LOCATION

From the north via Interstate 65 take Raymond Street exit; take Raymond Street east to Sherman; take Sherman south to Southern; go east on Southern. Enter the third driveway. From the south via Interstate 465 exit north on Emerson Avenue to Churchman; go west on Churchman, which turns into 13th Street. At 13th and Southern enter drive to retreat center.

114. Bethany Retreat House

2202 Lituanica Avenue
East Chicago, IN 46312
219/398-5047
bethanyrh@sprynet.com
http://www.Bethanyretreathouse.org
Catholic/Poor Handmaids of Jesus Christ

DESCRIPTION

Christians know Bethany as the hometown of Martha and Mary, mentioned in a New Testament story. It represented a place of hospitality where Martha served Jesus. Like its namesake, Bethany Retreat House intends to offer a place apart to spend time with God in an atmosphere of hospitality, beauty, and spiritual encouragement.

Situated in a pleasant subdivision in East Chicago, Indiana, Bethany's peaceful, homelike setting includes a backyard garden. The quiet neighborhood is pleasant for walking, with a park close by. The center is open to women and men of all faiths, to laity, clergy, and members of religious orders who seek its quiet atmosphere for prayer and reflection. Retreatants can meet with a professionally trained spiritual director, either during retreat or on an ongoing basis.

Directed retreats entail a daily meeting with a spiritual director who draws from a variety of resources to encourage and facilitate prayer: your experience, Scripture, journaling, dreamwork, artistic expression, guided imagery, fairy tales, and the *Spiritual Exercises* of Saint Ignatius.

ACCOMMODATIONS AND RESERVATIONS
Three private bedrooms, private kitchen and dining room. Private retreat suggested donation: (including room and food) $30 per day; individually directed retreat with spiritual direction: $37 to $47 per day (sliding scale based on ability to pay). When someone is unable to give the suggested amount, the sisters accept contributed services along with a donation within that person's means.

POINTS OF INTEREST
Library and bookstore with books on prayer, spirituality, journaling, loss, and grieving, and cassettes and CDs of liturgical music. Lake Michigan beaches are a fifteen- to twenty-five-minute drive. Eucharist daily at four locations within the neighborhood.

LOCATION
From Interstate 80/94 in Indiana: Take Cline Avenue north, take Columbus Drive exit left. Turn left at second light (Alder). Turn right at second stop sign. From Chicago: Take

Skyway to Indiana Toll Road. Exit Toll Road at Cline Avenue. Exit Cline Avenue at Columbus Drive. Follow signs through stop light to Columbus Drive, turning right. Turn left at next light (Alder). Turn right at second stop sign (Lituanica).

115. Fatima Retreat Center
P.O. Box 929
Notre Dame, IN 46556
219/631-8288
Fax 219/631-5239
ND.Fatima.1@ND.edu
http://www.nd.edu/~Fatima
Catholic/Holy Cross Fathers

DESCRIPTION

Adjacent to the University of Notre Dame campus, the retreat center takes full advantage of the spirit and resources of the school. Beautiful in any season, Fatima is on the edge of Saint Mary's Lake, which winds through the Notre Dame campus filled with ducks, Canada geese, and swans.

Guests may make a private retreat of any length. Spiritual direction is available.

ACCOMMODATIONS AND RESERVATIONS

The center has forty rooms, all with twin beds and private bathrooms. Linens and towels are provided. Rooms have individual heating and air-conditioning. They are handicapped accessible, but the showers are not.

Conference rooms, dining rooms, and the chapel are all handicapped accessible.

The suggested donation is $27 per person based on double occupancy. Meals are $6 for breakfast, $7 for lunch, and $11 for dinner. Cheese trays, vegetable trays, and soft drinks offered at reasonable prices. Coffee, tea, and home-made cookies can be provided.

A donation for spiritual direction is appreciated.

POINTS OF INTEREST

Guests have complete access to University of Notre Dame facilities such as swimming pool, indoor gym facility, and bookstore. There is the opportunity to wander around tree-surrounded lakes, both of which have pedestrian walkways around them.

LOCATION

Located on the west edge of the campus of the University of Notre Dame, Fatima is easily accessible by car. It is about three hundred yards from the Indiana Turnpike and a fifteen-minute drive from the airport and train and bus terminals.

 116. Fatima Retreat House
5353 East 56th Street
Indianapolis, IN 46226-1405
317/545-7681
Catholic/Archdiocese of Indianapolis

DESCRIPTION

Located on thirteen beautiful acres of wooded property in the northeast section of Indianapolis, the retreat house and its colorful gardens provide a secluded place for retreats.

Fatima offers day, evening, and overnight accommodations for groups and individuals. Persons wishing to make a private or directed retreat are welcome. Although it is primarily committed to serving individuals, parishes, and agencies of the Catholic community, the retreat house also welcomes people of other religious traditions.

ACCOMMODATIONS AND RESERVATIONS

The retreat house has sixty-seven private bedrooms with semiprivate baths. Each room has a sink and an easy chair. Rooms do not have televisions or telephones. Although it was built in 1963, the facility is well maintained. Rooms have been decorated within the past two years. A private retreat is $45 per day (three meals and overnight); a directed retreat is $60 per day (three meals, overnight, and a spiritual direction session).

Meals are served buffet style. Special dietary needs will be accommodated with advance notice. Snack items and beverages are available. The modern, air-conditioned building is handicapped accessible.

Private retreatants also have the use of the Sabbath House of Prayer, which is a three-bedroom private home on the property of the retreat house. The bedrooms will accommodate five people overnight. Guests may prepare their own meals in the kitchen, or they may eat in the main dining room. The overnight cost for one person is $40 per night; for two people, $60.

For groups, the retreat house provides audiovisual equipment at no additional charge. Tables, fax machine, and photocopier are also available. Meeting rooms are available for a charge.

POINTS OF INTEREST

A chapel that accommodates up to one hundred persons is used for liturgical and private prayer.

LOCATION

The retreat house is easily accessed from Interstate 465.

117. Kordes Enrichment Center
802 E. 10th Street
Ferdinand, IN 47532-9239
812/367-1411
Fax 812/367-2313
sisters@thedome.org
http://www.thedome.org/index.html
Catholic/Benedictine

DESCRIPTION

Kordes Enrichment Center is a retreat center nestled in the rolling hills of Ferdinand, Indiana. It is sponsored by the Sisters of Saint Benedict of Ferdinand, one of the largest Benedictine communities of women in the United States. (Their community is called Monastery Immaculate Conception.) The Ferdinand Benedictines currently number 243 women, 137 of whom live at the monastery. The facility, open to people of all faiths, serves groups and individuals, and offers space for retreats, meetings, prayer days, and time for rest, relaxation, and reflection. The 190-acre monastery grounds include a magnificent church with domed ceilings and beautiful stained glass windows. Its Romanesque dome rises eighty-seven feet over the town of Ferdinand and has earned it the name "Castle on the Hill." It has solid oak panels and pews hand-carved in Oberammergau, Germany, and stained glass windows depicting Benedictine saints and angelic figures. The church has been listed in the National Register of Historic Places.

ACCOMMODATIONS AND RESERVATIONS

The center offers hospitality through air-conditioned facilities and space for scheduled activities, quiet time, or prayer. Attractive, nutritious meals are prepared in the center's own kitchen.

POINTS OF INTEREST

Lourdes Grotto and outdoor Stations of the Cross. An expanded and relocated gift shop, For Heaven's Sake, recently opened. The shop features handcrafted items, from both the Ferdinand sisters and local artisans in Peru and Guatemala, where the sisters have missions; gift and religious articles; inspirational books; cards; and freshly baked bread and cookies. The grounds also have an outdoor swimming pool, lighted tennis courts, and space for hiking, walking, and bicycling.

Nearby is Saint Meinrad Archabbey, the Lincoln Boyhood National Memorial, Lincoln State Park, the Young Abe Lincoln Musical Outdoor Drama, Ferdinand State Forest, and Holiday World in Santa Claus, Indiana.

LOCATION

Ferdinand is located just off Interstate 64 between Louisville, Kentucky, and Evansville, Indiana. It is one hour from Evansville, Indiana; one and a half hours from Louisville, Kentucky; two and a half hours from Lexington, Kentucky; three hours from Cincinnati; two and a half hours from Indianapolis; and three hours from Nashville. Two regional airports (Evansville and Louisville) are located close to Ferdinand.

From the south take Exit 63 on Interstate 64. Turn north onto State Road 162. Proceed north on SR 162 for approximately one mile. Turn right on 10th Street onto the monastery grounds. At the top of the hill on the left are the stairs and ramp leading to the main monastery entrance.

From the north (the intersection of State Road 64 and State Road 162), proceed south on SR 162 into Ferdinand, turn left on 10th Street, and follow the directions as noted above.

118. Little Noddfa Retreat & Spiritual Life Center

1440 West Division Road
Tipton, IN 46072
765/675-3950
wwetli@tiptontel.com
http://www.sisters.jo-tiptontel.org
· Catholic/Sisters of Saint Joseph

DESCRIPTION

Little Noddfa—the Welsh word for "refuge" or "shelter"—is located on the grounds of Saint Joseph Center. The renovated turn-of-the-century house is wrapped in the sheltering arms of splendid old trees.

Visitors of all denominations are welcome at the center, which offers small group retreats for two to ten people, directed retreats for five to eight days, and private retreats for one or more days. Spiritual direction with a professionally trained spiritual director is available. Guests have the opportunity to participate in daily liturgy.

ACCOMMODATIONS AND RESERVATIONS

Comfortable air-conditioned accommodations for guests are in five bedrooms with baths. Soap, towels, and linen are provided. A living-room space holds ten people, and there is a fully equipped kitchen. Nutritional meals are served at Saint Joseph Center.

A private retreat (includes overnight and three meals) costs $38. Directed retreats (overnight, meals, and spiritual direction) are $45–$55. Spiritual direction is $25–$30 per session.

POINTS OF INTEREST
The center has beautifully landscaped grounds in a quiet rural setting, a simply furnished chapel, a small lending library, and a wide screened-in porch with rocking chairs and a swing.

LOCATION
The center is on the northern outskirts of Tipton, Indiana, which is north of Indianapolis off State Road 31 North. Call for detailed directions.

119. Mary's Solitude
Saint Mary's
Notre Dame, IN 46556
219/284-5599
Catholic/Sisters of the Holy Cross

DESCRIPTION
Just across the street from the University of Notre Dame is a comfortable, hospitable, and secluded environment that welcomes guests. The center is committed to interfaith ministry as it accompanies persons on their spiritual journey through prayer, retreat, spiritual direction, and study. Private and directed retreats are available. Hosted groups may come for a few hours, an overnight, or a weekend.

ACCOMMODATIONS AND RESERVATIONS
Overnight accommodations include sixteen single air-conditioned rooms. A comfortable lounge holds thirty to thirty-five people. The fee for a private retreat, which includes

meals in the dining room, is $20 per day or $40 overnight. A directed retreat, which includes meals and a session with a spiritual director, is $40 a day or $50 overnight. Spiritual direction sessions are $20 each.

Because weekends fill up quickly, call well in advance to reserve space.

POINTS OF INTEREST
The scenic, peaceful setting provides space for walking and enjoying nature. There is a large library and a lovely chapel, as well as an outdoor patio that overlooks a meadow and acres of wooded grounds.

LOCATION
Mary's Solitude is on the campus of Saint Mary's College on 933 (formerly US 33), just south of the Indiana Toll Road (Exit 77) across the street from the University of Notre Dame. Turn west into the main entrance of Saint Mary's College and follow the tree-lined avenue to the back of the campus and continue past the information/security booth. The road ends in a parking lot in front of Mary's Solitude.

 120. A Quiet Place
Contemplative Prayer Center
Camp Alexander Mack
P.O. Box 158
Milford, IN 46542
219/658-4831
Church of the Brethren

DESCRIPTION
Citing Jesus' invitation in Mark 6:31, "Come with me by yourselves to a quiet place and get some rest," this center offers "sacred space and solitude for any person seeking to answer the invitation of

Jesus," as its brochure notes. They offer "holy hospitality" in an environment of prayer, listening, and encouragement.

The center's house can accommodate up to five persons for private retreats, personal solitude, and spiritual direction. Pastors and other church leaders are encouraged to schedule a personal Sabbath day on Mondays, 9:00 A.M. to 3:00 P.M. Quiet days can be scheduled for daylong or overnight.

ACCOMMODATIONS AND RESERVATIONS
Private retreat rate is $20 per day. Overnight is $30 per night, which includes continental breakfast and a light lunch. Kitchen utensils allow guests to do their own cooking should they prefer. Directed retreat is $35 per day.

POINTS OF INTEREST
Picturesque Amish country nearby.

LOCATION
721 E 1150 North, Milford. Travel south from Milford on State Road 15 through Milford and around the curves. Turn east at the sign for Camp Mack on 1150 N, come to a stop sign, cross the railroad tracks, and follow 1150 N to the center (on the south side of the road). It is just over a mile from State Road 15.

121. Saint Meinrad Archabbey

Saint Meinrad, IN 47577
812/357-6585 or 812/357-6611
Fax 812/357-6977
con_ed@saintmeinrad.edu
http://www.saintmeinrad.edu
Catholic/Benedictine

Home to a large community of Benedictine monks, the archabbey rises amid the rolling hills and cornfields of a southern Indiana small town. It is the home to about 135 monks. Among their works are teaching at a graduate school for Catholic priesthood and lay ministry studies; Abbey Press, an international mail-order firm that markets inspirational gifts, cards, and books; and the guest house, which hosts retreats year-round. The campus, monastery, and guest house are surrounded by 2,500 acres, including 1,500 wooded acres and five lakes. The immediate campus of 250 picturesque acres sits on a hillside. Its massive buildings, carved from native stone, reflect the long traditions of the archabbey.

Saint Meinrad Archabbey offers a variety of retreat options for those seeking a more intimate relationship with God. Weekends (Friday evening through Sunday noon) and weekdays (Tuesday evening through Thursday noon) are host to varied group retreats, and private and directed retreats are encouraged.

The grounds surrounding the guest house include wooded rolling hills, lakes, and gardens. Retreatants and other guests are invited to join the monks for daily communal prayer and Eucharist.

It is no accident that Saint Meinrad Archabbey makes hospitality a priority. The saint after which the monastery is named was a monk and hermit who lived during the ninth century in what is now Switzerland. Though he was a hermit, people often sought him out for spiritual advice and the sacraments. While showing hospitality to two robbers, the pair responded to his generosity by killing him. He is known as the "Martyr of Hospitality."

ACCOMMODATIONS AND RESERVATIONS
The archabbey guest house has twenty-five air-conditioned rooms with private baths. Other facilities associated with the guest house include the Saint Jude Chapel, dining and conference rooms, and a lounge. Suggested donation for a private retreat is $50 per night, which includes meals, lodging, and taxes. For guided retreats an additional donation of $25 per day is suggested.

POINTS OF INTEREST
Saint Meinrad School of Theology is adjacent, as well as a well-stocked library rich with material on prayer and the spiritual life. Abbey Press sits on monastic property. It operates a large gift and book shop. The Scholar Shop offers for sale theological books and gift items.

Nearby is The Monastery Immaculate Conception [sic], the site of Kordes Enrichment Center (see above). Also within easy driving distance: Lincoln Boyhood National Memorial, Lincoln State Park, the Young Abe Lincoln Musical Outdoor Drama, Ferdinand State Forest, and Holiday World in Santa Claus, Indiana.

LOCATION
Seventy-five miles from Louisville, Kentucky, fifty-five from Evansville, Indiana.

By car: From the west take Interstate 64 East to Exit 63 (Ferdinand and Santa Claus); proceed south two and a half miles on Indiana 162 to flashing red light; turn left on Indiana 62 and proceed four miles to Saint Meinrad. From the east take Interstate 64 West to Exit 72 (Birdseye and Bristow); proceed south one block to Indiana 62; turn right and proceed eight miles to Saint Meinrad. From the north and south use US 231. Travel to Dale, turn onto SR 62 heading east and drive ten miles.

By plane: Saint Meinrad, Indiana, is served by Louisville International Airport and Evansville Regional Airport.

 122. Quaker Hill Conference Center
10 Quaker Hill Drive
Richmond, IN 47374
765/962-5741
quakrhil@infocom.com
Quaker

DESCRIPTION
Shaded lawns, woods, and hiking trails surround two houses, including one built in 1855, that serve the retreat needs of this Quaker center. While primarily oriented to group retreats, a solitude room is set aside for personal, self-directed retreats. Located on the Indiana/Ohio border between Indianapolis and Dayton, Ohio.

ACCOMMODATIONS AND RESERVATIONS
In addition to the solitude room, sixteen bedrooms and a dining room have air-conditioning. There is no charge for overnight use of the solitude room.

POINTS OF INTEREST
Outdoor amphitheater. Near Quaker Hill Bookstore, Earlham College, Earlham School of Religion, Quaker Meetings (churches), and historic Quaker sites.

LOCATION
Richmond is on Interstate 70 near the Indiana/Ohio state line. Indianapolis is seventy-two miles to the west. The Dayton airport is a forty-five-minute drive on Interstate 70. Traveling north or south on Route 27, take Waterfall Road west to Richmond Hill Road.

123. American Martyrs Retreat House

2209 North Union Road
P.O. Box 605
Cedar Falls, IA 50613-0605
319/266-3543
dbqamrh@impresso.com

DESCRIPTION

Set in the Cedar River Valley and surrounded by seventy-five acres of trees and rugged beauty, the center reflects "an atmosphere of peace and serenity." The retreat house is dedicated to the North American martyrs Isaac Jogues, Rene Goupil, and John Lalande.

Preached and individually directed retreats, spiritual direction, workshops, and simple quiet time for prayer are all possible.

ACCOMMODATIONS AND RESERVATIONS

The house has fifty-nine bedrooms, some with private baths.

LOCATION

North Union Road accessible off Highway 57 or County Road C57.

124. Emmaus Community

1437 Woodland Avenue
Des Moines, IA 50309
515/282-4839
Catholic/Jesuit

Near downtown Des Moines is a home that provides a setting and quiet place for prayer and reflection. The community offers guests opportunity for prayer, retreat, and spiritual direction. The house is open to any who wish to spend quiet time in prayer.

The staff provides spiritual direction and individually directed retreats. Staff members also serve as resource persons for groups at other centers: retreats, days of reflection, lectures, and workshops on spirituality, prayer, and spiritual direction.

ACCOMMODATIONS AND RESERVATIONS

Four rooms are available for guests. Additional guests can be housed nearby. Linens are provided.

An overnight private retreat with spiritual direction costs $50 per day for room and board. A day of private prayer without spiritual direction, but including lunch, is $25 per day.

POINTS OF INTEREST

The center has a library. A small chapel holds daily celebration of the Eucharist. Located in the Sherman Hill section of Des Moines, Emmaus is surrounded by many lovely Victorian homes.

LOCATION

On US 235 take Harding Road exit. Follow Harding to Woodland Avenue: Turn left. Emmaus Center is on the left, between 15th Street and 14th Street Place.

125. New Melleray Abbey

6500 Melleray Circle
Peosta, IA 52068
319/588-2319

266

http://www.osb.org/osb/cist/melleray/html/guestindex.html
Catholic/Cistercian

DESCRIPTION

Monks from Ireland began this Cistercian (Trappist) abbey in 1849. It graces the rolling farmland south of Dubuque, Iowa. Thirty-nine monks live, pray, and provide hospitality to guests. They also farm hundreds of acres of corn, soybeans, and organic cereal grain, and they tend a thousand-acre forest of black walnut, oak, pine, and European larch.

Seven times a day the monks gather for Liturgy of the Hours, and retreatants are always welcome to attend in the guest section of the chapel. An atmosphere of silence is guarded by the monks and requested of the guests in many sections of the monastic grounds.

ACCOMMODATIONS AND RESERVATIONS

In an effort to meet the needs of spiritually seeking people, New Melleray makes fourteen rooms with single beds and four rooms with double beds available to people who would like to make quiet, personal retreats. The guest house is attached to an impressive stone church. Bed linens and towels are provided. Meals are served three times per day. Fees are on a freewill donation basis, but $30 per day is appreciated. Schedule your stay well in advance. Rooms are more generally available on weekdays than on weekends.

POINTS OF INTEREST

A small, select collection of books on contemplation and monastic spirituality. Nearby Dubuque has an art museum, Mississippi River Museum, and an Arboretum/Botanical Gardens.

LOCATION
The monastery is located twelve miles southwest of Dubuque City in Vernon township. Accessible via Interstate 151 or 20.

 126. Prairiewoods Franciscan Spirituality Center
120 E. Boyson Road
Hiawatha, IA 52233-1206
319/395-6700
Fax 319/393-7602
ecospirit@prairiewoods.org
Catholic/Franciscan

DESCRIPTION
Seventy acres of unspoiled beauty created a home for this community of prayer, reflection, and education. Trails allow for quiet hikes and contemplation of the beauty of nature, including sightings of woodchucks, deer, and a resident red-tailed hawk. The prairie is currently under restoration to return it to its original native state, including bluestem, coneflower, wild rose, and blazingstar.

Private and directed retreats available, along with a day of prayer for those not wanting to stay overnight. Counseling is available, as are numerous workshops and programs.

ACCOMMODATIONS AND RESERVATIONS
Private and semiprivate overnight accommodations. Simple meals with an eye to holistic health are served.

POINTS OF INTEREST
The center has a library, art room, meditation room, and a large conference room. The dining area/atrium has a high vaulted ceiling with a cozy fireplace area and fountain. The

guest house is a very short walk from the center and has a small kitchenette area.

LOCATION

Just north of Cedar Rapids, Iowa, and just over a hundred miles from Des Moines. From Interstate 80 near Iowa City take Interstate 380/218 North to Cedar Rapids. Continue through Cedar Rapids and take the Boyson Road exit. Go east (not even a mile) and Prairiewoods is on the north side of the road.

Kansas

127. Manna House of Prayer

323 East 5th Street
P.O. Box 675
Concordia, KS 66901
785/243-4428
Fax 785/243-4321
mannahse@dustdevil.com
Catholic/Sisters of Saint Joseph

DESCRIPTION

Manna, as the brochure from this self-described "warm, loving community" states, "harks back to the significance of bread in the Hebrew and Christian Scripture. Manna was the breadlike substance God used to feed the children of Israel in the wanderings millennia ago. It prefigured and foreshadowed the·Bread of Life in Jesus and the bread of the Eucharist in Christian worship. It also signifies hospitality, bread shared with others.

Once a hospital run by the Sisters of Saint Joseph, the three-story brick building was converted in 1978 to a retreat center to become Manna House of Prayer. It is a place for all people to come "for personal and/or group prayer, ongoing learning, quiet time, or counseling," as the brochure states.

The house schedules an array of workshops and retreats, including Marriage Encounter weekends or retreats for the divorced and separating. Also available: eight-day directed retreats; shorter directed retreats on request; Magnificat Program, a two-week program of spiritual renewal to help women integrate twelve-step recovery into their lives; and Sarah Sabbatical, an eight-week spiritual renewal program for women in their sixties, seventies, and eighties wanting insight, guidance, and personal and spiritual growth.

ACCOMMODATIONS AND RESERVATIONS
The spacious brick building includes a dining room, parlor, chapel, and meeting space. The second floor houses not only staff but private rooms for retreatants. Suggested fee is $40 per day including room, meals, and spiritual direction.

POINTS OF INTEREST
Library, kitchenette, exercise room, reflection room, chapel, laundry facilities. Next to a parish church where daily liturgy is available. Far enough into the outskirts of town to allow for solitary walks in the nearby country.

LOCATION
Within walking distance of downtown Concordia.

128. Shantivanam House of Prayer
22019 Meagher Road
Easton, KS 66020-7038

913/773-8255
shanti@lvnworth.com
Catholic/Archdiocese of Kansas City

DESCRIPTION

Shantivanam, a Sanskrit word that means "Forest of Peace," is located on 120 acres of rolling timberland. The environment provides nourishment of body, mind, and spirit. While Catholic in orientation, the house is open to people of all faiths. There are several retreat options. A private retreat can last a day, a weekend, or a week or longer. A directed retreat lasts six or eight days. A solitude sabbatical retreat lasts one to six months.

ACCOMMODATIONS AND RESERVATIONS

Three styles of accommodations are available. Guests may choose guest wing rooms, which are designed for the disabled. There are also guest cabins in the woods with full facilities and simple one-room wooden hermitages also in the woods, with electric heat and light but no plumbing.

Guests share meals and times of prayer with the resident staff. The well-balanced meals have no red meat. Thursdays are Forest Days, with no common meals or prayer. Simple food is available to take to one's dwelling.

The suggested donation for two days with one overnight in the guest wing or a hermitage is $70; a cabin is $85. A six-day directed retreat is $275 in the guest wing or a hermitage and $300 in a cabin.

POINTS OF INTEREST

A small library has spiritual books from a variety of perspectives as well as periodicals on prayer, spirituality, and well-

ness. Swedish and Lomilomi (Polynesian technique) massage
are available by appointment.

LOCATION
Shantivanam is about fourteen miles west of Leavenworth,
Kansas. From Country Road 17 (207th Street) take Mount
Olivet Road (the first crossroad) for about a half mile until a
fork in the road. Take Meagher Road, which is to the left.
Continue past a small bridge, then around the bend and up
the hills. Shantivanam is on the left.

129. Sophia Spirituality Center
751 South 8th Street
Atchison, KS 66002-2784
913/367-6110
Fax 913/367-3886
jkputnam@juno.com
http://www.benedictine.edu/sophia.html
Catholic/Benedictine

DESCRIPTION
Situated on forty acres of rolling hills in northeastern Kansas along the bluffs of the Missouri River,
the center is an ideal setting for prayer and reflection. Sophia Center was established in 1990 on the
beautiful and spacious grounds of the 138-year-old
Mount Saint Scholastica Monastery. The monastic
community consists of 230 women devoted to a
communal life of prayer, work, and hospitality
based on the Rule of Benedict.

Retreatants may take private, directed, or
thirty-day retreats. The duration and content of
guests' programs is determined by their special

needs. The peaceful setting and the hospitable surroundings are conducive to prayer, reflection, learning, and discovery. Also offered: Advent and Lenten
days of prayer; days of recollection and more.

ACCOMMODATIONS AND RESERVATIONS

Guests stay in simple, quiet, and private rooms in the Benedictine spirituality center. Monastic prayers and meals are
shared with the Benedictine sisters of Mount Saint Scholastica Monastery.

The center is air-conditioned and handicapped accessible. The cost per day for an overnight retreat is $40.

POINTS OF INTEREST

Retreatants have the use of excellent libraries: Benedictine
College Library, the Monastic Library, the Sophia Center
Library, and the Center for Benedictine Studies Library.
Also, tours of spots of cultural interest are included in
guests' stays. Atchison's history dates back to July 4, 1804,
when the Lewis and Clark Expedition traveled up the Missouri River. In the 1930s, Atchison gained notoriety from
the aviation prowess of Amelia Earhart (the first woman to
fly solo across the Atlantic; see http://www.ionet.net/~
jellenc/ae_intro.html), who was born July 24, 1897, in her
grandparents' home at 223 N. Terrace.

Also nearby: Atchison County Historical Society Museum, the Muchnic Art Gallery, the Evah Cray Historical
Home Museum, and Amelia Earhart's birth home. All are
open to the public.

LOCATION

The center is located fifty miles north of Kansas City in
historic Atchison, Kansas. It is thirty-five minutes north of
Kansas City International Airport and twenty-five minutes
south of downtown Saint Joseph, Missouri.

130. Spiritual Life Center
7100 East 45th Street N.
Wichita, KS 67226
316/744-0167
Fax 316/744-8072
spiritlife@feist.com
http://www.feist.com/~spiritlife
Catholic/Catholic Diocese of Wichita

DESCRIPTION

The quiet, pastoral setting of the Spiritual Life Center encourages thought and reflection among its guests. The retreat center's brochure states that the center is the most comprehensive and unique retreat center in Kansas. It is owned by the Catholic Diocese of Wichita and administered by the Redemptorist Community, Saint Louis Province. It provides opportunities for adult education, lay leadership development, and spiritual direction to non-profit groups.

Directed and private retreats are available upon request. On a directed retreat, a guest meets daily with a spiritual director: Meals, daily Eucharist, and opportunities for the sacrament of reconciliation are available.

ACCOMMODATIONS AND RESERVATIONS

Overnight accommodations are available: double or single occupancy with private baths. Food service for complete meals, refreshments, or appetizers is provided for guests. The cost for a private retreat is $40 per day; $50 per day for a directed retreat. The Spiritual Life Center is designed so that each meeting will be isolated from all other visitors for privacy and serenity for all guests.

Coffee bar open at all times. Lovely grounds, walking pathways, and adjacent five-acre reservoir. Services also include a
gift shop, featuring a wide array of books, audiotapes, and
religious articles.

LOCATION
Convenient access to the Spiritual Life Center in Northeast
Wichita from Highways K-96 and K-254, or from Interstate
135 and Interstate 235. Call for detailed instructions.

131. Tall Oaks Conference Center
12797 189th Street
P.O. Box 116
Linwood, KS 66052-0116
800/617-1484 or 913/723-3307
Fax 913/723-3213
director@talloaks.org
http://www.talloaks.org
Christian Church (Disciples of Christ)

DESCRIPTION
The Christian Church (Disciples of Christ) of
Greater Kansas City envisions the 350 acres of Tall
Oaks as perfectly suited to fostering prayer, spiritual
growth, and the renewal of faith for both clergy and
laity, young and old. "We care for our guests," the
promotional material states, "in ways that foster
spiritual renewal, enlarge the social conscience, and
model environmental stewardship."

ACCOMMODATIONS AND RESERVATIONS
A wide variety of cabins and lodges and carpeted buildings,
some with private baths and air-conditioning or fireplaces,

offer a number of options for retreatants. Two overnights and a full day's stay, including six delicious meals and the use of the grounds is $80.

POINTS OF INTEREST

Matthews Memorial Chapel, Vesper Circle (an outdoor campfire area with seating for groups), Inspiration Point (another outdoor campfire area atop the highest point of the campus and overlooking the Kaw River Valley), and a swimming pool with heated showers and male and female dressing rooms. Volleyball and basketball nets are available.

LOCATION

From the Kansas City International Airport/North Kansas City take Interstate 29 North from the airport to Interstate 435 South. Follow Interstate 435 to the State Avenue exit (Highway 24/40). Turn right onto Highway 24/40 to Leavenworth County Road 2. Turn left. Proceed to Highway K-32. Turn right. Follow K-32 to Leavenworth County Road 26 and turn left. Tall Oaks is located on the immediate left.

From Interstate 70 West take Interstate 70 East to Interstate 435 South. Follow Interstate 435 South to K-32 West, continue on K-32 right (west) past K-7 and through Bonner Springs. (In Bonner Springs K-32 makes a 90-degree right turn as it goes through town. This turn is right after the Walnut Street/K-32 intersection.) Proceed on K-32 for approximately eight miles to 189th Street/Leavenworth County Road 26. Turn left on County Road 26/189th Street. Tall Oaks is located on the immediate left.

From Interstate 70 East take Interstate 70 West to K-7 South (this is the last free exit before the turnpike). Take K-7 to K-32 West through Bonner Springs. Follow directions as above.

132. The Hermitage

11321 Dutch Settlement
Three Rivers, MI 49093
616/244-8696
Mennonite/Interdenominational

DESCRIPTION
Sixty-five acres of heavily wooded hills in southwest Michigan provide the setting for two cabins in the woods, a renovated barn with eight sleeping rooms and a common dining room, an apartment, a chapel, a library, and trails for leisurely walking. Retreatants may spend a few hours, a day, a week, or a month—even longer. Internships and sabbatical experiences (including directed study and spiritual direction) are possible. Usually retreatants begin their time by meeting with one of the directors to discuss their spiritual longings and hopes.

ACCOMMODATIONS AND RESERVATIONS
The Hermitage depends on the contributions of a range of friends. Guests are asked to pay $45 a day for hospitality and $35 a day for spiritual direction with a declining scale for longer stays. Some physical labor (grounds chores and maintenance) is urged for those staying several days, adaptable to people of all ages, strength, and health.

POINTS OF INTEREST
Within driving distance of Elkhart County, Indiana's Amish country.

Two hours east of Chicago, two hours west of Detroit,
thirty minutes south of Kalamazoo. Coming north or south
on Interstate 131: Turn west on Hoffman Road in Three
Rivers. Follow to Abbey Road, then Dutch Settlement
Road. Watch for Hermitage sign on left. Coming south or
north on Michigan Road 40: Go east four miles on Dutch
Settlement Road.

 133. Saint Augustine's House

3316 East Drahner Road
P.O. Box 125
Oxford, MI 48371
248/628-5155
Staughouse@aol.com
http://www.svare.com/augustine
Lutheran

DESCRIPTION

Located on a hillside amid forty rural acres, this is
the only Lutheran monastery in the United States.
Seven liturgical offices plus the Eucharist are observed each day. Prayer is central to the life of the
community. Notes one friend writing on behalf of
the monastery, "The observance of the [daily] offices
and the Eucharist are the heart of Saint Augustine's
House. They are the primary activities for which
people come to it. . . . One subordinates all other
activities to prayer and turns one's attention toward
God."

The community, including retreatants, observes
several daily periods of silence.

Six men can stay in single rooms in the guest house, all with shared bath. There are also accommodations for one or two women. Three meals served daily, with lighter fare typical on Wednesdays and Fridays. Suggested donation is $20–$25 per day.

POINTS OF INTEREST
Library. A new chapel is being planned.

LOCATION
Traveling from the south (Detroit) take Interstate 75 North to Pontiac. Exit onto M 24 (Exit 81). Travel north to Oxford and turn east (right) onto East Drahner Road. The house is located on the north side of East Drahner Road two and a half miles east of M 24 (not US 24). It is between Barr and Hosner Roads.

134. Saint Gregory's Abbey
56500 Abbey Road
Three Rivers, MI 49093
616/244-5893
Episcopal/Benedictine

DESCRIPTION
Located on 604 acres of farmland in southern Michigan in a parklike setting of woods, this is the oldest Episcopal Benedictine monastery in the United States. Men and women retreatants are welcome throughout the year.

Individual retreatants, or small, quiet groups of up to four stay at Saint Anthony's and eat with the monks in the refectory. There is also a guest cottage, Saint Benedict's, which is a little less than half a mile away from the main buildings. This house can be used for families or groups.

Supper is the light meal at the monastery; the main meal is at noon. The kitchens in both Saint Denys' and Saint Benedict's are fully equipped with appliances and utensils.

Guests are welcome at all services in the abbey church and are expected at the Eucharist and vespers each day.

ACCOMMODATIONS AND RESERVATIONS
Room for ten men in single rooms in Saint Anthony's Guest House and six women in single rooms in Saint Denys' Guest House. Three meals served daily to men in the monastery; women's meals are self-prepared in the guest house. Fees by donation.

POINTS OF INTEREST
Near Kalamazoo. Surrounded by Michigan farmland.

LOCATION
If driving take Interstate 94 to Kalamazoo, then US 131 South. At Three Rivers take Route 105 right, then right again on Abbey Road (Route 103).

 135. Weber Center
1257 E. Siena Heights Drive
Adrian, MI 49221-1793
(517) 266-3400
http://www.op.org/adrian/weber/htm
Catholic/Adrian Dominican Sisters

DESCRIPTION
Weber Center is located on the historic ninety-five-acre campus of the Adrian Dominican Sisters, amid

the natural beauty of gardens, hills, and wooded areas. The six-story facility has 170 single and double bedrooms with common bath facilities, an auditorium seating 175 people, two large meeting rooms, and eight smaller breakout rooms.

Weber Center offers programs on spirituality and theology; sabbatical programs; directed, private, and preached retreats; serenity retreats; and personal growth and development programs.

ACCOMMODATIONS AND RESERVATIONS
Single and double rooms with shared bath facilities. There are four bedrooms with private baths for the physically challenged.

POINTS OF INTEREST
Circle garden, chapel, outdoor prayer areas, bookstore. Lake Erie is forty miles to the east. Lake Hudson State Recreational Area is a short drive away.

LOCATION
Southwest of Detroit, northwest of Toledo, Ohio, near the intersections of Routes 52 and 34.

Minnesota

136. Center for Spiritual Development
211 10th Street
P.O. Box 538
Bird Island, MN 55310-0538
320/365-3644
Fax 320/365-4042
centerbi@willmar.com

Catholic/School Sisters of Notre Dame

DESCRIPTION

Situated in the rich farmland of western Minnesota, the sisters here "believe the world can be changed through the transformation of persons." To this end they offer retreats, programs, and renewal experiences for groups and individuals. "Integral to this call of transformation," they write, "we desire to reach out to those in need of justice and compassion. Surrounded by God's creation we nurture an appreciation of the earth and its resources through simple, creative beauty and reverent stewardship."

Retreats include directed and conference-oriented offerings.

ACCOMMODATIONS AND RESERVATIONS
Twenty attractive, tastefully furnished single bedrooms (one room of which has a private bath). Call for rates.

POINTS OF INTEREST
Chapel, library with resource materials for personal and spiritual growth.

LOCATION
Ninety-five miles west of Minneapolis, five miles east of Olivia. Take Highway 212 and turn south on 10th Street just east of Highway 71.

137. Christ the King Retreat Center
621 South First Avenue
Buffalo, MN 55313
612/682-1394
Fax 612/682-3453

Catholic/Missionary Oblates of Mary Immaculate

DESCRIPTION

Resting on a bluff overlooking Buffalo Lake, the retreat center and its tree-covered grounds provide a sacred place for meditation and quiet time. According to legend, the area was occupied by Native Americans, who called the place *Dabinawa,* meaning "a sheltered, quiet place."

Spiritual direction and directed and private retreats are available throughout the year. The center's primary ministry is providing silent retreats. Retreat facilities are open to nonprofit groups and organizations and to individuals.

ACCOMMODATIONS AND RESERVATIONS

There are sleeping accommodations for 131 (sixty-three double rooms with full baths and five single rooms). Linen, towels, and meals are provided. The fee for private retreats is $40 per day; directed retreats are $50; silent retreats are $85; and a day of prayer is $15.

The center is air-conditioned and handicapped accessible.

POINTS OF INTEREST

Retreatants will enjoy walks along the shore of Buffalo Lake and on the beautiful grounds. There is a spacious chapel and a library. Spiritual resources include videotapes, audiotapes, and a gift shop/bookstore.

LOCATION

The center is about forty-five minutes west of the Twin Cities off Highway 55 West. At the intersection of 55 and Highway 25, turn left. Drive through the town on 25 and

turn right on County Road 12 (Montrose Boulevard). Drive
two blocks, turn right on 7th Street South, then right to
parking.

 ## 138. Franciscan Retreat House

16385 Saint Francis Lane
Prior Lake, MN 55372
612/447-2182
Fax 612/447-2170
Franciscan_Retreats@Juno.com
Catholic/Franciscan

DESCRIPTION

The Franciscan Retreat House is built around a praying community of Franciscan friars. Their facility
rests amid sixty-five acres of land, with woods and
fields. An adjoining suburban neighborhood also
provides a quiet place for an invigorating walk up
and down the hills. Two parks (one with a prairie
lake, the other hilly and wooded) provide space for
walking, bicycling, roller skating, outdoor swimming, and cross-country skiing. Deer sightings and
bird-watching are common. While groups often reserve use of the retreat facilities, private retreatants
are welcome. They often join the friars for morning
and evening prayers and Mass. If time allows, private
retreatants can also meet with our staff for confessions and spiritual consultation.

ACCOMMODATIONS AND RESERVATIONS

Fifty-eight people can be housed in twenty-nine suites. Each
suite divides into two private bedrooms with lavatories, and
a shared bathroom and shower. The monks provide towels
and bedding. "Our guests need to bring," the brochure

notes, "comfortable clothes, walking shoes, toiletries, and a disposition for quiet. You might want to bring your journal, or to start one while you are here."

The monks do not charge a set fee (though they suggest $35 a night), asking simply that donations to cover expenses be generous.

POINTS OF INTEREST
Wooded grounds and two nearby scenic parks. Bookstore and library.

LOCATION
From Minneapolis take 169 South, crossing Minnesota River. After crossing river, exit to MN 18 and travel south out of the valley. Turn left on CR 42, right on CR 27. Where CR 27 turns right, continue directly onto CR 44 (a half mile). Turn left at Franciscan Retreat House sign.

From Mankato and Jordan take 169 northbound; exit CR 18 South and follow above directions.

From Interstate 35E southbound out of Saint Paul take CR 42 West; turn left on CR 27. Where CR 27 turns left, go straight onto CR 44. Proceed a half mile to Franciscan Retreat House sign, turn left.

139. Holy Spirit Retreat Center
3864 420th Avenue
Janesville, MN 56048
507/234-5712
Catholic/Sisters of Saint Francis Rochester

DESCRIPTION
Thirty acres of woods surround the retreat center on Lake Elysian, which offers natural beauty and solitude conducive to inner reflection.

Groups and individuals are welcome, and can receive spiritual direction.

ACCOMMODATIONS AND RESERVATIONS

Eighteen bedrooms sleep thirty-three people. Common restrooms and showers are located down the hall from the bedrooms. Guests must bring their own bed linens and towels, as well as food to do their own cooking in the fully equipped kitchen. Blankets are provided. A sitting and dining room have a lake view. Retreatants are asked to determine their own donation for an overnight stay.

A year-round hermitage is available for private retreats seven days of the week. It is located in a wooded area facing the lake and has heating, plumbing, and kitchen facilities.

Reservations for all of the center's accommodations are recommended as early as possible.

POINTS OF INTEREST

Guests have plenty of space for walking in the woods or being quiet near the lake. The center has a chapel.

LOCATION

Coming from Minneapolis/Saint Paul take 35W South to Faribault. Connect with Highway 60. Go approximately twenty miles to Waseca County Road #3 South. Go approximately three miles to entrance of retreat center.

 140. House of Prayer

P.O. Box 5888
Collegeville, MN 56321
320/363-3293
Fax 320/363-2074
Episcopal/Benedictine

DESCRIPTION

Five acres of wooded land provided by the monastic community of Saint John's Benedictine Abbey in Collegeville Mission are home to this house of prayer. The buildings display award-winning architecture of wood, glass, and stone surrounded by miles of walking trail. The mission of the house is "to guide and support its guests in their desire to seek God in the midst of busy lives, to offer opportunities for spiritual growth and transformation, and to challenge guests to manifest God's presence, delight, and compassion in a complex world."

Guests are welcome to join the monastic community at Saint John's Abbey or Saint Benedict's Monastery for worship.

ACCOMMODATIONS AND RESERVATIONS

Nine single and four double rooms with individual sinks, desk, chair, reading lamp, towels, and sheets. There are separate toilet and bath facilities for women and men, but no private baths. For groups, the university dining service caters the meals and guests assist in serving and dish washing. Individuals may eat at the dining facilities nearby on the university campus.

POINTS OF INTEREST

Meditation room at the end of the residential wing. Saint John's Benedictine Abbey, a short walk away, houses a famed abbey church, monastic manuscript library, and miles of wooded walking paths.

LOCATION

Seventy-six miles northwest of the Twin Cities and ninety minutes from the Minneapolis/Saint Paul International Airport. Take Interstate 94 to Exit 156 (Saint John's University). Head south on County Road 159 one mile. Turn right (west) on Fruit Farm Road and proceed a half mile. Watch for the first gravel drive on the left after the bend in the road and an inconspicuous sign.

141. McCabe Renewal Center
2125 Abbotsford Avenue
Duluth, MN 55803-2219
218/724-5266
Catholic/Duluth Benedictine Sisters

DESCRIPTION

The building that houses the center, a three-story brown-brick Georgian-style home built in 1914, has had a history of various uses: a family home, a senior citizen residence, a college dorm. In 1977 new life was breathed into the charming nineteen-room structure when it became a facility devoted to retreats and programs promoting spiritual and personal growth.

ACCOMMODATIONS AND RESERVATIONS

Room for eighteen guests in single-, double-, or triple-occupancy rooms, with shared baths. Suggested fees or donations: day of quiet/prayer/self-care: by donation. Individual retreats per day (includes overnight lodging and three meals): $45. Retreat direction: $20 per session.

LOCATION

From Interstate 35 going north take 21st Avenue East exit. It turns into Woodland Avenue. Take a left at Lewis at the stone church and turn right onto Abbotsford.

 142. Pacem in Terris
P.O. Box 418
Saint Francis, MN 55070
612/444-6408
Catholic/Franciscan

DESCRIPTION

This retreat center, whose name means "Peace on Earth," covers 180 acres, seven of which are tall-grass prairie. Silence reigns here: Hermitages (prayer cabins) have no telephones and no electricity; they overlook Lake Tamarack and views capture morning rays of sun.

Guests determine their length of stay and pattern of visit. If possible, they should allow at least two nights at the center. The heart of the hermitage experience is the freedom to become "quiet and still" within. Protection for the silence and solitude of all hermitage guests is very important. A staff member is always close by to protect the privacy of all guests.

ACCOMMODATIONS AND RESERVATIONS

The hermitages are simple, one-room cabins with a bed, rocking chair, end table, and altar. Gas lamps provide lighting. An outhouse is only a short walk away. There is also a portable commode in each hermitage. A shower is available at the community house.

Linens and towels are provided, as are a Bible, soap, a flashlight, a rain poncho, and an umbrella. The food is simple: a basket of bread, cheese, and fruit. Dinner is available with the staff Monday through Friday.

The approximate cost of providing a twenty-four-hour hermitage retreat is $35. The retreat center appreciates a donation to meet this cost. Reservations are required.

POINTS OF INTEREST

The hermitages are located in beautiful wooded areas. Trails throughout the woods and prairie invite leisurely walks and enjoyment of the abundant wilderness and wildlife.

LOCATION
Pacem in Terris is located twenty minutes north of Anoka
on Highway 47 and Isanti County Road 8.

 143. Saint Francis Center
116 SE 8th Avenue
Little Falls, MN 56345-3597
320/632-2981
Fax 320/632-1714
Catholic/Franciscan Sisters of Little Falls

DESCRIPTION
The brick buildings on the large campus of this
facility run by Franciscan nuns once housed a hospital, orphanage, nursing home, and girls' high
school. Today it hosts a music center (a school for
performing arts), a food pantry for the poor, and a
custom candle shop. And its Hospitality Services
provide a variety of retreat house and hermitage
accommodations. Daily Mass is offered, as is spiritual
direction.

ACCOMMODATIONS AND RESERVATIONS
Overnight housing for up to fifty-three people, a few rooms
with private baths. Meals provided. The hermitage, a two-
unit winterized log cabin nestled in a pine grove clearing on
the Saint Francis campus, provides a stay for persons who
want more privacy and who do their own cooking and
cleaning. Each cabin contains a bed, small desk, chair, half
bath, small stove, and refrigerator. Rates vary depending on
facility used. Private overnight accommodations, for example, are $21.50 per night, with meals extra. Stays at the
hermitage are $18 per night.

The Health and Recreation Center on site has a swimming pool, gym, whirlpool, exercise and weight room, tennis courts, and sauna available to retreatants for a small fee. Sacred Heart Chapel, built in 1943, carries remnants of a Romanesque influence with pillars, rounded arches, and stained glass symbolism.

LOCATION
One hundred miles northwest of Minneapolis, one hundred and forty-three miles southeast of Fargo, North Dakota. On the campus of the Franciscan sisters at the south end of Little Falls. On US 10 (now County Road 76) near the intersection of Highway 210.

144. Saint John's Abbey
Spiritual Life Program
P.O. Box 7500
Collegeville, MN 56321
320/363-3929 or 320/363-2573
Fax 320/363-2504
Guestmaster@csbsju.edu
http://users.csbsju.edu/~physplnt/index.html
Catholic/Benedictine

DESCRIPTION
Saint John's University shares with the monastery 2,400 acres of grounds (and indeed was founded by the monks). The abbey and campus are set amid lush woodland on a quiet lake. Both private and directed retreats are offered. Private retreats focus on rest, reading, reflection, and prayer (including joining the monks for corporate prayer if you wish). Directed retreats include regular meetings with a spiritual director, to "help you recognize how God

is leading you to deeper understanding and spiritual growth," as the abbey brochure states. Also available: a Benedictine day of prayer held on the final Friday of each month from 6:45 A.M. to 3:30 P.M. Included is a group conference with one of the monks on praying with the Bible, periods of silence and prayer, optional group prayer experiences, and breakfast and lunch.

ACCOMMODATIONS AND RESERVATIONS
Rooms are simply furnished and provide a private bath. Cost per day runs around $42, including meals, for single or $67 double.

POINTS OF INTEREST
Art Center, Hill Monastic Manuscript Library, Liturgical Press, and Saint John's University Bookstore.

LOCATION
Ninety miles northwest of Minneapolis/Saint Paul and twelve miles west of Saint Cloud at Exit 156 off of Interstate 94. A shuttle service runs from Minneapolis/Saint Paul airport.

 ## 145. Tau Center
511 Hilbert Street
Winona, MN 55987
507/454-2993
Fax 507/453-0910
Catholic/Franciscan
  (limited)

DESCRIPTION
The Tau Cross (named after the Greek letter shaped like our capital T) was the primary symbol for Fran-

cis of Assisi in thirteenth-century Italy and continues to be a symbol for many Franciscans worldwide. "The sign [of this cross]," explain the sisters who sponsor this center, "calls us to mission and reminds us that Christ became our servant. The Tau is an invitation to deep hospitality and profound peace." Begun in 1973, the retreat ministry shares its Franciscan values with all people "seeking renewal of spirit and life in the presence of God." The center offers spectacular views of the bluffs lining the Mississippi River.

In addition to private and group retreats to all interested persons, the center offers a twelve-week sabbatical to members and friends of Franciscan communities.

ACCOMMODATIONS AND RESERVATIONS
More than fifty bright bedrooms, some with double beds, have a sink, wardrobe, writing desk, chair, and lamp. Two rooms have private baths. The dining room serves delicious meals and snacks.

POINTS OF INTEREST
Circular stained glass chapel, intimate icon chapel, Franciscan life library.

LOCATION
Accessible by car, bus, Amtrak, or train. Located off Highway 61, the center is two hours southeast of the Twin Cities, thirty miles north of La Crosse, Wisconsin, and forty-five miles east of Rochester, Minnesota. From Highway 61, take Villa north to Mark Street and turn right on Hilbert.

146. Assumption Abbey
RR 5 Box 1056
Ava, MO 65608-9142
417/683-5110
Fax 417/683-5658
http://www.cistercian-usa.org/assump.htm
Catholic/Cistercian (Trappist)

DESCRIPTION

Monks from New Melleray Abbey in Iowa founded this monastery in 1950 in the rugged woods of the Ozark Mountains in southwest Missouri. The thousands of acres of land surrounding the monastery were donated. Over the years the monks have supported themselves through tending orchards and vineyards, making concrete blocks, and, most recently, through baking fruitcakes, which are sold through Williams-Sonoma stores, Midwestern specialty stores, mail order, and at their gift shop. "We are faithful," the monks note, "to Saint Benedict's insistence that monasteries be places of unique hospitality. Treating strangers as if they are Christ is our way. And so we invite you to 'taste and see' the monastic alternative."

ACCOMMODATIONS AND RESERVATIONS

The guest house has nine single rooms for men or women. Meals are served in the guest dining room.

POINTS OF INTEREST

A gift shop sells the monks' renowned dark fruitcakes. The grounds are crisscrossed with miles of old logging roads for hiking. Mark Twain National Forest is nearby.

Seventy-five miles southeast of Springfield, about thirty miles from the Arkansas border off State Road 14.

147. The Cenacle

7654 Natural Bridge Road
Saint Louis, MO 63121
314/381-7070
Fax 314/381-2370
Catholic

Limited day and evening programs. See Marianist Retreat and Conference Center, Eureka, Missouri (below), for more retreat offerings of the Cenacle Sisters.

148. Conception Abbey

P.O. Box 501 Highway 136 & VV
Conception, MO 64433-0501
660/944-2821
Fax 660/944-2811
abbeys@netins.net
http://www.conceptionabbey.org
Catholic/Benedictine

DESCRIPTION

Six hundred and forty acres in rural northwest Missouri host the abbey's retreat extension, the Center for Prayer and Ministry. Dedicated in 1891, the basilica on the property is one of thirty minor basilicas in the United States. The basilica's Romanesque decoration includes eighteen Beuronese-style murals depicting the life of Mary and four scenes from the life of Saint Benedict. Conception Seminary College shares the property.

A full range of individual and group retreats are offered. Topics for the latter include developing prayer and meditation in daily life, experiencing the sacred presence of God in vocation, opening the Sacred Scriptures so that God's Word may speak powerfully.

ACCOMMODATIONS AND RESERVATIONS
Suggested donation for a private retreat is $35 per day, which includes room and meals. Suggested donation for a directed retreat is $60 per day.

POINTS OF INTEREST
Printery House, sponsored by the abbey, prints a fifty-six-page color catalog with a selection of high-quality greeting and prayer cards, notes, and religious art. Included are icons, as well as fine sculpture made by a monk who lived at Conception Abbey until he died at age eighty-five. The Basilica of the Immaculate Conception is the spiritual center of Conception Abbey/Seminary College, and is the heart of the monastic community.

LOCATION
Rural northwest Missouri, ninety miles north of Kansas City. One hundred and twenty miles from Omaha, Nebraska; 125 from Des Moines, Iowa. From Kansas City take Interstate 29 North to US 71 North to Route M. Turn east (right) and proceed seven miles to Route AH, turning north (right). Proceed seven miles to Route VV. Turn east (right) and proceed one mile to the abbey.

 149. Cordis House
648 South Assisi Way
Republic, MO 65738

417/732-8602

Catholic/Little Portion Franciscan Sisters

DESCRIPTION

In the Missouri countryside, Cordis House focuses on prayer, particularly silent prayer.

Spiritual direction, guided retreats for three to six persons, private days of prayer, and contemplative retreat days are available to retreatants. Guests have the option of praying vocally with the Franciscan sisters and the opportunity to join sisters in silent prayer.

ACCOMMODATIONS AND RESERVATIONS

Five private rooms and a hermitage are available for retreatants. Linen and towels are provided, and meals are taken in silence.

An overnight with meals and spiritual direction has a suggested offering of $40. A day and night without meals is $20. A thirty-day retreat is $1,000.

POINTS OF INTEREST

Retreatants will enjoy walking among the trees and the flower and herb gardens. There is a spring near the edge of the property. Birds abound.

The center has an extensive number of books and a prayer space for quiet meditation.

LOCATION

From Saint Louis on Interstate 44 West: At Springfield, take MM (Exit 70); turn right on 60 and go two and a half miles. Turn left on Hines, turn right on Lynn, then turn left on Miller. Turn right onto gravel driveway.

150. Maria Fonte Solitude

(See also Queen of Heaven Solitude, below)
6150 Antire Road
High Ridge, MO 63049-2135
314/677-3255
Catholic/Sons of Our Mother of Peace

DESCRIPTION

Founded in 1966, the Sons and Daughters of Our Mother of Peace strive to combine a contemplative simple life with a commitment to evangelize and help people grow spiritually.

This retreat on a ridgetop is designed to allow retreatants to "withdraw from the noise and clutter of everyday life and to spend time alone with the Lord." Retreats may be scheduled at all times of the year and can be as short as a day or as long as a month.

ACCOMMODATIONS AND RESERVATIONS

Each retreatant occupies a simple hermitage that includes linens, shower, toilet, heat, and air-conditioning. Three meals are provided but taken privately. The hermitage buildings are designed for retreatants desiring a solitary experience. Strong walking or hiking shoes recommended. Fees by donation.

POINTS OF INTEREST

Library with books and tapes. Ample acreage for walking, praying, and reading.

LOCATION

Twenty miles southwest of Saint Louis. The brothers will provide detailed directions by car or meet retreatants at the airport.

151. Marianist Retreat and Conference Center

4000 Highway 109
P.O. Box 718
Eureka, MO 63025-0718
314/938-5390
Fax 314/938-3493
Catholic/Marianist

DESCRIPTION

The center graces 120 acres of hillsides in southwest Saint Louis County, about forty minutes from downtown Saint Louis and Lambert Airport. Three miles of walking trails wind through the property, including a wonderful path along the Meramec River.

In addition to an active schedule of group retreats for youth and adults, the center hosts private retreatants. Also, the Cenacle Sisters of Saint Louis host a variety of retreats at this facility, including directed and nondirected private retreats.

ACCOMMODATIONS AND RESERVATIONS

Forty-four private rooms with complete baths house mostly groups, often youth. Marycliff, a residence for the brothers, is also on the grounds. Two of the rooms have private baths and are used for private retreats. Call for rates.

LOCATION

Take Interstate 44 West to Highway 109, Eureka exit (264). Make a right onto Highway 109. The sign for Marianist Center/Marycliff is two and a half miles north, on the right.

152. Queen of Heaven Solitude
12494 Highway T
Marionville, MO 65705-9739
417/477-2011
Catholic/Daughters of Our Mother of Peace

See description under Maria

Fonte Solitude, above.

ACCOMMODATIONS AND RESERVATIONS
Each retreatant occupies a simple hermitage that includes
linens, shower, toilet, heat, and air-conditioning. Three
meals are provided but taken privately. Retreatants are invited to join in the Liturgy of the Hours in the chapel. The
hermitage buildings are designed for retreatants desiring a
solitary experience. Fees by donation.

POINTS OF INTEREST
Library with books and tapes. Ample acreage for walking,
praying, and reading. Strong walking or hiking shoes recommended.

LOCATION
About twenty miles west of Springfield. The sisters will pick
up retreatants from bus depot or airport.

$\mathcal{N}ebraska$

 153. The Crosier Renewal Center
P.O. Box 789
223 East 14th Street
Hastings, NE 68902-0789
402/463-3188

DESCRIPTION

This center, located on twenty acres of land in eastern Hastings, has as a part of its mission statement the desire to be "committed to the dignity, worth, and sacredness of every individual person and the development of his or her personal and spiritual growth." The center offers day, evening, and weekend retreats, workshops, support groups, private retreats, and spiritual direction. Liturgies with the Crosier Fathers are available if desired. The Crosier Renewal Center features a twenty-four-hour "desert day" for those who desire to spend time alone with God in complete surrender. Further, through different programs and services, the center pays specific attention to the needs of Hispanics in mid-America.

ACCOMMODATIONS AND RESERVATIONS

Hermitage is $20 per day. The fee for the desert day is $35 without spiritual direction, $55 with spiritual direction. Nonrefundable deposit of $15 to confirm directed retreat reservations.

POINTS OF INTEREST

Chapel, large conference rooms, lounge area, private dining room, book and gift shop, gym, tennis court, twenty acres for walking or hiking, Asmat Museum of New Guinea artifacts, *Poustinia* (the brochure describes this small hermitage as being dedicated to "prayer, penance, mortification, solitude, and silence"). The center is open seven days a week for programs to the public.

LOCATION
Located at the Monastery of the Immaculate Conception in
the eastern part of Hastings.

 ## 154. Knowles Mercy Center

2304 Campanile Road
Waterloo, NE 68069-6838
402/359-4288
Catholic/Sisters of Mercy of the Americas

DESCRIPTION
Twenty acres of wooded area adjacent to the beautiful Platte River surround this center that hosts individuals wishing quiet and reflective time, as well as
groups. Retreatants may come for spiritual direction, directed retreats, or private days of prayer.

ACCOMMODATIONS AND RESERVATIONS
The center has nine bedrooms that can be single or used to
accommodate up to eighteen persons. Some bedrooms
share a half bath, and some have a private bath. Large restrooms with a shower and tub are available.

The building is completely heated, air-conditioned, and
handicapped accessible. There is a sunporch with a patio and
a gas grill. The center has a fully equipped kitchen and
provides meals for groups of ten or more.

POINTS OF INTEREST
The Knowles Mercy Center has bicycles for guests to pedal
along its country road. In the woods, there are paths with
park benches for sitting and meditating.

LOCATION
Approximately twenty minutes from west Omaha.

155. Niobrara Valley House of Renewal

Box 117
Lynch, NE 68746
402/569-3433
Catholic

DESCRIPTION

Approximately two hundred miles northwest of Omaha in a valley nourished by the Niobrara River, this center is surrounded by a beauty that symbolizes, as the brochure says, God's invitation to come and be renewed by "living water." The center is sponsored by Assumption Parish in Lynch and Saint Mary's Parish in Spencer, Nebraska.

Retreats, activities, and spiritual direction are offered for adults and youth. Spiritual direction for private retreats is available.

ACCOMMODATIONS AND RESERVATIONS

Private rooms and multiple-occupancy rooms available, some with private baths. Meals may be prepared in the conference room with kitchen or provided by the center on contract. Typical suggested offering for a stay is $20 the first night and $10 thereafter (meals additional). Individuals or families welcome. Children under twelve stay for less.

POINTS OF INTEREST

Chapel, educational media library. Niobrara State Park is nearby.

LOCATION

West of Interstate 81 near the intersection of Routes 12 and 14.

156. Saint Benedict Center
P.O. Box 528
Schuyler, NE 68661-0528
402/352-8819
Fax 402/352-8884
Benedict.center@navix.net
http://www.megavision.com/benedict
Catholic/Benedictine

DESCRIPTION

Retreatants and guests can enjoy a lake and park for walking, praying, and meditating at the retreat center. Across the street is Christ the King Priory, where visitors are welcome to participate with the monks in the scheduled hours of worship.

Saint Benedict Center welcomes guests of all Christian denominations for a quiet day of prayer, individual directed retreats, or group retreats. Priests in the Benedictine community and center staff are available for spiritual direction and for listening to those who are searching.

ACCOMMODATIONS AND RESERVATIONS

The air-conditioned center has a large chapel, meeting rooms, dining rooms, solarium with a library and a fireplace, media room, gift shop, and spacious lobby. Thirty-six guest rooms are furnished with twin beds, chairs, and private bathrooms. Linens are supplied.

A room, single occupancy, is $46 per night; double occupancy is $39 per night. Meals are included. A directed retreat, which requires seven days' notice, is $46 per day (room and meals) plus $10 a day for direction.

The center has an elevator and is handicapped accessible. Two bedrooms are available for those with disabilities.

The center has an outdoor amphitheater for guest use. A permanent exhibit inside the center provides information on the history of the Missionary Benedictine Congregation. For guest reading, some books are available in the solarium. The center also has a well-stocked book section and a selection of Christian art in the gift shop.

LOCATION

Schuyler is sixty miles west of Omaha at the junction of US Highway 30 and Nebraska Highway. Saint Benedict Center and the monastery are located four miles north of town from the intersection of Highways 15 and 30.

North Dakota

157. Benedictine Spirituality Center

Sacred Heart Monastery
Box 364
Richardton, ND 58652
701/974-2121
sacheart@richardton.ctctel.com
http://www.rc.net/bismarck/shm
Catholic/Benedictine

DESCRIPTION

This gentle monastic rural community of several dozen Benedictine women feels "called together to witness God's presence among and within us." They trace their existence to the early 1900s when the Benedictine tradition was "brought to western North Dakota from Saint Mary's, Pennsylvania."

Ample walking areas and natural prairie beauty contribute to the retreat experience.

The community gathers three times daily to pray the Divine Office, and once to celebrate Eucharist. Guests are always welcome at such services. A monthly Taize (pronounced Ty-zay) prayer worship, modeled on the Taize prayer community in France and incorporating song, Scripture readings in several languages, silence, and spontaneous prayer, is also open to all.

Directed retreats provide a time of silence "for increasing one's awareness of God's unique presence and action in one's life. Daily the retreatant meets individually with the director to receive appropriate scriptural material for prayer, to reflect on one's prayer, and to discern the guidance of the Holy Spirit in one's life."

· The sisters also offer thirty-day retreats patterned after the *Spiritual Exercises* of Ignatius of Loyola. A day of recollection allows an individual or group to spend a day at the monastery for personal renewal. Audio and videotapes on Scripture and spirituality are available. Also offered are an eight-month "Journey to Spiritual Growth" program using the *Spiritual Exercises* of Ignatius and sabbaticals of varied lengths and purposes.

ACCOMMODATIONS AND RESERVATIONS
Single and double rooms with linens, towels, and soap are provided. Meals are available in the monastic dining room.

Llamas (which the sisters raise for income), deer, other wild-life.

Richardton is located seventy miles west of Bismarck directly off Interstate 94. From the west take the Taylor exit, drive the one mile north until you reach Taylor, then take a right turn driving through Taylor, and continue about four miles east. Turn right and you will be at Sacred Heart Monastery. From the east take the Richardton exit, drive the one mile north until you reach Richardton, then take a left turn driving through Richardton (the towers you see in town are the abbey, not us). Continue one mile past Richardton on old Highway 10. Turn left.

158. Maryvale Spiritual Life Center
11550 River Road
Valley City, ND 58072-9620
701/845-2864
Fax 701/845-0805
Catholic/Sisters of Mary of the Presentation

Set in a valley, Maryvale is surrounded by rolling hills, a spring, and the Sheyenne River, making it well suited to meditative walks. The physical layout of the building, with the chapel in the center, is a symbol of the God-centered lives that all are called to lead, according to the brochure.

In addition to group retreats and days of prayer, a retreatant may have spiritual direction, a directed retreat (a silent retreat that focuses on the personal prayer of the individual and includes meetings with the spiritual director), or a private retreat, in which retreatants choose their own material for prayer each day.

ACCOMMODATIONS AND RESERVATIONS
Simple bedrooms are private, and most baths are shared (three rooms have private baths). Retreatants may take their meals with the community or in private, as they desire.

A donation of $15 a day is suggested for private retreatants, $35 a day for a directed retreat, and $20 per spiritual direction session.

The facilities are air-conditioned and handicapped accessible, with elevators. There is a no-smoking policy.

POINTS OF INTEREST
Indoor private space for prayer and reflection is available in two chapels, and retreatants are welcome to participate in morning and evening prayers and Mass. The center also has books available for retreatants.

LOCATION
Valley City is just off Interstate 94, sixty miles west of Fargo. Maryvale is north of town. Take any Valley City Interstate 94 exit and proceed to Main Street. Follow to Central Avenue North; take Central Avenue to 12th Street. Turn right and proceed downhill to stop sign (5th Avenue Northeast) and turn left. Travel under railroad bridge and turn left on River Road. Follow about two miles to the Maryvale sign.

Ohio

 ## 159. Bergamo Center for Lifelong Learning
4400 Shakertown Road
Dayton, OH 45430

937/426-2363
Fax 937/426-1090
bergamo@erinet.com
Catholic/Marianist

DESCRIPTION

Quiet and comfortable, Bergamo Center is set on 180 wooded acres. While the center provides an ideal setting for large groups or conferences, it also makes individual retreats available to its visitors. This self-described "place where learning and nature mingle" was named for Pope John XXIII's childhood home. Among its various program offerings are Sabbath mornings, finding God in marriage, feminine images in prayer, and exploring biblical images.

ACCOMMODATIONS AND RESERVATIONS

Air-conditioned rooms accommodate ninety-six people. Single or double occupancy. Private baths, lovely views from rooms. Full food service. Laundry facility. Call for prices.

POINTS OF INTEREST

Included in the landscape is an eighty-acre nature preserve, which has walking trails and areas for reflection. Six conference rooms. Two indoor basketball/volleyball courts, racquetball and handball court. Fireplace lounge. The center is well known for its chocolate chip cookies.

LOCATION

On the outskirts of downtown Dayton. On the campus of Mount Saint John. South of Interstate 35. Easily accessible from Interstate 675. Twenty-three miles from Dayton International Airport.

160. The Franciscan Renewal Center
321 Clay Street
Carey, OH 43316
419/396-7970
Catholic/Franciscan

DESCRIPTION
Situated on the campus of the National Shrine of Our Lady of Consolation, the renewal center has as its mission "providing an environment which will enhance a person's spiritual, intellectual, emotional, and physical wholeness." Weeklong retreats may be made in the summer. Year-round the center features days of reflection and various sponsored retreats, which explore Franciscan themes, and topics such as Mary, aging, prayer, bereavement, and growth and intimacy in relationships. The center's Basilica of Our Lady of Consolation, in addition to being the site for Masses, is open twenty-four hours a day for quiet reflection and prayer.

ACCOMMODATIONS AND RESERVATIONS
Thirty-seven bedrooms, each with vanity and mirror. Air-conditioning, private baths in some rooms. Rooms, $25 per person per day. Room and three meals, $42.50 per person per day.

POINTS OF INTEREST
Gift shop. Thirty-acre Shrine Park located two blocks west of the center. Stations of the Cross. Public swimming pool close by. Snack room.

LOCATION
From Interstate 75 North and South, take Route 15 East to Carey. From Cleveland, take Interstate 71 South to Route 224 West to Route 23 South. From Columbus, take Route 23 North.

161. Milford Spiritual Center

5361 S. Milford Road
Milford, OH 45150
513/248-3500
Fax 513/248-3503
Catholic/Jesuit

DESCRIPTION

Begun in 1925, Milford Spiritual Center has a mission to nurture the spirituality of its visitors by "providing programs, facilities, and an environment which help them find God in all things and live a life of compassionate service." The center is set on thirty-seven acres on the shores of the Little Miami River. Vital to the center's purpose are its personally directed retreats, designed to foster spiritual development and personal growth in individuals. Directed retreats, which are held year-round, may last a weekend or up to eight days. Conference retreats, days of reflection, and training for spiritual directors are also available. The daily liturgy is communal. Almost half of the center's seven thousand annual visitors are high school students.

ACCOMMODATIONS AND RESERVATIONS

Two retreat buildings, both with central air. Total of 110 individual rooms. Each building with chapel, meeting rooms, and dining room. The Loyola Youth Retreat Center, specifically designed for the burgeoning Milford Youth Ministry Program, has forty-six private rooms, chapel, meeting areas, and dining room.

Weekend retreats commence Friday at 7:00 P.M. and finish Sunday at 4:00 P.M. Directed retreats, $50 nonrefundable registration deposit. Directed retreats, one night, $75;

two nights, $145; three nights, $185; four nights, $225.
Weekend retreats, $135 per person; $250 per married couple.
Scholarship assistance available.

POINTS OF INTEREST
The center is within a few blocks of the Little Miami River
State Park, which has a fifty-mile trail for hiking or biking.
Bicycles available at retreat house.

LOCATION
Fifteen miles from downtown Cincinnati. Northeast of Ter-
race Park. East of Wooster Pike and Little Miami River.
South of Mill Street in Milford.

 **162. Sacred Heart Retreat and Renewal
Center**
3128 Logan Avenue
P.O. Box 6074
Youngstown, OH 44501
330/759-9539
Fax 330/759-8235
sacredheartctr@worldnet.att.net
Catholic/Missionaries of the Sacred Heart

DESCRIPTION
Located on twenty-six beautiful acres of lawn and
woods one mile north of Youngstown, Ohio, this
diocesan retreat center is a year-round facility. The
grounds are perfect for walking or jogging on the
paved path through the woods or around the lawn,
and offer a place to rest under the trees or near a
peaceful pond.

Center staff provides twenty-four-hour hosting
for guests from any denomination and educational

group. Guests may take individual private retreats.
Spiritual direction is available.

ACCOMMODATIONS AND RESERVATIONS
Sleeping quarters have individual rooms with a half bath
and showers on each floor. Linens are provided. A house of
prayer is available for small groups of seven or for individuals.

A full kitchen staff serves three meals a day in a dining
room that seats sixty overlooking the spacious front lawn.
The cost for an overnight stay per person is $35 per day
including meals.

POINTS OF INTEREST
The center has two chapels. The retreat house chapel has
capacity for fifty people in a traditional environment. The
community chapel has a separate Eucharistic chapel for private prayer and a communal liturgy chapel.

The retreat center is within ten miles of two major
malls, Mill Creek Park, and many restaurants.

LOCATION
Directions from Interstate 80: Go south on Belmont Avenue,
five lights to Gypsy Avenue. Turn left to the end, to Logan
Way. Turn left, go about one mile. The center is on the left.

163. Saint Joseph Christian Life Center
18485 Lake Shore Boulevard
Cleveland, OH 44119
216/531-7370
Fax 216/531-0629
http://www.StJosephChristianLife.com
Catholic

DESCRIPTION
Since 1947, this center set on the banks of Lake Erie
has welcomed thousands of visitors for workshops,

programs, and private retreats. Twelve well-landscaped acres include contemplative garden areas and a shoreline walkway of 360 feet. Program retreats, which may last from one afternoon to a week, address various topics, including prayer-filled living, wellness and the spiritual journey, marriage, mystics, journaling, and contemplative outreach. Private retreatants are welcome, and spiritual direction is available.

ACCOMMODATIONS AND RESERVATIONS

Overnight accommodations for as many as 105 visitors. Single- and double-occupancy rooms, a number with a view of the lake. Most rooms with private baths. Air-conditioned meeting rooms and dining room for up to two hundred.

Prices for program retreats vary. Nonrefundable deposit of $25 required for overnight programs. Private rooms for overnight retreats, add $20 per night. Call for further price information.

POINTS OF INTEREST

Book and gift store.

LOCATION

Take the East 185th Street exit off Interstate 90. North on East 185th to Lakeshore Boulevard. Left (west) on Lake Shore. First or second driveways on right lead to the center grounds.

164. Saint Joseph Renewal Center

200 Saint Francis Avenue
Tiffin, OH 44883
419/443-1485
Fax 419/447-1612

SJRC@bright.net
Catholic/Sisters of Saint Francis

DESCRIPTION

Subjects for the renewal center's day retreats include rest and renewal, aging, prayer, parenting, music, and Mary. Situated on the order's Motherhouse Grounds, the center also offers private and guided retreats, spiritual direction, group retreats, and days and evenings of recollection. Retreats may be for six days, eight days, or thirty days. Here, a brochure from the center says, one can find a place to "celebrate life in God and continuing conversion in love." The spacious campus provides one a chance to commune with God through God's creation.

ACCOMMODATIONS AND RESERVATIONS

Retreats available year-round. Twenty-two rooms with full beds; eleven with single beds. All rooms are private and have sink and closet. Showers centrally located in each hall. Linens, towels provided.

Cost varies depending on type of retreat. Call for further price information. Scholarships available.

POINTS OF INTEREST

Chapel for prayer, reflective music accessible. Opportunities for therapeutic massage. Books are available for purchase.

LOCATION

From the west or south take State Route 224 to State Route 231. Turn left on 231. Proceed one mile to Saint Francis Avenue; go right on Saint Francis, right at Saint Francis Home. The center is on the left as one comes up the drive.

From the east take State Route 224 to State Route 100.

Turn right on 100. Proceed one mile north to Saint Francis Avenue. Turn left at first drive. The center is on the right.

From the north take State Route 53 to Tiffin. Turn left at Washington Street; proceed two miles through town. Turn left at church onto Melmore Street and go one mile to Saint Francis Avenue; turn right. Take left at first lane into convent grounds. The center is on the right.

165. Saint Thérèse's Retreat Center
Catholic Diocese of Columbus
5277 East Broad Street
Columbus, OH 43213
614/866-1611
Catholic

DESCRIPTION
Although the retreat center welcomes mainly groups for scheduled retreats, private retreats may be made on a limited basis (one week per month). Group retreats are intended for men, women, priests, youth groups, senior citizens, and others.

ACCOMMODATIONS AND RESERVATIONS
Fifty-four rooms, twenty of which have double beds. Each room has a dresser or desk and a sink. Several rooms share a bathroom. The center provides linens and towels. The main conference room and the dining room are air-conditioned.

POINTS OF INTEREST
Rooms are offered only for those on retreat.

LOCATION
Call for directions.

166. Sisters of Charity Spirituality Center
5900 Delhi Road
Mount Saint Joseph, OH 45051
513/347-5453 or 513/347-5456
Fax 513/347-5467
scspirctr@aol.com
http://members.aol.com/RKUHNsc/sespirctr/html
Catholic/Sisters of Charity

DESCRIPTION

This center just west of Cincinnati offers a variety of retreats: parish missions, days of reflection, weekends or days of retreat, and workshops. Among the themes the center explores are compassion, the paschal mystery, women of wisdom, and praying with Scripture. The staff wants to "unite faith with life experience in a holistic approach" and help "feed the hungers of [one's] heart." In addition to group retreats, spiritually directed retreats for individuals are available. The well-landscaped, spacious outdoors result in a quiet and serene atmosphere.

ACCOMMODATIONS AND RESERVATIONS

Private rooms, each with a sink and a fan. Air conditioners in hall. Common baths. Overnight space for thirty. Various offerings for retreats are suggested, depending on the type of retreat made. A directed retreat for women ranges from $90 to $110 (two nights, five meals, and individual direction).

POINTS OF INTEREST

Motherhouse chapel, small prayer room for private or communal prayer. Library with books and tapes.

Take US 50 (River Road) West of Cincinnati. Right at Fair-
banks Avenue, which becomes Delhi Road after a curve to
the left. Follow Delhi to its end at the entrance to Sisters of
Charity Motherhouse (past Bender Road). Turn right into
Motherhouse driveway to post office entrance.

167. Yokefellow Retreat and Renewal Center
2603 Evansport Road
Defiance, OH 43512
419/428-2891
mmsafe@williams-net.com
Quaker

DESCRIPTION
Quaker minister and philosopher Elton Trueblood
started a discipleship movement known as the Yokefellow Movement. As a result, the staff say, Yokefellow House was begun in 1960 as "a Christian oasis
where groups or individuals could come . . . to
build or renew themselves in their Christian walk."
The center is found in the countryside encircled by
grain fields and backed by the Tiffin River.

ACCOMMODATIONS AND RESERVATIONS
The rustic house, more than a hundred years old, was once
a dairy barn. Central air-conditioning.

LOCATION
Northwest Ohio. Accessible from the north, east, and west
via US 6. From the south, reachable by Ohio State Route 66.
South of Evansport on Evansport Road.

168. Blue Cloud Abbey

P.O. Box 98
Marvin, SD 57251
605/432-5528
Fax 605/432-4754
abbey@bluecloud.org
http://www.bluecloud.org
Catholic/Benedictine

DESCRIPTION

The northeastern South Dakota abbey, founded by Indiana's Saint Meinrad Archabbey in 1950, is surrounded by lakes and hills overlooking the large prairie of Whetstone Valley. A blue cloud, one of the abbey's postcards says, is "a cloud of blessing, bringing moisture to the Dakota plains." The abbey strives to be a place "to come aside, to think, to pray, to be quiet before God and . . . listen." Visitors are welcome to join the monks in the Eucharist and in communal prayer. The abbey offers group retreats, days of recollection, directed private retreats, and individual private retreats. Private retreats may last from one day to a week or more. In addition, the abbey offers its Associate Program that allows men between the ages of nineteen and fifty to fully experience the monastic life for anywhere from two weeks to three months.

ACCOMMODATIONS AND RESERVATIONS

Twenty-one double-occupancy rooms, all with private baths. Days of recollection, $20 per person (includes lunch).

Private retreat is $35 per person per night. Double occupancy, $30 per person per night. Spiritual direction, add $20 per day. Meals, towels, bedding provided. The monastery will not turn away anyone due to lack of finances.

POINTS OF INTEREST
American Indian Culture Research Center, created by members of fourteen reservations in the Upper Midwest. The research center exists to help Native American leaders and educators rebuild their community, and to make non–Native American people aware of the culture of the American Indian. The abbey's Camp Mahpiyato, set in a large ravine behind the abbey, affords opportunities for swimming, fishing, hiking, tennis, football, and indoor games. Resource room with books and tapes is available.

LOCATION
Thirteen miles west of Milbank, two miles south of Highway 12. From Interstate 29 North, Exit 201 East to Blue Cloud Abbey (seven and a half miles).

W i s c o n s i n

 169. The Bridge Between Retreat Center
4471 Flaherty Drive
Denmark, WI 54208
920/864-7230
Catholic/Dominican

DESCRIPTION
Located about twenty minutes from Green Bay, the center provides guests with a time to let go of schedules and enjoy the solitude of a comfortable facility in a rural setting, offering a place to be alone

to rest, reflect, and recreate. Guests may bring bikes and ride the country roads, stroll along the nature trails, or pause in the natural bird sanctuary. Guests of all religious denominations are invited to join in prayer, share simple meals, study, and enjoy the recreation and natural silence of the center.

One may also request a spiritual guide to share with and to suggest resources. Groups are welcome and may be self-directed or guided according to their needs.

ACCOMMODATIONS AND RESERVATIONS

The silo has private rooms and baths. A cottage offers a one-room dwelling located in an orchard. The 1890 Granary Lodge accommodates groups. None of the rooms are air-conditioned. The suggested donation for individuals, which includes meals, is $32. Day of reflection is $15 and spiritual direction is $20 per session. The donation for individuals in a group is $15 for a directed day of reflection and $12 for a self-directed day of reflection. Retreatants should bring walking shoes, boots, layered clothing, and a flashlight for night walking.

POINTS OF INTEREST

In winter, snowshoeing is possible. Persons may wish to share talent or contribute in needed areas in return for a program offering.

LOCATION

Coming from the north take 41S to 172E to GV. Turn right on GV to stop sign. Turn left on G or Dickinson Road and go past Shirley two miles to intersection. Turn left onto Cooperstown Road to Fairview. Turn right. Watch for Bridge sign. Turn left on Flaherty to buildings. Coming from the south, use Interstate 43 and exit at Maribel. Turn left on Z. Stay on Z to NN. Turn right on NN. Follow to Cooperstown Road. Left on Cooperstown Road to Fairview. Turn left on Fairview. Watch for Bridge sign. Turn left on Flaherty to buildings. Or use 41 North to 96. Follow 96 to Lark. Go straight through Lark. Turn left on Fairview. Watch for Bridge sign. Turn right on Flaherty to buildings.

 170. Franciscan Spirituality Center
920 Market Street
LaCrosse, WI 54601-8809
608/791-5295
FSCenter@juno.com
Catholic/Franciscan Sisters of Perpetual Adoration

DESCRIPTION

The mission of this center located in the heart of LaCrosse, its brochure states, "is to provide . . . a sacred space where persons can be supported in their search for God, meaning, or fullness of life." A variety of directed programs and daylong retreats are offered to groups throughout the year. Individually directed retreats for the person who wishes to meet God in prayer and solitude are also offered. The retreatants meet daily with a spiritual director. For large groups the center offers the preached retreat and for smaller groups, the guided retreat. Both retreats consist of daily conferences, reflection, and Eucharistic liturgy.

In addition to its LaCrosse facility, the center also runs three hermitages known as Solitary Ridge, located next to a woodland on the property of the Sisters' Villa Saint Joseph in the village of Saint Joseph, thirteen miles south of the center.

Rooms at the center are air-conditioned. Some have private baths. A nonrefundable deposit of $20 is requested. Suggested donations: $25 per day; $260 for six-day directed retreat; $25 per hour for individual spiritual/retreat guidance. No pets.

Each of the three hermitages at Solitary Ridge is equipped with electric and wood stove heat, water, bath, stove, refrigerator, and phone. Bed linens are provided, but guests are asked to bring their own towels and personal grooming items. They are also advised to bring good walking shoes, boots, and slippers for inside. Guests provide and prepare their own food.

POINTS OF INTEREST
LaCrosse is nestled between the Mississippi River and soaring bluffs. The area includes Mississippi River attractions, parks, and great restaurants.

LOCATION
Call for directions.

171. Redemptorist Retreat Center
Our Mother of Perpetual Help
1800 North Timber Trail Lane
Oconomowoc, WI 53066-4897
414/567-6900
Fax 414/567-0134
Catholic/Franciscan

DESCRIPTION
Located near Oconomowoc, this center sits beside the beautiful and secluded Crooked Lake and amid the rolling hills of Wisconsin's Kettle Moraine region. Thirty-five minutes west of Milwaukee, it of-

fers group retreats, silent weekend preached retreat, and a hermitage experience of *Poustinia* (from the Russian word that can be translated as "hermitage" and which forms the name for the center's hermitage building). "The *Poustinia*," notes the center's materials, "is limited to those who desire to encounter God in a retreat setting in complete silence and solitude. . . . [It] is not intended as merely a vacation or resting place but rather as a holy place of silence, fasting, and reflection."

ACCOMMODATIONS AND RESERVATIONS

Rooms for regular retreatants have private bath and writing desk and lamp. Linens and towels provided. The *Poustinia* features a kitchenette, full bathroom, living room, and bedroom. Call for various rates. Scholarships available.

POINTS OF INTEREST

Within driving distance of numerous lakes and the Kettle Moraine State Forest.

LOCATION

An hour drive from Madison and two-and-a-quarter-hour drive from Chicago. Driving west from Milwaukee on Interstate 94 take Exit 283 (Sawyer Road), turn left at the bottom of the ramp, and take the first right onto County Road DR (Delafield Road). Turn at North Timber Trail (about one mile up on the left) and take to the end. Driving east from Madison take Exit 282, turn right at the top of the ramp onto State Highway 67 (South). At the first intersection turn left onto County Road DR (Delafield Road). Turn at North Timber Trail (about one mile up on the right) and take to the end.

172. Saint Anthony Retreat Center
300 East Fourth Street
Marathon, WI 54448
715/443-2236
Fax 715/443-2235
sarc@dwave.net
http://www.dwave.net/~sarc
Catholic/Capuchin Franciscan

DESCRIPTION

Nestled on the bank of the Rib River amid pines, maples, and birches, Saint Anthony Retreat Center is open to people of all denominations who seek God and spiritual growth. The monks care for retreatants, lead them in prayer, listen to their needs, and help shoulder their burdens. Retreatants experience the tranquillity of the scenic gardens and walkways of the forty-five acres that surround the center.

While the center hosts retreats for groups that have their own presenters, it also offers retreats throughout the year that are planned specifically for families, couples, or individuals.

ACCOMMODATIONS AND RESERVATIONS

Delicious meals are served in the dining room. Several of the lounges and conference rooms are air-conditioned. Seven bedrooms have private bathrooms adjoining.

LOCATION

The center is in Marathon City, thirty-five minutes from Central Wisconsin Airport and eleven miles west of Wausau, Wisconsin. It is accessible by Highway 29.

173. Saint Benedict Center

P.O. Box 5070
Madison, WI 53705-0070
608/836-1631
Fax 608/831-9312
Catholic/Benedictine

DESCRIPTION

The spacious grounds at the center include a small glacial lake and wooded nature trails. Natural beauty and a welcoming environment invite entry into the inner space where God dwells, a brochure reads.

Retreat options include a day of retreat (meeting with a spiritual guide), and directed retreats for several days, also including meetings with a spiritual guide. Guests are welcome to participate in the Benedictine Liturgy of the Hours and centering prayer with the Sisters of Saint Benedict.

Directed retreats are available on a limited basis, and advance arrangements must be made with one of the spiritual guides.

ACCOMMODATIONS AND RESERVATIONS

Personal retreatants are welcome for a day, an overnight, a weekend, or longer. A comfortable private room is provided at the monastery. Rooms are air-conditioned and have private baths. In addition, an ecumenical Retreat and Conference Center hosts larger gatherings.

An overnight stay for an individual is $30. Use of a private room for the day only is $12.50. Continental breakfast is included with an overnight stay; lunch is $4.50 and dinner is $6. Guests may bring their own food. The suggested fee for one hour with a spiritual guide is $30.

Retreatants will enjoy and value the nature trails, pond, orchards, woods, and wildlife. Coyotes, fox, deer, wild ducks, and raccoons live in the rolling fields and woods. Efforts are under way to restore native prairie plants.

The oratory in the monastery, a chapel, a monastic library, and bookstore, a fire circle, volleyball net, swimming pool, and a view/meditation area are also available.

LOCATION

The center, which is fifteen minutes away from the Dane County Regional Airport, is on County Highway M on the northwest side of Lake Mendota. It is three and a half miles east of the junction of County Highway M and US Highway 12, or four miles west on M from the junction of M and State Highway 113.

174. Saint Francis Friary and Retreat Center

503 South Browns Lake Drive
Burlington, WI 53105
414/763-3600
Catholic/Franciscan

DESCRIPTION

This peaceful refuge bears the name of a saint known for centuries as a peacemaker, and the center's carefully tended gardens, grottoes, and statues reflect his spirit. Built on 170 acres three miles north of Burlington, Wisconsin, this center welcomes individuals and groups of varied backgrounds in an atmosphere of Christian hospitality. A team of Franciscan friars, sisters, and laypeople is committed to sharing the spirit of Francis with its guests.

There are other Franciscans living at the friary who add a special flavor to the center: men involved in teaching, woodworking, and ministering to the handicapped.

Individuals will enjoy the solitude of a private retreat, or one may choose to meet with a spiritual director during this time. Groups can also experience a directed retreat. Participants meet with a director in a private setting for daily sessions. Married couples are welcome.

ACCOMMODATIONS AND RESERVATIONS
Each room has a desk and sink; common baths. The center supplies linens and towels. Fee for a private retreat is $26 without meals or $38.25 with meals. Fee for directed retreats is $36 without meals, $48.25 with meals. Fee for couple's weekend: $39 per couple, without meals. Add $24.50 per day for meals. Fee for couples receiving a directed retreat is $54 per night. The Greccio Hermitage is available for one person or small groups of up to twelve people. Meeting rooms are air-conditioned.

POINTS OF INTEREST
Nearby bike trail.

LOCATION
On Wisconsin Highway 36, at the intersection of County W three miles north of Burlington, Wisconsin.

175. Saint Joseph Retreat
3035 O'Brien Road
Bailey's Harbor, WI 54202
920/839-2391
Fax 920/839-2391

Catholic/Priests of the Sacred Heart and School Sisters of Saint Francis

DESCRIPTION

On a 440-acre working farm, the retreat offers a variety of atmospheres: pasture, grain fields, animals, woods, and a lake. It provides, according to its brochure, space and beauty that invite retreatants to recognize the glory of God revealed through all of creation.

Guests may come for private, directed or guided retreats, weekend workshops, or days of reflection. Spiritual direction is available all year.

ACCOMMODATIONS AND RESERVATIONS

Comfortable rooms, which have a combination of twin and double beds, have desks and rocking chairs. Linen and towels are provided.

The per-day cost for a private retreat, including meals, is $45. A thirty-day experience is $1,200, which can be lowered if an hour or two of work each day would fit into the retreat experience. Registrations are only accepted in writing and must be accompanied by partial payment, $25 of which is nonrefundable and nontransferable.

POINTS OF INTEREST

Retreatants can walk, ski, or snowshoe on marked trails through the woods. The retreat also provides bicycles and a mile of lakeshore. There is a kivalike chapel built in a silo, a library, and outdoor Stations of the Cross.

LOCATION

From the south take Route 43 North to Green Bay. Take Exit 185 to Sturgeon Bay (Route 57). Continue on Route 57

North through Jacksonport. Go one mile, turn left on
Logerquist Road. The retreat is two and a half miles off
Route 57.

 176. Siena Center
5635 Erie Street
Racine, WI 53402-1900
414/639-4100
Fax 414/639-9702
Catholic/Dominican

DESCRIPTION

In a beautiful sylvan setting on the shore of Lake
Michigan guests are able to retreat from the concerns of everyday living and for a time be nourished
and refreshed. The Dominican sisters intentionally
share the tranquillity of their home with women
and men of all faiths. While the large complex with
its forty-plus-acre site is available to individuals for
private retreats or to large groups who bring their
own speakers, the center also sponsors retreats that
wrestle with issues of concern in today's world. The
center is open year-round except three weeks in
August.

ACCOMMODATIONS AND RESERVATIONS

Seventy-six single rooms and four double rooms with central bath facilities. The chapel and auditorium are air-conditioned, but the breezes of Lake Michigan sometimes act as a
natural air conditioner. Four meeting rooms can accommodate up to eighty persons. There are several small conference rooms. Retreatants enjoy their home-cooked meals
with the community in the cafeteria-style dining room.

$35–$45 per night includes meals. Elevator access to all floors. Siena is a smoke-free facility.

Library with over fifteen thousand books, tapes, videos, periodicals, and newspapers. On the grounds is a labyrinth, an ancient meditation tool. The sandy beach on Lake Michigan's shoreline and the natural wildlife setting afford recreational opportunities.

From the Milwaukee area exit Interstate 94 at Highway 100 (Ryan Road), go left on 100 to Highway 32 (almost four and a half miles), turn right on Highway 32 to Four Mile Road (six and a half miles), go left on Four Mile Road to Erie Street (just over one mile). Turn left on Erie Street to Siena Center (just over a half mile). Driveway is on right.

From Chicago area exit Interstate 94 at Highway 20, go right on Highway 20 to Highway V (one mile), left onto V. Follow V north (four and a half miles) to Four Mile Road (residence on northeast corner). Turn right onto Four Mile Road to Erie Street (seven and a quarter miles), then turn left onto Erie Street to Siena Center (just over a half mile). Driveway on right.

177. Sinsinawa Mound
Sinsinawa, WI 53824
608/748-4411
Catholic/Dominican

The land on which the center rests was considered sacred by Native Americans. The Mound is still considered a holy place by the sisters who minister there and by those who come to receive ministry.

Guests are free to enjoy the natural beauty of the 450 acres of lush woodlands, vineyards, gardens, and nature trails. The harvest from the orchards and gardens is shared with guests at the dinner table, and dairy products, beef, and pork are provided by the Mound farm. Water is pumped fresh from artesian wells deep under the Mound.

The center hosts both private and group retreats. A phone interview is required with the program director for first-time retreatants. A specially trained staff member is available for those retreatants desiring to meet with a spiritual guide to pray and reflect on the spiritual journey.

ACCOMMODATIONS AND RESERVATIONS
Almost all rooms are dorm style. There are two bedrooms that have private baths. Bedrooms are not air-conditioned. The entire facility is smoke-free indoors. Outside there are designated smoking areas. Cost for individual (private) retreats: $50 per day: 3 days or less; includes 3 meals. $45 per day: 4 days or more; includes 3 meals. $15 per day: day of reflection; includes noon meal. Suites that include private bath and sitting room are $5–$10 per day additional.

POINTS OF INTEREST
Ongoing displays in the Mound Gallery of Art. Exhibit of vintage scientific equipment used by the Mound's founder to teach astronomy and principles of electricity.

LOCATION
Sinsinawa Mound is located approximately ten miles east of Dubuque, Iowa, and thirty minutes from the Dubuque Regional Airport in the very most southwestern corner of Wisconsin. Traveling west on Highway 11, turn left on County Road Z and proceed one mile.

Pacific and Northwest

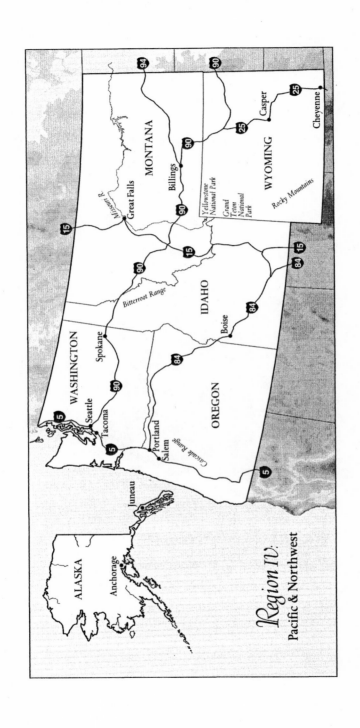

Region IV:
Pacific & Northwest

178. Holy Spirit Retreat House

10980 Hillside Drive
Anchorage, AK 99516
907/346-2343
Fax 907/346-2140
Catholic/Jesuit

DESCRIPTION

This retreat center finds home amid twenty acres in the foothills overlooking Anchorage and Denali. Sightings of moose and eagles are frequent. As a spirituality center in the Jesuit tradition, the *Spiritual Exercises* of Ignatius of Loyola, a Spanish saint and spiritual theologian, provide the foundation for programs and retreats. Guests of all religious traditions are welcome. Directed retreats are offered, as well as conference retreats for men and women and couples. Mass is held weekdays at noon and on Sunday mornings.

ACCOMMODATIONS AND RESERVATIONS

Single or twin rooms with shared bathrooms. Two cabins with private baths are also available. Lodging is $35–$55 per night, not including meals. Self-serve meals for individual retreatants are $10 per day when buffet-style meals are not available. The latter run $27 for three meals per day. Reservations are required and are taken up to one year in advance, with 50 percent deposit required, nonrefundable ninety days before the stay.

Stations of the Cross. Resurrection Chapel provides a panoramic view of Anchorage and a beautiful setting for prayer. Common areas include a library and sitting room. The Alaska Zoo is two miles away. Hiking available in Chugach State Park a mile and a half away.

LOCATION
Seven miles from the Anchorage International Airport.

 ## 179. Shrine of Saint Thérèse

5933 Lund Street
Juneau, AK 99801
907/780-6112
Catholic

DESCRIPTION
The retreat center is located twenty-three miles north of Juneau on the island shores of Lynn Canal. It honors the nineteenth-century French nun, Thérèse of Lisieux. Known for her "little way" of everyday spirituality, she wrote the popular *Story of a Soul*. The grounds offer breathtaking views of the Chilkat Mountains and the northern Pacific waters of Pearl Harbor. The chapel is built of beach stone, creating a striking profile. The lodge is built of natural logs. The shrine is surrounded by fourteen Stations of the Cross, used by Catholics to commemorate and remember Jesus' journey to his crucifixion. Some spiritual direction is available.

ACCOMMODATIONS AND RESERVATIONS
Retreatants stay at a lodge (with ten bedrooms and three bathrooms), the Post Office Cabin (private rooms with pri-

vate baths), or two cabins heated by wood-burning stoves and lacking running water. The cabins are usually available at short notice. Couples and children are welcome. Rates are comparable to those of other retreat houses.

POINTS OF INTEREST
Wildlife abounds—sea lions, whales, and other creatures. Salmon is fished from the shore in early spring and summer and can be seen spawning in August.

LOCATION
Accessible from the Egan Expressway and Glacier Highway (Mile 23).

Idaho

180. Monastery of Saint Gertrude

HC 3, Box 121
Cottonwood, ID 83522-9408
208/962-3224
Fax 208/962-7212
webmasterjmb@juno.com
http://www.rc.net/boise/st_gertrude/index.html
Catholic/Benedictine

DESCRIPTION
The monastery traces its beginnings to 1882, when three nuns were sent from Switzerland to begin a new community in the U.S. They eventually settled on a wooded butte overlooking prairie. Much of the 1,400 acres they own is timberland with stands of ponderosa pine, fir, and spruce. Some is used for grazing, farming, and orchards. Wildflowers and songbirds abound. The sisters nurture both a close

337

relationship to the land and invite others to experience the "natural beauty, solitude, and restful quiet" of the land. The monastery's presence stands out with its blue porphyry and red-domed twin towers. "We are a religious community of ninety sisters," they write, "who follow the Rule of Benedict at the monastery . . . and the other places where we live and serve. . . . Through a balance of prayer, work, and leisure we commit ourselves to bringing hope to the world by doing what Jesus did. This commitment is expressed through our present ministries of prayer, health care, parish ministry, retreats, hospitality, care of the land, education, social services, counseling, development, administration, and preservation of tradition."

The celebration of the Eucharist, the Liturgy of the Hours, and *lectio divina* provide a framework for the monastery's life and work.

Individualized retreat experiences are available: a private retreat of a few hours, several weekdays, or a weekend. Or an individually directed retreat in which the retreatant uses Scripture-centered prayer, with the help of a prayer companion, to explore his or her relationship with self, God, and others.

ACCOMMODATIONS AND RESERVATIONS
Suggested donations range between $40 and $50 per night for one night (individual), less for multiple nights. One night for a couple ranges between $65 and $80 for the first night. Meals included.

POINTS OF INTEREST
Saint Gertrude's Museum is a corporate ministry of the sisters, a permanent, public, nonprofit educational institu-

tion that provides for the systematic collection and care of its artifacts. It is located on the monastery grounds. Several portions are of special historical interest; the Polly Bemis exhibit displays items that belonged to a Chinese slave girl brought to the Warren gold mining camp in 1872. There are handcrafted utensils made by Buckskin Bill (Sylvan Hart), who lived in Idaho's Primitive Area along the Salmon River for fifty years. Other attractions include mineral collections, exquisite handcrafted lace and embroidery.

LOCATION
Two miles south of Cottonwood off of US 95.

M o n t a n a

181. Sacred Heart Renewal Center
26 Wyoming Avenue
P.O. Box 153
Billings, MT 59103-0153
406/252-0322
Catholic

DESCRIPTION
In the heart of the largest city in Montana, the center is within walking distance of the legendary Moss Mansion, Yellowstone Art Museum, Western Heritage Center, and great dining and shopping. The mission of this renewal center, housed in a former convent built in the late 1950s, is to be a place for spiritual renewal and growth and a quiet house of prayer, spiritual reflection, and solitude.

Individuals and groups are welcome at the center's overnight retreats or evening programs. Spiritual direction, an opportunity to talk about one's relationship with God with a certified spiritual director, is offered.

ACCOMMODATIONS AND RESERVATIONS
Thirty-four single and double bedrooms lodge guests. Linens, towels, and soap are provided. Four rooms have private bathrooms. A dining room seats fifty, and a kitchen is available for catering.

Two large meeting rooms and five small meeting rooms can be used. Guest fees depend on facilities used.

POINTS OF INTEREST
The Marian Library, located on the first floor of the center, contains Christian classics as well as a variety of reference books. Inspirational books, tapes, and videos can be checked out for personal study.

LOCATION
The center is in the heart of Billings, between 24th Street West and 27th Street. Call for directions.

O r e g o n

 182. Brigittine Priory of Our Lady of Consolation
23300 Walker Lane
Amity, OR 97101
503/835-8080
Fax 503/835-9662
http://www.brigittine.org
Catholic/Brigittine

DESCRIPTION
A small Roman Catholic monastery that offers private, nondirected retreats to individuals or married

couples, the retreat facility is located in rural farm country in the Willamette Valley of Oregon. Brigittine monks in their dark grey habits go about their rhythmic style of life creating an atmosphere conducive to prayer and reflection. Retreatants are welcome to attend the daily Mass as well as the Liturgy of the Hours, which is chanted seven times a day.

ACCOMMODATIONS AND RESERVATIONS
The retreat house has six bedrooms and three baths. Each bath is shared by two bedrooms. One of the bedrooms will accommodate a married couple. The air-conditioned retreat house has a living room and a conference room. Suggested donation is $35 per day, which includes three meals.

POINTS OF INTEREST
Books for spiritual reading are available at the retreat house and at the monastery reception area.

LOCATION
Forty-five miles southwest of Portland. Take Highway 99W to Amity and watch for large blue direction signs to the monastery. The monastery is five miles west of Amity.

183. Christian Renewal Center
22444 North Fork Road SE
Silverton, OR 97381
503/873-6743
Fax 503/873-8300
CRCRetreat@aol.com

DESCRIPTION
Located on a beautifully forested forty-acre hillside, the Christian Renewal Center is a favorite weekend retreat site for churches and Christian organizations.

Opportunities for individual retreats are available for those who are able to come weekdays. Open all year, the center sponsors family retreats at Thanksgiving, New Year's, Memorial Day, and Labor Day, and a weekend retreat for couples around Valentine's Day. The staff is available to serve individuals or groups through pastoral leadership, prayer, counseling, and teaching.

ACCOMMODATIONS AND RESERVATIONS
There are four lodges and two cabins on the site. All buildings except the two cabins have bathroom facilities in the building. A bath house is near the two cabins. Trailer hookups are also available. The center can accommodate up to 130 people.

POINTS OF INTEREST
Adjoins Silver Falls State Park. Several nature trails wind through the property. Other recreational opportunities include a swinging bridge, a rope swing, and a tree house.

LOCATION
From Portland take Interstate 5 to Woodburn exit. Follow Highway 214 through Mount Angel and Silverton to Silver Falls State Park, fourteen miles southeast of Silverton.

From the south take Highway 22 East from Salem, then Highway 214 all the way through the park to the north end (twenty-six miles from Salem). Turn on the gravel road opposite North Falls parking area and go one mile, following signs to the center.

184. Franciscan Renewal Center
0858 SW Palatine Hill Road
Portland, OR 97219

503/636-1590
Fax 503/636-8099
Catholic/Franciscan

DESCRIPTION

Surrounded by attractively landscaped grounds, orchards, and evergreens, the center is a contemplative place for private and group retreats. Individuals may arrange for quiet retreats for journaling, reading, and listening to tapes. Groups may wish to participate in a thematic retreat led by a retreat director with opportunity for reflection and group interaction. Comfortable conference rooms, two with fireplaces, and a breakout room enhance retreatants' experience.

The facility schedules educational workshops/ seminars throughout the year that respond to the spiritual, personal growth, and psychological needs of the people.

ACCOMMODATIONS AND RESERVATIONS

Single and double rooms. Some have private baths. Bed linens, towels, and wash cloths are provided. Delicious home-cooked meals served in the large dining room. Cost for an overnight stay, $30; meals, $17 per day; spiritual direction, $35 per session.

POINTS OF INTEREST

At the entrance to the facility's twenty-acre site is a mansion of French chateau-style architecture. Known as Our Lady of Angels Convent, the mansion has been used for retreats and a residence of the Sisters of Saint Francis since 1943. Adjoining the complex is Lewis and Clark College.

North or south on Interstate 5: Take Terwilliger exit (297). Follow Terwilliger Boulevard and Lewis and Clark College signs. Continue past the college campus (now Palatine Hill Road). Turn right at first driveway.

North or south on Macadam Street (43): Turn at Taylor's Ferry Road. Turn left at Terwilliger and follow same directions as above. (Other approaches from Macadam are Palatine Hill Road, Military Road, or Terwilliger Boulevard.)

185. Menucha Retreat and Conference Center

38711 E. Crown Point Highway
P.O. Box 8
Corbett, OR 97019
503/695-2243
Fax 503/695-2223
Presbyterian Church (USA)

DESCRIPTION

Menucha comes from a Hebrew word that means "rest" or "repose." This site was purchased in 1950 by Portland's First Presbyterian Church to provide a place that would nurture just such rest in retreatants. It is envisioned as a place where individuals and groups can come for study, reflection, and spiritual renewal. Its one hundred acres sit on a bluff above the Columbia River and offer views of the great falls gorge. There are trails throughout the property and several views of the gorge and the mountains in the distance. It was once home to the governor of Oregon. Private retreatants are welcome.

ACCOMMODATIONS AND RESERVATIONS

Ample accommodations for men, women, and children in private or semiprivate rooms in a homelike atmosphere. Private baths available in most rooms. Delicious homemade meals are served, including freshly baked bread and cookies. A private retreat space allows for retreatants to prepare their own meals. Fee is $23 per day for the facility plus the cost of meals. Rates vary for other accommodations. There is a seven-day-per-person-per-year limit on stays, as guests commonly are eager to return.

POINTS OF INTEREST

Swimming and tennis. Hiking around gorge and vicinity. Seacoast attractions are within a two hour's driving range. A prime windsurfing area is one hour away. Portland is a half hour's drive.

LOCATION

Twenty-two miles east of Portland via Interstate 84 to Corbett. Take Exit 22. Take Corbett Hill Road to Crown Point Highway and turn left. The east gate is one and a quarter miles to the left.

186. Our Lady of Guadalupe Trappist Abbey

9200 N.E. Abbey Road
Lafayette, OR 97127
503/852-0107
Catholic/Cistercian (Trappist)

DESCRIPTION

"You are invited to withdraw from the more hectic rhythm of your normal life," says the brochure of this center, "into a special period of prayer and silent reflection." The surrounding woods and hills provide opportunities to the retreatant for quiet walks and meditation. Retreatants may also wish to read or listen to tapes in the quiet room that overlooks the pond. Some find that a portion of their day spent in work affords balance to the rhythm of their retreat.

Located at the foot of a lovely wooded hillside, the abbey is a monastery of Trappist, or Cistercian, monks who are devoted to a life of contemplation in a cloistered atmosphere. The community in recent years has numbered between thirty-five and forty. Abbey guests may request conversation with one of the monks.

ACCOMMODATIONS AND RESERVATIONS
Private and small group retreats not exceeding one week. There is no stated regular charge, but donations according to one's means are expected. Operating expenses per day amount to about $25. Rooms have no air-conditioning and no private bathrooms. Two retreatants share a bathroom. To reserve space, telephone between 9:00 A.M. and noon, weekdays.

POINTS OF INTEREST
Guest library. A thirty-day monastic-life retreat within the monastery is also offered.

LOCATION
From Portland drive south on Interstate 5 to the Tigard/Highway 99W exit. Turn right and stay on Highway 99W for twenty-six miles to Lafayette. In Lafayette, drive to the west end. Turn right off 99W onto Bridge Street (sign also says "Trappist Abbey"). Go north for three miles, staying on the surfaced road. Abbey is on the right.

187. Shalom Prayer Center

840 South Main Street
Mount Angel, OR 97362-9527
503/845-6773
Fax 503/845-6585
shalom@open.org
Catholic/Benedictine

DESCRIPTION

In the heart of the lush, green Willamette Valley with its mild winters and gentle summers, the prayer center offers a place set apart for persons of all faiths. The center is on the Queen of Angels Monastery grounds in a quiet, rural setting. Close by are the foothills of the Cascade Mountains and the beauty of Mount Hood.

Personal retreatants are welcome. Guests may make a day or several days of retreat, meeting with a spiritual director during that time. On retreat, guests are welcome to participate in the prayer life of the monastery.

ACCOMMODATIONS AND RESERVATIONS

The prayer center has overnight accommodations as well as day space and meeting rooms. Guests and staff gather for meals with healthful, low-fat food. Many fruits and vegetables are grown in the monastery orchards and gardens.

The fee for a private retreat is $40 per day (overnight and meals). For meetings with a spiritual director, an additional donation of $40 is suggested. Day use of a private room plus one meal is $20. Arrangements for individual spiritual direction must be made in advance.

The building is handicapped accessible and has a no-smoking policy.

Shalom has a library and bookstore. Serious scholars have access to the Mount Angel Abbey Library. Also, fifteen acres of flower and vegetable gardens, fruit and nut orchards, and a wooded area provide places to walk or just to sit and enjoy the beauty. If they wish, guests are welcome to help garden or pick fruit and berries according to season.

LOCATION
The town of Mount Angel is located off Interstate 5. Go through the town and stay to the right at the fountain, where the street forks. Turn left at last driveway before going out of town. Shalom is in the two-story brick building on the right.

Washington

 188. Immaculate Heart Retreat Center
6910 South Ben Burr Road
Spokane, WA 99223
509/448-1224
Fax 509/448-1623
Catholic

DESCRIPTION
At the foot of Tower Mountain, the retreat center commands a view of rolling countryside to the west.

Private retreats are available when guests need to spend one day or several days on their own. Staff brings a wide variety of backgrounds and experience to spiritual direction, which is available upon request. Also offered are group retreats for special interests, annual quiet retreats, days of prayer, and personalized retreats and programs for a particular group.

Several buildings on the retreat property can house guests. The main wing contains a dining room, a picturesque lounge, thirty-four rooms equipped with double beds, and fourteen rooms with a single bed. Each room has a chair, a desk, a half bath, and a view of the grounds.

Rosage Hall is connected to the main wing. It contains a conference room, small chapel, and twenty rooms with two single beds and a half bath.

The Monastery is the original farm house on the property. It has a chapel and seven bedrooms and is an ideal spot for small groups. A complete kitchen allows meal preparation.

The Red House has three apartments. The two upper level areas offer a living room with couch, desk and chair, a bedroom with a single bed, and bathroom. The lower level consists of a bedroom with two single beds, a full bath, a complete kitchen, and combined living-dining room.

The White House has four units each with a bed, couch, table, bathroom, kitchenette, and porch. It is an ideal place for those who wish solitude and privacy.

POINTS OF INTEREST
Guests will enjoy walking on the center's sixty-five acres. The main wing contains a chapel, a bookstore, and a library.

LOCATION
The center is two miles southeast of Spokane's city limits.

189. Kairos House of Prayer

W. 1714 Stearns Road
Spokane, WA 99208

509/466-2187
Catholic

DESCRIPTION

Located on twenty-seven acres of forested hills, Kairos House of Prayer provides a place for anyone called to a prayerful, reflective, and contemplative environment for any length of time. It has been established within the Diocese of Spokane. Although spiritual direction is available, there is no imposed structure, only the freedom and creativity of solitude. Since Kairos has no resident chaplain at this time, celebration of the Eucharist and reconciliation will be contingent on the availability of a priest.

ACCOMMODATIONS AND RESERVATIONS

Kairos has nine private rooms, seven hermitages, and a large chapel prayer room. Hermitages, open-ended retreats, and group retreats are available. Schedule well ahead of time. For those who wish, there are two group meditations each day except on hermit days.

Meals are provided and may be taken (in silence) at the main house. Those in hermitages may wish to prepare their own meals. Food will be furnished.

Kairos is completely dependent on donations for its ministry of prayer. Therefore, the cost per day, which includes overnight accommodations and home meals, is $30. In order that no one is denied a Kairos time because of finances, please inquire about price reductions prior to coming.

POINTS OF INTEREST

Kairos House of Prayer sets retreatants in a landscape filled with forests and beautiful meadows, which provides a natural beauty and solitude conducive to the total prayer experience.

LOCATION
Kairos House of Prayer is eleven and a half miles north of downtown Spokane. Leave Interstate 90 at Exit 281. Drive north on Division Street (US 2-395). Pass Wandermere Golf Course. Take first left, which is Dartford Drive.

190. The Priory Spirituality Center
500 College Street NE
Lacey, WA 98516-5338
360/438-2595
Fax 360/438-9236
prioryspc@juno.com
Catholic/Benedictine

DESCRIPTION
Retreatants will value the hospitality offered in this guest house situated in a contemplative wooded environment near Olympia, Washington, and run by Saint Placid Priory. Lovely grounds and wooded trails make a perfect setting for prayerful reflection, rest, and relaxation away from the busyness of daily life.

A retreat may last from a few hours to a week. Individual directed, nondirected, and group retreats are available. Also, the center offers a variety of spiritual growth opportunities through its programs. Retreatants may participate in the priory's daily prayer and worship.

ACCOMMODATIONS AND RESERVATIONS
Private rooms have a bed, desk, chair, and sink. All linens are provided. Bathrooms are shared. Meals may be taken with the sisters or in silence.

Fees are on a sliding scale. The suggested range for an overnight stay per person is $35–$55 including meals. For a day only, the range is $10–$20 (includes a meal). The center welcomes, but does not require, an additional donation of $25–$40 for spiritual direction. Gift certificates are available. The center is handicapped accessible.

POINTS OF INTEREST
The library of Saint Placid Priory is open for guests' use. Books, cards, compact discs, and other items are available in the Priory Store.

LOCATION
Coming south on Interstate 5: Take exit 109; turn right onto Martin Way. Take a right turn at the next light onto College Street NE. Turn right at the second driveway. Coming north on Interstate 5: Take exit 109; Turn left onto Martin Way. Turn right at second light onto College Street NE.

$\mathcal{W}yoming$

 191. Thomas the Apostle Center
45 Road 3CX-S
Cody, WY 82414
Phone and fax 307/587-4400
thomap@wave.park.wy.us
http://www.shoshoneriver.com/tac
Episcopal Church/Diocese of Wyoming

DESCRIPTION
Thomas the Apostle Center is located on Dinosaur Ridge, overlooking Cody, Wyoming, near the East Gate to Yellowstone National Park. It provides stunning views of the adjacent wilderness area, as well as places for fishing and hiking.

While supported by the Episcopal Diocese of Wyoming, the center remains open to groups and individuals from widely varied backgrounds.

A six-bedroom guest house, with twin and double beds, a full kitchen, conference room (accommodates ten), bathrooms, and a large art and craft studio with kiln and work tables. Guests have open access to a chapel, recreation area, plus two hundred acres of open grounds for scenic walks or meditation. A suggested donation per night includes a self-serve breakfast.

POINTS OF INTEREST
Nearby Yellowstone National Park provides geological wonders (there are more geysers and hot springs here than in the rest of the world combined), the colorful Grand Canyon of the Yellowstone River, fossil forests, and Yellowstone Lake.

LOCATION
Yellowstone Regional Airport is located not far from the center, with flights daily. Billings, Montana, is the nearest international airport, a scenic two-hour drive away.

192. San Benito Monastery
859 Main Street
Dayton, WY 82836
307/655-9013
Fax 307/655-9052
Catholic/Benedictine Sisters of the Perpetual Adoration

DESCRIPTION
As its brochure notes, this community of Benedictine sisters "lives, prays, works, and attempts to create an environment in which others may share in

their prayer and way of life." The monastery is located on thirty-eight acres near the Bighorn Mountains and the Tongue River Canyon. Private, directed, or guided retreats are available.

ACCOMMODATIONS AND RESERVATIONS
Six private rooms, most with private bath. Guests should bring casual clothing and comfortable walking shoes. Suggested offering is $25 per day.

POINTS OF INTEREST
Bighorn National Forest and Medicine Wheel National Historical Site are within driving distance.

LOCATION
Approximately 170 miles northwest of Casper. From Casper take Interstate 25 North to Interstate 90 West. Proceed west on Highway 343. Sheridan, Wyoming, has the nearest airport, and the guests can be met there for the forty-minute drive to the monastery.

West and
Southwest

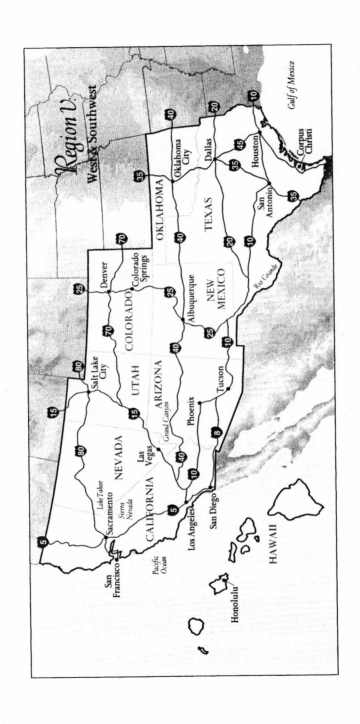

193. Desert House of Prayer

7350 W. Picture Rocks Road
Tucson, AZ 85743
or P.O. Box 570
Cortaro, AZ 08652 (mailing address)
520/744-3825
Fax 520/744-0774
Catholic

DESCRIPTION

As the name suggests, Desert House of Prayer is designed for prayerful solitude. "The solitude," the brochure of the house suggests, "has to do, to an uncommon degree, with its location. The buildings are located on thirty-one acres of primitive, high desert land, profusely covered with desert growth, plants, flowers, and trees." While the surrounding three mountain ranges convey a rugged grandeur, staff members say they most prize the area for its solitude, "as surely as Jesus prized the mountains and deserts of Judea into whose company 'it was his habit' to go in search of the solitude he desired for communion with his Father."

Each day the Eucharist is celebrated and morning and evening prayers are chanted. Twice daily the staff offers a one-hour session of group centering prayer for those interested. They also encourage retreatants to practice *lectio divina* (spiritual, reflective reading of Scripture).

Staff also consults with retreatants about prayer. Retreats can last one day or as long as a year.

$34 per day for regular rooms (three days or less; $31 per day for longer stays). $39 for hermitage stays. Retreatants bring bath soap and other personal items.

POINTS OF INTEREST
Near Saguaro National Monument-West. Library of ten thousand literary works and spiritual-life books, numerous audio and videotapes presenting teachings on prayer.

LOCATION
Accessible from Interstate 10 to Ina Road exit to Picture Rock Road. Arizona Stagecoach Shuttle serves Tucson, Arizona shuttle serves Phoenix.

194. Holy Trinity Monastery
P.O. Box 298
Saint David, AZ 85630
520/720-4016, ext. 17
or 520/720-4642, ext. 17
Fax 520/720-4202
Catholic/Benedictine

DESCRIPTION
The ninety-two-acre monastery, founded in 1974, is near the San Pedro River and has an ecumenical outreach, hosting various visitors for spiritual retreats throughout the year. Members of the community also participate in ministries outside of the monastery. The wooded grounds and high desert climate afford retreatants the chance to experience silence, solitude, and personal prayer. Retreatants may also take part in community prayer. Further, the monastery offers days of reflection.

ACCOMMODATIONS AND RESERVATIONS

Eleven rooms, single or double occupancy. A room, Casa de Bernardo, provides space for prayer and reading. Breakfast and supper are taken in silence. A "Grand Silence" is observed from the end of compline (evening prayer) until the conclusion of breakfast the next morning. Retreatants should bring a flashlight and alarm clock. The monastery provides basic linens and towels. Three meals a day are provided.

Suggested donation: double occupancy, $30 per person per day or $55 per couple per day. Meals are $10 per day or $5 per meal. If cost is an issue, contact the guest coordinator.

POINTS OF INTEREST

San Pedro Valley Center for the Arts is set on the monastery grounds. In addition to a museum, it hosts workshops in sculpture, painting, pottery, and other forms of art. Throughout the year various concerts feature internationally acclaimed musicians. A one-and-one-tenth mile bird sanctuary trail provides opportunities for walking. The grounds have an adobe chapel, outdoor Stations of the Cross, and a Meditation Garden.

Also on site: monastic library, Trinity Bookstore and Gift Shop Gallery, Trinitas (art gallery and museum), and Benedict's Closet (a thrift shop). Two annual festivals are held to raise funds for building and expansion.

LOCATION

Fifty-eight miles southeast of Tucson. Take Interstate 10, follow Exit 303 at Benson, proceed nine miles on Highway 80 to Saint David. After leaving Saint David, look for a large cross on the west side of the highway. Greyhound and Amtrak are both accessible in Benson, as is an airport in Tucson.

195. Living Water Worship and Teaching Center

P.O. Box 529
Cornville, AZ 86325
520/634-4421 (reservations at 602/951-9494)
Fax 520/634-0005
http://www.sierranet.net/~living
Interdenominational

DESCRIPTION

This center two hours north of Phoenix is described as "a lush oasis in the heart of the vast and beautiful desert mountains of Arizona." Nearby are the flowing waters of Oak Creek, green pastures with grazing horses, and a tranquil pond. The staff, working from an evangelical and interdenominational perspective, strive to provide "a peaceful place to escape the hectic world of meetings, deadlines, and responsibilities." Goals include helping retreatants "focus on the Lord's peace, grow in spiritual strength, share in God's grace, experience his Holy Spirit, and build lasting relationships" in a climate of solitude. Wooded hiking trails allow opportunities for quiet. A retreat master and materials are available.

ACCOMMODATIONS AND RESERVATIONS

Private and twin-bedded rooms combine with sectional dorm-style rooms. Bed linens are provided. Individual retreats welcome, as are families.

Suggested donation is $50–$60 a night, which includes three meals.

POINTS OF INTEREST

Prayer chapel, prayer garden, library of Christian classics, fishing, other outdoor sports. Also numerous local attractions: the Grand Canyon is two and a half hours away. Flagstaff, Arizona, at the base of the San Francisco peaks and site of snow-skiing facilities, is one hour north of the Center. Sedona, Arizona, is twenty minutes from the center. Nestled in beautiful red-rock formations, it is an ideal place for hiking. Nearby Camp Verde and Cottonwood house ancient ruins and Native American cliff dwellings. Historic Fort Verde is open daily. Also nearby: Jerome, Arizona, a booming mining town in the late 1880s, now home to a thriving artists' community.

LOCATION
From Phoenix take Interstate 17 North from Phoenix past Camp Verde to Exit 293 (McGuireville, Montezuma Well). Go left at top of exit ramp. After eight miles pass Casey's Corner at Page Springs Road. Continue half mile to Aspaas Road (gravel). Turn right. Drive almost half mile, turn left at Living Waters sign at bottom of the hill.

Shuttle buses available from Phoenix Sky Harbor Airport will leave you ten minutes from the center. With advance notice, staff can meet you at the shuttle stop.

196. Our Lady of Solitude Contemplative House of Prayer
P.O. Box 1140
Black Canyon City, AZ 85324
602/374-9204
Catholic

DESCRIPTION
Forty miles north of Phoenix, surrounded by mountains and Sonoran desert, the house rests on a desert mesa overlooking Black Canyon City. An adjacent knoll provides more solitude and a vista of miles of rugged land.

Staff members describe the house in this way: "Our Lady of Solitude welcomes guest retreatants who come for prayer and solitude for the purpose of closeness to God. Men and women of Christian faith find here a place where God is All-Important. Their faith gives them the courage and freedom to face untamed deserts within and without."

Housing, grounds, clothes, food, prayer, and work reflect the nuns' communal attachment to simplicity. Even the daily liturgical prayer is "simple, austere, low-keyed," yet full of praise for "God alone."

A hat and sturdy shoes for walking are recommended. Retreats may last a day (in which case retreatants are asked to bring a sack lunch) or a month.

ACCOMMODATIONS AND RESERVATIONS

Three hermitages, each with bath, is a self-contained unit, complete with a kitchen with refrigerator, crock pot, microwave, toaster, and utensils. Retreatants bring their own food. For those flying in, a stop at a general store can be arranged for stocking up on fruit and produce. Those driving in need to supply their own bed linen.

There is a suggested per-day rate, a donation according to one's means, though retreatants are asked to keep in mind the house's operating expenses.

POINTS OF INTEREST

The main building houses a prayer chapel, meditation and reading room with fireplace, and library, a kitchen, and a dining room.

LOCATION

Taking Interstate 17 North from Phoenix, exit at 242. Go to far right (frontage road), travel to first dirt road marked by tall transformer, and turn right. Continue up hill on Saint Joseph Road (using lowest gear). Served by Greyhound buses and Phoenix Sky Harbor Airport (with shuttle by Sedona Transportation Company).

California

(Northern)

197. The Bishop's Ranch

5297 Westside Road
Healdsburg, CA 95448
707/433-2440
Fax 707/433-3431
Episcopal/Benedictine

DESCRIPTION
Located in the vineyard country of Sonoma, California, seventy-five miles north of San Francisco, this center, owned by the Episcopal Diocese of California, offers expansive views of forests and valley farms. The ranch has 240 acres of gardens, pasture, and woodland for walking and solitude. Trails lead to a three-story tree house, creeks, a lake, and more views of the surrounding hills. At the center of the grounds, accented by a single white bell tower, is the Chapel of Saint George, open for individual prayer when services are not in progress. Group retreats are sponsored by the ranch and individual retreatants are welcome.

ACCOMMODATIONS AND RESERVATIONS
A number of buildings house retreatants, including a historic, two-story Spanish-style ranch house built in 1930.

There are also several cottages for overnight guests. Linens are provided. Individuals pay $35 per night; double occupancy is $60. Three meals, served buffet style, run approximately $23 per day per person. The ranch schedules individual retreats up to two weeks before a proposed visit, as space permits.

POINTS OF INTEREST
Small library and a shop for books, cards, and T-shirts. Swimming pool in season.

LOCATION
Southwest of Healdsburg on Westside Road. From the south take 101 North to the Central Healdsburg exit. At the second stop light make a hard left onto Mill Street, which becomes Westside Road. Drive about five miles. Just beyond the Bucher Dairy look for the sign on the right. From the north take 101 South to the Westside Road/Guerneville exit. Turn right onto Westside Road and proceed five miles to the entrance.

 ### 198. The Carmelite Monastery House of Prayer
20 Mount Carmel Drive
P.O. Box 347
Oakville, CA 94562
707/944-2454, ext. 4
Fax 707/944-8533
Catholic/Carmelite

DESCRIPTION
Situated in a serene setting bordered by vineyards at the foot of Mount Saint John, the House of Prayer provides guests a setting to find silence and solitude. Private retreats, group retreats, and days of rec-

ollection are available. Although preference is given to Roman Catholics, all denominations are welcome. Guests are invited to participate in Mass and morning and evening prayers.

ACCOMMODATIONS AND RESERVATIONS

Individual retreatants stay in a cottage thirty yards from the monastery. They prepare their own breakfast and lunch in a fully stocked, common kitchenette.

The group facilities can comfortably accommodate fifteen retreatants. This limit assures each retreatant a separate room. Monday through Saturday, the evening meals are prepared and served in the monastery. Also, breakfast, lunch, and dinner are prepared and served in the monastery. The cottage area and air-conditioned third floor of the monastery (accessible by elevator) are used for groups.

All guests must stay a minimum of two nights. Individual retreatants are asked to begin retreats on weekdays, since no evening meal is provided on Sundays. The fee for individuals and groups is $47.50 per person per day. Reduced rates are available to individuals who stay Monday through Friday. A deposit of half the amount of the full stay is required two weeks in advance for individuals and two months in advance for groups.

POINTS OF INTEREST

The House of Prayer is an impressive Georgian-style building in a beautiful natural environment. There is a gift shop, and the monastery chapel is available for guests' use.

LOCATION

The House of Prayer is located in California's Napa Valley. Call for directions.

199. Jesuit Retreat House and Conference Center

300 Manresa Way
Los Altos, CA 94022
650/948-4491
Fax 650/948-0640
ElRetiro@Retreat.scu.edu
http://www.Retreat.scu.edu/Jesuit
Catholic/Jesuit

DESCRIPTION

Surrounded by thirty-five acres of landscaped gardens and groves of oak and eucalyptus, nestled in the hills above Los Altos with a majestic view of the San Francisco Bay and the Santa Clara Valley, the Spanish-style buildings of this center reflect a California ambience. Spiritual retreats in the tradition of Ignatius of Loyola (sixteenth-century Spanish priest) are scheduled most weekends of the year, along with retreats with Advent and Lenten, twelve-step recovery, divorce recovery, and midlife transition themes.

Also provided are days of recollection, private retreats, individually directed retreats, and thirty-day Ignatian retreats.

ACCOMMODATIONS AND RESERVATIONS

Eighty-two rooms with private baths. $35 deposit required for registration for singles, $50 for married couples. Limited scholarships are available.

POINTS OF INTEREST

One mile from the quaint town of Los Altos.

From Highway 101 exit at San Antonia Road, turn left at Foothill Expressway, turn right at El Monte (first signal), turn right at University (first signal), proceed half mile to Manresa Way. Turn left. From Highway 280 exit at El Monte/ Moody Road, turn left at University (third signal), proceed as above.

200. The Marianist Retreat and Conference Center

22622 Marianist Way
Cupertino, CA 95014
408/253-6279
Fax 408/253-1834
Catholic/Marianist

 .

DESCRIPTION

Gardens surround the spacious conference rooms, bedrooms, and guest houses of the Marianist Center. Close by, the nature trails of San Antonio Park and Stevens Creek Park beckon visitors for day hikes. The Marianist Center is dedicated to a spirituality of wholeness. It offers comfortable meeting and overnight facilities in a beautiful, tranquil setting for private and group retreats.

ACCOMMODATIONS AND RESERVATIONS

The twenty-two guest bedrooms each have a garden patio and intercom phone. Guest houses include a reading room, a living room with fireplace, private patio, and garden.

Overnight use, which includes a full breakfast, a furnished meeting room, coffee and tea throughout the day, lunch, baked cookies in the afternoon, dinner, pool, Jacuzzi, garden, and tennis court use, is $60 for private retreatants.

The center serves delicious home-cooked meals and snacks. Indoor and outdoor dining is available.

POINTS OF INTEREST

The center's architecture has been integrated with the natural beauty of the center's grounds, which include acres of lush gardens and waterfalls. Flagstone paths wind through the front gardens to the Seat of Wisdom Chapel, and earthtones predominate in the decor.

A full-size indoor pool, with a retracting ceiling for natural light and year-round use, is surrounded by a tropical garden. Inside, guests can enjoy the extensive libraries.

LOCATION

From Highway 280 take Foothills Expressway/Grant Road Exit. Go right if coming from San Francisco; go left if coming from San Jose. Turn right on Voss; take an immediate left on Merriman. The Marianist Center driveway is on the right-hand side.

 ## 201. New Camoldoli Retreat House/ Hermitage

Big Sur, CA 93920
408/667-2456 or 667-2341
Fax 408/667-0209
Catholic/Camoldolese

DESCRIPTION

This five-hundred-acre tract of land at 1,300 feet above sea level in the Santa Lucia Mountains provides an almost otherworldly retreat experience. Panoramic views of the Pacific and craggy canyons below take the breath away. The Camoldolese monks live as a community of hermits and reside mostly in quiet in their own cells. Founded as a reform in the early eleventh century by Italian saint Romuald, the Camoldolese are known for their scrupulous adherence to monastic silence and extreme solitude.

The monks meet in the chapel four times a day to chant the liturgy and always welcome guests to join them.

A monk is available on request for limited guidance, but guests are mostly on their own.

ACCOMMODATIONS AND RESERVATIONS

A guest building houses nine single hermitages, each with a toilet and wash basin (showers are shared) and a view looking to the sea. Hermitage stays are for three days to one week. For meals guests help themselves to hearty soups, salad, and freshly baked bread, which are eaten in retreatants' own rooms. Also, the grounds have two trailers—one for men and one for women—for those wanting longer stays.

The monks ask for $30 per day for room and meals.

POINTS OF INTEREST

Big Sur coastal scenery along Route 1, the scenic road that traverses much of the California coastline.

LOCATION

Off Pacific Coast Highway (Route 1) about twenty-five miles south of Big Sur and fifty-five miles south of Monterey. Guests who take plane or bus to Monterey can be met on Friday afternoons between 5:00 and 7:00 P.M. The entrance on the inland side of the highway is marked by a large wooden cross.

202. Presentation Center

19489 Bear Creek Road
Los Gatos, CA 95030-9519

408/354-2346
Fax 408/354-5226
Catholic/Sisters of the Presentation

DESCRIPTION

Set in the Santa Cruz Mountains, Presentation Center is a retreat and educational conference center. Meeting rooms and bedrooms that look out on mountains and trees provide a setting for guests to think, pray, relax, and be revitalized.

The center is primarily offered for groups that bring their own programs and facilitators, but individuals are welcome and special retreat programs are periodically offered. People of all faiths are welcome.

ACCOMMODATIONS AND RESERVATIONS

Presentation Center has bedroom accommodations for one hundred double occupancy or fifty single. The center sets rates for both groups and individuals and for nonprofits and for-profits. The rates generally increase by 5 percent at the first of each year.

Individuals may stay in the retreat center's cottages (each houses four to six people) or Saint Martha's Guest House for $50 per night with a meal or $40 without. Meeting room capacity runs from fifteen to 195 people, with three rooms in the fifty-person range.

POINTS OF INTEREST

The natural beauty of Presentation Center, with the availability of hiking trails and other outdoor opportunities, helps renew the body and spirit. A lovely chapel is available for private prayer and celebration of the Eucharistic liturgy.

North of Santa Cruz on Highway 17 twenty miles. Left on
Bear Creek Road just over two miles; Presentation Center is
on the left.

203. Quaker Center

Box 686
Ben Lomond, CA 95005
831/336-8333
qcenter@cruzio.com
Quaker

DESCRIPTION

Towering redwoods dwarf this retreat center on
eighty acres of mountainous terrain on the eastern
slope of the California coastal range. A network of
hiking trails beside running creeks and under majestic trees provide places for reflection. The center
intends to offer people time away from the ordinary
routine and the opportunity for writing, meditation, reading, and study that a personal retreat will
give them.

ACCOMMODATIONS AND RESERVATIONS

Personal retreatants may stay in the Sojourners' Cottage,
which sleeps a maximum of four people in one double bed
and a sleeper sofa. The small cottage is fully equipped and
self-contained. Bed linens and bath and kitchen towels are
provided. The minimum weekend fee on the center's sliding
scale is $20 per night for single occupancy.

The Redwood Lodge, which accommodates up to eight
in bunk beds in two bedrooms and is wheelchair accessible,
is also available for personal retreats. The small kitchen is
fully equipped, and wood is provided for the wood stove.

Linens are not provided. The weekend fee is $15 per night single occupancy.

All guests bring their own food and are responsible for cleaning the facilities prior to departure. Reservations may not be made more than two months in advance.

POINTS OF INTEREST
The Redwood Circle, a large clearing surrounded by cathedral redwoods with bench seating for 100 people, provides an inspirational setting for outdoor gatherings.

Quaker Center maintains a self-guided nature trail, a volleyball court, and a play structure.

LOCATION
From San Jose and the Bay Area take Highway 17 South toward Santa Cruz. Go over the summit and down the mountain to the second Scotts Valley exit (Mount Herman Road, Felton, Big Basin). Go right at end of ramp. Call for detailed instructions from this point on.

 204. Saint Anthony Retreat Center
P.O. Box 249
Three Rivers, CA 93271
209/561-4595
Fax 209/561-4493
Catholic/Franciscan

DESCRIPTION
Cradled in foothills of the Sierra Nevada mountains, the gateway to Sequoia National Park, the center is a quiet, comfortable facility. Spectacular views of the Sierra Nevada Mountains greet retreatants.

ACCOMMODATIONS AND RESERVATIONS
The air-conditioned retreat center has semiprivate accommodations for housing ninety persons. Each unit has a pri-

vate bath; there are also semiprivate rooms with shared bathrooms. One room is handicapped accessible, as are all public areas. An experienced kitchen staff provides excellent meals served buffet style.

The rate for a semiprivate room including meals, use of facilities, and insurance, is $55 per person. Private rooms are an additional $25 per night. A one-day group conference, which includes continental breakfast, lunch, coffee breaks, and use of the facilities is $20 per person.

All arrangements for a conference or retreat must be made with the conference coordinator prior to the requested date.

POINTS OF INTEREST
The main chapel, a place for group worship or quiet meditation, can also be used for respectful meetings. Audiovisuals, a tape deck, and cassettes are in place for guests' use.

LOCATION
Highway 99 (North or South) to Highway 198 East through Visalia to Three Rivers. The nearest airports are in Visalia and Fresno.

205. Saint Francis Retreat Center
549 Mission Vineyard Road
P.O. Box 970
San Juan Bautista, CA 95045
408/623-4234
Fax 408/623-9046
Stfranret@aol.com
http://www.sbfranciscans.org/
Catholic/Franciscan

DESCRIPTION
The center sits on the outskirts of the historic and quaint town of San Juan Bautista in Northern Cali-

fornia. "We are nestled in the spacious, wooded hill-sides on a seventy-three-acre site," center materials note, "with a small lake and vistas overlooking the San Juan Valley. This beautiful, natural setting offers peace and serenity to all our guests. . . . Our purpose is to offer a place of spiritual growth, healing, and renewal, both personal and communal."

A ranch house, central to the beauty and charm of the retreat center, was built in the 1860s. Various families lived here until 1947, when the Franciscans purchased the property to create a retreat house. The ranch house now has the administrative offices, a major conference room, kitchen facilities, and the dining rooms. A large chapel and conference rooms have been added in recent years. Retreatants can join the monks for communal prayer and worship services.

ACCOMMODATIONS AND RESERVATIONS

Groups commonly use the facilities, but private retreats are offered as space allows and only on a midweek basis. The suggested donation is $60 per night for a private room.

POINTS OF INTEREST

Spacious grounds, including a four-acre lake, provide a haven for a wide variety of birds and wildlife. Gift and book shop, volleyball and basketball court.

LOCATION

Forty-five minutes south of San Jose, or east from the Monterey Bay cities and west of I-5 and points in the Central Valley. Less than two hours from San Francisco, twenty minutes from either Salinas or Gilroy, or forty-five minutes to Monterey Bay/Carmel area. Also conveniently proximate

to communities of the Central Valley, from Stockton to
Fresno.

206. San Damiano Retreat
P.O. Box 767
Danville, CA 94526
510/837-9141
Catholic/Franciscan

DESCRIPTION

Located thirty miles east of San Francisco on sixty
acres of oak-wooded hillside overlooking the San
Ramon Valley. Mount Diablo also stands in majestic
view. The center is named after the church in Italy
where centuries ago Francis of Assisi received his
mission to renew the church. Spanish-influenced architecture highlights the roomy facilities. Throughout the gardens and grounds are private meditation
areas and shaded footpaths.

Programmed retreats, private retreats (with or
without spiritual direction), and opportunities for
group use of facilities are offered.

ACCOMMODATIONS AND RESERVATIONS

Seventy-eight guest rooms, private or double, each with
private bath.

POINTS OF INTEREST

Chapel, gift shop, bookstore.

LOCATION

Highway 680 to Danville, exit Diablo Road West. Turn left at
Hartz Avenue, take a short block to Prospect, bearing left at

both forks in the road. At second fork Prospect becomes Highland Drive, which you take up the hill one mile.

 207. Santa Sabina Center
25 Magnolia Avenue
San Rafael, CA 94901
415/457-7727
Fax 415/457-2310
Sntasabina@aol.com
Catholic/Dominican

DESCRIPTION

Catholic in history and heritage, this center welcomes people of all faiths. It adjoins the wooded hundred-acre campus of Dominican College, seventeen miles north of San Francisco. The elegant building with European monastic touches includes an arched doorway and dark wood-paneled interior. "From the quiet of Santa Sabina's inner courtyard garden," notes the brochure, "the spirit of tranquillity and simplicity permeates the center."

Group retreats take place through the year and private retreats are available, space permitting. Also offered: Monthly days of prayer (from 9:00 A.M. to 2:30 P.M.). The sisters meet for community prayer at 6:30 A.M. each morning and retreatants are welcome.

ACCOMMODATIONS AND RESERVATIONS

In addition to regular rooms, a hermitage is available for day, weekend, or monthlong retreats. Both women and men welcome. Rate is $40 per night, exclusive of meals. Retreatants usually bring their own food or can walk to the college dining room nearby.

Adjacent campus of Dominican College. Fire trail leads to a lookout called "Rim of the World," which offers a panoramic view of the San Francisco Bay and beyond. Seasonal concerts in the chapel on Sunday afternoons.

LOCATION
From San Francisco take Interstate 101 North to the Central San Rafael exit to Irwin Street. Turn right on Mission Street, left on Grand Avenue, right on Acadia, then right on Locust/Magnolia.

California

(Southern)

208. Center for Spiritual Development
434 South Batavia Street
Orange, CA 92868-3907
714/744-3175
Fax 714/744-3176
Catholic/Sisters of Saint Joseph of Orange

DESCRIPTION
Beautifully tended flower gardens and simple, graceful buildings create a tranquil setting for retreatants at the ecumenical Center for Spiritual Development (CSD). The CSD is open year-round, seven days a week. Private retreats are offered all year. The center also offers seven six- to eight-day silent retreats yearly in a variety of styles: directed, guided, preached, contemplative, and private.

ACCOMMODATIONS AND RESERVATIONS

The air-conditioned and handicapped accessible center can accommodate up to fifty-two people a night in beautifully decorated rooms with twin beds and private baths. It also offers daytime meeting rooms (complete with audiovisual equipment). Nutritious, well-prepared meals are served.

Rooms for private retreats may be reserved on a space-available basis one week in advance. The private retreat suite offers guests a private bedroom and bath, comfortable sitting room, and a well-stocked kitchen. Breakfast is taken in the suite, and a hot meal is provided elsewhere for lunch and dinner. The weekday rate is $40 per night; the weekend rate is $45 per night. For those on directed retreats, spiritual direction is $10 per session.

In addition, a "personal day away," at $10 per day, provides a room for a day retreatant's time for personal reflection and careful solitude. No meals are served, but crackers and beverages are available.

POINTS OF INTEREST

The center has a heated outdoor pool, an oratory, and peaceful gardens. Disneyland, Knott's Berry Farm, cultural centers, beaches, and mountains are all close by.

LOCATION

The center is in the Southern California city of Orange, approximately thirty-six miles from Los Angeles. From Los Angeles take Interstate 405 to Highway 22 East past Interstate 5 to the Main Street exit. Turn east (right) onto La Veta Street, then north (left) on Batavia Street. The nearest airport is Orange County/John Wayne Airport. Shuttle buses are available at a minimal cost.

 209. Immaculate Heart Retreat House
3431 Waverly Drive
Los Angeles, CA 90027
213/664-1126

Fax 213/664-2215
Catholic/Sisters of the Immaculate Heart of Mary

DESCRIPTION
Built in the style of a medieval Renaissance castle, the residence of the Sisters of the Immaculate Heart of Mary sits on eight and a half acres in the middle of Los Angeles. The retreat house, formerly a private residence, offers a place of peace in the surrounding city. It is an urban sanctuary available to individuals or groups for a few hours or a day of reflection and prayer.

Overnight retreats are not offered, but directed and private day retreats are available. For those seeking spiritual direction, a spiritual director is available.

ACCOMMODATIONS AND RESERVATIONS
Open seven days a week, the air-conditioned retreat house can accommodate up to fifty day guests.

POINTS OF INTEREST
Immaculate Heart Retreat House has a beautiful chapel, a lounge, library, dining room, conference rooms, patios, and a swimming pool for retreatants' use and enjoyment.

The interior of the entrance tower was furnished as a replica of the prayer room of the Pope in the Vatican in Rome.

LOCATION
From Golden State Freeway go west on Los Feliz to Griffith Park Boulevard. South on Griffith Park to Rowena, turn left. Left on Waverly Drive, up to the parking lot.

210. La Casa de Maria
800 El Bosque Road
Santa Barbara, CA 93108
805/969-5031 or 805/969-2474
Fax 805/969-2759
casadema@rain.org
http://www.rain.org/~casadema
Catholic heritage, ecumenical and multidenominational

DESCRIPTION

Twenty-six acres in the oak-studded foothills of Monteceito, bordered by San Ysidro Creek and forest land with sycamores, flowering acacias, and eucalyptus and alder trees surround this house of prayer and retreat center. The land has a long history: it was part of a 1780 land grant of the king of Spain to the Franciscan mission, a lemon grove, an opulent estate, and now a retreat and conference grounds.

The center offers a wide array of group and individual retreats, including contemplative retreats and twelve-step workshops.

ACCOMMODATIONS AND RESERVATIONS

Forty-two retreat rooms with private baths. Call for rates. Accommodations for individuals and married couples.

POINTS OF INTEREST

Massage available. Hiking, swimming, Ping-Pong, tennis, volleyball, and basketball.

LOCATION

South of Santa Barbara. Off US Highway 101 take the San Ysidro Road exit. Turn right on East Valley Road, then left

on El Bosque Road. The airport in Santa Barbara is fifteen
miles from La Casa. Amtrak and Greyhound also serve the
center.

211. Mater Dolorosa Passionist Retreat Center
700 North Sunnyside Avenue
Sierra Madre, CA 91024
626/355-7188
materdolorosa@compuserve.com
www.passionist.org/materdolorosa/index.htm
Catholic/Passionist

DESCRIPTION
Located on eighty acres of foothills, with a breathtaking view of Southern California's San Gabriel
Valley, the retreat center boasts open fields, groves
of trees, and lawns with ample walkways. Programs
include weekend retreats for men or women and
days and evenings of recollection. Also retreats for
married couples, priests, and AA/AlAnon. The
"preached retreat" programs include conferences,
worship services (including the Stations of the
Cross), and opportunities for confession and private
counseling. Both group and individual retreatants
are welcome.

ACCOMMODATIONS AND RESERVATIONS
Three large meeting rooms and a chapel. Ninety rooms with
private baths. Handicapped accessible rooms available.

LOCATION
North Sunnyside Avenue is accessible from the Michillinda
exit off the 210 (Foothill) Freeway.

212. **Mission San Luis Rey**
4050 Mission Avenue
Oceanside, CA 92057-6402
760/757-3659
Fax 760/757-8025
http://www.sanluisrey.org
Catholic/Franciscan

DESCRIPTION
Located only four miles from the Pacific Ocean and thirty-two miles north of San Diego, the retreat center occupies the grounds of the Old Mission San Luis Rey, founded in 1798 by Franciscan friars. It was the eighteenth of twenty-one missions established in California. The fifty-six acres of historical grounds are carefully landscaped, providing a peaceful setting.

A full range of midweek and weekend group retreats are offered.

ACCOMMODATIONS AND RESERVATIONS
Fifty-two single or double guest rooms. Private retreatants pay $50 per night with three meals ($30 without meals). Couples stay for $70 per night with meals ($40 without). Due to natural ocean breezes, rooms are not air-conditioned.

POINTS OF INTEREST
The mission is a National Historic Landmark. Sunken gardens and an arched colonnade recall everyday life of the padres and Indians who inhabited the mission more than a century ago. The museum houses exhibits relating to the history of the mission and of early California, including artifacts from Native American and Spanish mission periods.

A gift shop offers Native American, mission, and other religious articles, including books and collectibles.

The annual early-summer fiesta commemorates the founding of the mission with arts and crafts booths, food, entertainment, and carnival rides.

LOCATION
Four miles east of Interstate 5 on Mission Avenue. Forty-five minutes from San Diego airport.

213. Mount Calvary Monastery and Retreat

P.O. Box 1296
Santa Barbara, CA 93102
805/962-9855, ext. 10
Fax 805/962-4957
mtcalvary1@aol.com
http://www.mount-calvary.org
Episcopal/The Order of the Holy Cross

DESCRIPTION

Perched atop a rocky ridge in the foothills of the Santa Ynez Mountains with a commanding view of the Pacific seacoast, this out-of-the-way Episcopal monastery and retreat house offers views of Point Magoo to the north and the Channel Islands to the south. The monks offer "a ministry of Benedictine hospitality." Central to each day at Mount Calvary is the "work" of prayer (*Opus Dei*), as Benedict called it. Three services daily, to which retreatants are invited to praise God and intercede for the needs of the world.

Individual and group retreats are available, for one day or several days, during the week or on a weekend. States the retreat house brochure, "Solitude, silence, conducted meditations, discussions, and reading are elements which you may choose to include in your experience. Monks of the community are available for guidance when needed."

The retreat program also encourages study retreats, where the atmosphere of monastic prayer, work, and study feed into a retreatant's time of reflection and study. The library offers excellent resources in the Bible, church history, biography, spirituality, and literature.

A "working retreat" is offered those unable to pay the suggested donation for a stay; they instead donate skills and time.

ACCOMMODATIONS AND RESERVATIONS
Throughout the spacious, tastefully decorated facility, picture windows offer stunning views of the Pacific.

POINTS OF INTEREST
Bookstore and gift shop; the monks, through a friendship with a local coffee roaster, have developed their own blend of fine coffee and teas, which they sell by phone, mail order, and E-mail.

LOCATION
Take Highway 101 through Santa Barbara to Mission Street. Turn right. Follow signs to "Old Mission Santa Barbara." After passing the mission, take second right (tight blind corner) on Mountain Drive. Make sure you stay on Mountain Drive. At Sheffield Reservoir bear left. Stay on Mountain Drive to fork. At fork, take Gilbraltar Road. Stay on Gilbraltar Road. Continue to climb mountain and follow Mount Calvary signs to Mount Calvary driveway. Turn left to the monastery and guest house.

214. Pro Sanctity Spirituality Center
205 South Pine Drive
Fullerton, CA 92833-3227
714/956-1020
Fax 714/525-8948
Catholic/Apostolic Oblates

DESCRIPTION

Staffed by Apostolic Oblates, who are consecrated laywomen, the spirituality center offers a calm place where recollection is possible for anyone who wants to deepen their spiritual life. Pro Sanctity is a world-wide movement of people based in Catholic traditions seeking holiness in everyday life. The contemporary building of the center is attractively landscaped and gives retreatants the opportunity to stay overnight or to use one of the simple rooms during the day.

The Pro Sanctity Spirituality Center is available for group retreats; days of prayer and reflection on Scripture, seminars, and spiritual direction. Guests can spend time in peaceful silence.

ACCOMMODATIONS AND RESERVATIONS
Retreatants may take one-day, three-day, or five-day retreats. The center can accommodate twenty-seven overnight guests and forty day guests.

POINTS OF INTEREST
The center offers vocational guidance.

LOCATION
Fullerton is approximately twenty-five miles southeast of Los Angeles, accessible via Interstate 5 (Santa Ana Freeway) or State Road 57 (Orange Freeway).

215. Saint Andrew's Abbey

P.O. Box 40
Valyermo, CA 93563
805/944-2178
standrab@ptw.com
http://www.networkone.net/~standrab/index.html
Catholic/Benedictine

DESCRIPTION

Valyermo is situated in the northern foothills of the San Gabriel Mountains on the edge of the Mojave Desert at an altitude of 3,600 feet. The change of seasons is very much a part of the life at Valyermo. Warm days and cold nights are typical.

The monks of Saint Andrew's Abbey gather for prayer five times a day and guests are welcome to join the monks in chanting the services. "Indeed," notes the brochure, "guests are welcome to participate in all the liturgical celebrations of the monastic community; however, intercommunion at Mass with members of other churches is at this time only a fervent hope for the future." Additional time during the morning and evening is spent in a slow, contemplative reading of the Scriptures that helps participants enter more fully into the texts, its meanings, and the presence of God.

Conferences and workshops on various subjects are held at the monastery throughout the year, especially during the summer.

ACCOMMODATIONS AND RESERVATIONS

The retreat house facilities include seventeen rooms with twin beds and private baths. Linens, towels, and soap are provided. The rooms are air-conditioned in the summer and heated in the winter. Homestyle food is shared with the monastic community. Breakfast is taken in silence. A chapel stays open all the time for prayer or meditation.

Rooms are more readily available during the week, at a suggested donation of $55 per night for single occupancy and $50 per person per night for double occupancy (includes lodging, linens, and three meals).

POINTS OF INTEREST

The resources of the monastery library, a thirty-thousand-volume research library emphasizing early Christian and mystical writings, can be made available to retreatants.

Saint Andrew's Abbey Ceramics is a monastic workshop established in 1969, which financially supports the Benedictine community of Saint Andrew's Abbey. The monks sell handmade ceramic plaques along religious themes with over three hundred designs. There is also a gift and art shop.

Following a medieval tradition, the monks of Valyermo sponsor an Arts and Crafts Festival on the monastery grounds during the last weekend in September each year. Artisans and craftspersons from Southern California display their products.

LOCATION

From Los Angeles take Route 14 (Antelope Valley Freeway) to Pearblossom Highway (Route 138) exit. From San Bernardino take Route 15 to 138 and proceed thirty miles to Pearblossom. Take Longview Road South to Ave. W, which becomes Valyermo Road.

216. Serra Retreat Center

3401 Serra Road
P.O. Box 127
Malibu, CA 90265
310/456-6631
srmalibu@aol.com

http://www.sbfranciscans.org
Catholic/Franciscan

DESCRIPTION

Overlooking the Pacific Ocean to the south and movie star mansions to the west, Serra Retreat Center is perched atop the Santa Monica Mountains. The winding road up to the center, the eucalyptus grove, and the rugged terrain nevertheless maintain a rustic flavor to the surroundings. The layout of the grounds, including carefully tended flower beds, statues, fountains, and ornate tile provide an inspirational setting while panoramic views betoken the love of nature of the order's founder, Francis of Assisi. The center is named after Junípero Serra, the founder of California missions.

ACCOMMODATIONS AND RESERVATIONS

A maximum occupancy rate of one hundred makes this Serra Retreat Center appropriate for both group and individual retreats. Weekend retreats normally begin on Friday afternoon and conclude with lunch on Sunday. Individual private retreats are usually made during the week. There is a small library and gift shop, two large conference rooms, and five small meeting rooms. People of all faiths are welcome. Friars are available for spiritual direction.

POINTS OF INTEREST

Located in proximity to major Southern California cities and attractions.

LOCATION

Serra Road turns north off of Pacific Coast Highway north of Santa Monica and south of Santa Barbara, just west of the Malibu Pier.

217. Spiritual Ministry Center

4822 Del Mar Avenue
San Diego, CA 92107
619/224-1082
Fax 619/224-1082
spiritmin@aol.com
http://members.aol.com/spiritmin/SMCWebPage.html
Catholic/Religious of the Sacred Heart

DESCRIPTION

The center is designed to be an oasis of prayer and hospitality in a coastal Southern California city. "We welcome people of diverse faiths and cultures," notes material from the center, "who seek to deepen their relationship with God and others. Our programs facilitate personal integration in the light of Gospel values and the insights of contemporary theology and psychology."

While located in a residential area, the center is just one block from the Pacific Ocean. While the property is small, the surroundings provide a variety of places to walk, bike, or just sit. Bicycles, beach chairs, and mats are available to take to the ocean. One-on-one directed retreats, including thirty-day Ignatian retreats, are provided. The center also accommodates persons interested in sabbatical retreats, provided they are prepared for the aloneness and can design their own experience.

ACCOMMODATIONS AND RESERVATIONS

The four spacious retreat rooms are located in a double duplex in a residential neighborhood. Retreatants stay at $50 per night no matter the amount of time (one night only is $60). Each retreatant has his or her own private room with bath. Retreatants do their own meals in stocked, equipped kitchens. Linens and laundry facilities supplied. Thirty-day retreats cost $1,500. A $50 deposit is due with registration.

POINTS OF INTEREST

A chapel provides space for prayer. The library offers books, tapes, and CDs. Each retreat room has a Bible and a CD/tape player with headphones. San Diego is nearby and the Pacific Ocean, including a fishing pier, is a block away. Catholic services are offered daily at the nearby parish church. Churches of other denominations are within easy walking distance.

LOCATION

Approximately twenty minutes by shuttle or taxi from Lindberg Field International Airport. Highway 8 West to end, exit left onto Sunset Cliffs Boulevard; follow south about one mile to Del Mar Avenue, turn right. Center is on the right.

 218. Villa Maria House of Prayer

1252 N. Citrus Drive
La Habra, CA 90631
562/691-5838
Fax 562/691-2572
Catholic/Sisters of Saint Joseph

DESCRIPTION

Twenty-five miles east of downtown Los Angeles, this suburban house of prayer opens its five single rooms to persons desiring "an atmosphere of quiet for prayer and solitude" for a day or a weekend. A patio and garden provide space for walking and parks are ten minutes away. Spiritual direction is offered.

$15 per day (room and meals); overnight retreats are $30 per day, with $15–$30 additional for spiritual direction, if requested.

POINTS OF INTEREST
A resource library with books, tapes, and videos. Eucharistic liturgy is celebrated at Our Lady of Guadeloupe Catholic Church less than a mile away.

LOCATION
Accessible from the Artesia Freeway (Beech Boulevard to Whittier, west to Citrus) or the Pomona Freeway (Hacienda Boulevard to Avocado Crest to Citrus). Accessible by Amtrak (Fullerton Station) and the Ontario or Los Angeles International Airports.

C o l o r a d o

219. Benet Pines Retreat Center
15870 Highway 83
Colorado Springs, CO 80921-1519
719/495-2574
Fax 719/471-0403
Catholic/Benedictine

DESCRIPTION
The center occupies a beautiful rustic setting amid thirty acres of pine in the Black Forest, thirty minutes north of Colorado Springs and one hour south of Denver. The center is attached to a monastery and the monastic Liturgy of the Hours, *lectio divina*, solitude, and interaction with a small community

provides what the center's brochure called "a gentle peace and tranquillity."

Directed retreats (with daily meetings with a director for reflection and prayer) and private retreats (no direction) for a day, week, or month are options. Monastic days, a community experience of reflection on Scripture and faith sharing, are scheduled each week for those who want to spend a day (or portion). Reiki massage offered for an additional donation.

ACCOMMODATIONS AND RESERVATIONS
Suggested donations are $45 per day/night with meals, $35 without. Hermitage stays slightly less. Sabbaticals are $600 per month (room and board) plus one hour of work each day. Spiritual direction available daily: first session free, $15 per session thereafter. 25 percent nonrefundable deposit with registration. The monks turn no one away for lack of funds.

POINTS OF INTEREST
See points of interest for Glen Eyrie Conference Center below.

LOCATION
From Denver take Interstate 25 South to Monument Exit 161. Take Highway 105 East to Highway 83. Turn right and drive two and three quarter miles. From Colorado Springs take Interstate 25 North to Exit 156 A. Go east to Highway 83. Turn left and drive two miles.

220. Glen Eyrie Conference Center
P.O. Box 6000
Colorado Springs, CO 80934
719/594-2285 or 800/944-GLEN (4536)

requests@gleneyrie.org
http://www.gospelcom.net/navs/gleneyrie
Independent Evangelical

DESCRIPTION

Built in 1904 by General William Jackson Palmer, founder of Colorado Springs, an English Tudor–style castle forms the centerpiece of this conference and retreat site of 750 acres, now owned by the Navigators, an evangelical Protestant Christian group. The sixty-seven-room castle has twenty-four fireplaces and many unique features that were well ahead of their time when the castle was built. Retreatants can hike the trails that wander through the towering rock formations, waterfalls, lush lawns, and hidden valleys of oak and pine. As you quietly wind your way through the valley, you'll see the eagle's nest housed in the majestic rock formations. For all the comforts and paved roads, abundant wildlife and clear mountain air make for a rugged outdoor experience.

Situated in the eastern foothills of the Rocky Mountains in Colorado Springs, the glen's location has a surprisingly temperate climate. In the summer, evenings are cool, and brief rain showers may be expected in the afternoons.

ACCOMMODATIONS AND RESERVATIONS

Glen Eyrie has 104 guest rooms, including luxurious, turn-of-the-century rooms in the castle and specially appointed rooms in four other locations on the property. Twenty-four rooms have one bed and a private bath. Seventy newly renovated rooms have two beds and a private bath. All rooms have clock radios and private direct-dial phones.

Rates vary from $50 to $80 per night per person, depending on season and choice of room. Breakfast is included, other meals extra.

POINTS OF INTEREST
In addition to seven hundred acres of beautiful scenery, hiking trails, horseback riding, fitness room, tennis court, bookstore, and other attractions, Glen Eyrie is within driving distance of many Colorado points of interest, including the Cave of the Winds, Cheyenne Mountain Zoo, Focus on the Family Headquarters, Garden of the Gods Park, Olympic Training Center, Pike's Peak, Royal Gorge Bridge, Seven Falls, and Factory Shops at Castle Rock.

LOCATION
The glen is three miles from the Interstate 25 Freeway and easily accessible by car. The Colorado Springs Airport is twenty-five minutes away; Denver International Airport is one and a half hours away. The Colorado Springs Airport serves the following airlines: American, America West, Continental, Delta, Mesa, Northwest, Reno Air, TWA, and United. Low-cost shuttle and taxi services are available to and from the airport.

221. Marycrest Retreat and Conference Center
2852 West 52nd Avenue
Denver, CO 80221-1259
303/458-6270, ext. 120
Fax 303/433-5865
Catholic/Sisters of Saint Francis

DESCRIPTION
The center, and its affiliated Queen of Peace Oratory (place of prayer), provide a twenty-six-acre oasis in

the midst of busy Denver streets, including a mountain view and lovely natural surroundings. "Our mission," the sisters say, "is to welcome persons of all faiths and cultures by providing space and opportunities for spiritual and personal growth in an atmosphere of Franciscan hospitality." Spiritual direction (where a director listens to a retreatant wherever he or she is on the spiritual journey and guides with gentle suggestions) and daily liturgy provided. Several sisters provide spiritual direction, each bringing unique perspectives and strengths.

ACCOMMODATIONS AND RESERVATIONS
Comfortable, simply furnished rooms (a few with private baths) and home-cooked meals are included. Suggested donation is $40 per day (for one to two days; $35 per day thereafter). Average donation for spiritual direction is $20 to $45.

POINTS OF INTEREST
Chapel, library of books and tapes. Attractions of Denver nearby.

LOCATION
From Interstate 70: exit at Federal Boulevard. Proceed to 52nd Avenue. Turn right and continue one block. From Interstate 76 West: exit at Federal Boulevard. Go south to 52nd Avenue, turn left and continue one block.

222. Nada Hermitage
Spiritual Life Institute
Crestone, CO 81131
719/256-4778
Catholic/Carmelite

The relative austerity of this retreat center only serves to underscore its spectacular views of fourteen-thousand-foot Kit Carson Peak. "Guests to Nada," notes a recent article in *Newsweek*, "live in one of sixteen austere but serviceable hermitages tucked among the pinyon pines. . . . The seven Carmelite monks who run this monastery-retreat . . . are pleasant; helpfully but respectfully remote."[2] The retreatant is largely left on his or her own but hiking trails and opportunity for vespers services beckon. "Our life," notes the hermitage brochure, "is a rhythm of work and play, solitude and togetherness, fast and feast, discipline and wildness, sacrifice and celebration, contemplation and action. Retreatants participate in our monastic rhythms or choose solitude in their own hermitages."

A monk is usually available at the beginning of a retreat for minimal direction. Retreatants work with monks and other guests doing chores on Saturday mornings.

ACCOMMODATIONS AND RESERVATIONS

Each hermitage has its own kitchen and bathroom facility. Bedding and simple food is provided but most meals must be prepared by the retreatant. Typically one week is the minimum stay and guests should plan on arriving on a Thursday between one and four P.M. and depart by a Wednesday by noon. Retreatants may stay as long as a month.

Charges: $50 for the first day and $40 for each additional day.

Scenic views and hiking trails amid aspen meadows and forests.

By car, four hours south of Denver, three and a half hours southwest of Colorado Springs, and five hours north of Albuquerque. Crestone is one hour north of Alamosa or one hour south of Salida on Colorado 17.

223. Saint Benedict's Monastery Retreat Center

1012 Monastery Road
Snowmass, CO 81654
970/927-1162
retreat@rof.net
http://rof.net/wp/theophan/index.html
Catholic/Cistercian

Situated in a lovely valley beneath the Colorado Rockies' Elk Range at an elevation of eight thousand feet, the grounds of the monastery and retreat center include a chapel, cattle ranch, aspen forests, streams, and rolling meadow lands. Cabins and other buildings are constructed of stone, giving a rustic feel appropriate to the rugged, high-elevation terrain. The monastery is three quarters of a mile from the retreat center.

Individual solitary retreats, group communal retreats, and "Centering Prayer Intensive Retreats" are available to guests. Retreatants can arrange conferences with monks but directed retreats are not available. Guests can also attend prayer services with the monks at times throughout the day.

ACCOMMODATIONS AND RESERVATIONS
Guest facilities are primarily designed for private retreats by either men or women (or couples). All units have private kitchen and bath (with the exception of the gatehouse, which has shared facilities). Guests are responsible for their own meals. Kitchenettes come stocked with nonperishable items (salt, sugar, coffee, some spices), but guests need to bring all other food.

The main building houses a small reading lounge, community kitchen and dining room, and a meditation hall with a view of the Elk Range. Because the center is located near a prime wild game migration route (and subject to county regulations) no pets are allowed. Given the elevation, nighttime temperatures in the summer can dip into the forties. In winter subzero temperatures are rare but possible.

Charges are based on donation, though a fee of $35 per day single or $50 per couple is suggested.

POINTS OF INTEREST
Scenic country and spectacular views of mountains. Also a bookstore with an eclectic selection of reading material and cookies from the monastery kitchen. Nearby Aspen is an old silver-mining town and ski center.

LOCATION
Twenty miles from Aspen. From Denver, Interstate 70 to Glenwood Springs, then Highway 82 to Old Snowmass. Contact the center for further directions.

224. Saint Raphael's Retreat House
P.O. Box 43

Evergreen, CO 80439
Episcopal

DESCRIPTION

Located in a small mountain community about 7,200 feet above sea level on land that hosts a cascading creek, Raphael means "God heals," and this house is offered as a place of healing for body, mind, and spirit. Retreats, whether for individuals or groups, focus on spiritual growth through journaling, centering prayer, healing prayer, spiritual direction, Bible study, worship, and rest. The directors offer a special ministry to clergy and clergy couples who are "battle-scarred and weary."

Retreats for clergy are offered in three formats: A weekend at $67 per person, a weeklong retreat at $160 per person, or a three-week format at $335 per person (deduct 10 percent for clergy couples).

ACCOMMODATIONS AND RESERVATIONS

Simple, tasty, and healthful meals are served daily. The retreat house accommodates up to fourteen people. Next to the house is a small chapel and across the creek is the sponsoring parish church, Episcopal Church of the Transfiguration.

Suggested offering for individual or group retreat is $35 per day with meals; $22 without. Special bed-and-breakfast rates are offered to clergy families during the ski season and summer family months. Clergy from any denomination are welcome.

POINTS OF INTEREST

Prime ski areas nearby. Denver and environs is home to many tourist attractions. Nearby also is Episcopal Confer-

ence Center, where Episcopal Renewal Ministries holds its
conferences and leadership training institutes.

LOCATION
Thirty minutes west of Denver between two major highways. Call for directions.

 225. Spes in Deo
Franciscan Family Retreat Center, Inc.
21661 Highway 550
Montrose, CO 81401
970/249-3526
Catholic/Franciscan

DESCRIPTION
This small center can boast of some of the most
contemporary architecture likely to be found in a
retreat center. The retreat house is a four-bedroom,
two-bathroom geodesic dome, located on eight
acres in the beautiful Uncompahgre Valley at the
base of the San Juan Mountains.

The lay Franciscan family that directs the center
note a special affinity for centering prayer and the
arts. They provide spiritual direction for those interested.

ACCOMMODATIONS AND RESERVATIONS
Suggested donations vary. Individual retreat with meals and
spiritual direction, for example, have a suggested rate of $45.
Without meals and direction: $35.

There is a fully equipped kitchen available for those
who wish to prepare their own meals. Nonrefundable deposit: 25 percent of total cost.

Library, chapel, gardens, orchards, hikes on neighboring state lands. Nearby lake and campground of Dutch Charlie, wildlife sanctuaries, the Black Canyon of the Gunnison, and the historical town of Ouray with its hot springs pools.

LOCATION
Two hundred and eighty-five miles west of Denver, a six-hour drive by car, one hour by air. For pickup or drop-off at airport or train or bus depots at Grand Junction: $12. For pickup at airport at Montrose: no expense.

226. Xavier Jesuit Center
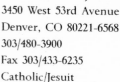
3450 West 53rd Avenue
Denver, CO 80221-6568
303/480-3900
Fax 303/433-6235
Catholic/Jesuit

DESCRIPTION
This center provides private and group retreats— "lots of silence and Ignatian contemplation, especially on divine love," notes one of the priests on staff. Mass and daily prayers combine with "time in high, beautiful Rockies retreat places" to provide an atmosphere of silent listening to God bathed in awareness of God's love.

ACCOMMODATIONS AND RESERVATIONS
Fifteen single rooms and two double rooms, air-conditioned and all with private baths, are available. Rates by donation.

POINTS OF INTEREST
Colorado's Rocky Mountain Range is nearby.

LOCATION
Accessible via Interstates 70 or 76.

227. The Spiritual Life Center
1020 S. Beretania Street
Honolulu, HI 96814
808/523-1170

DESCRIPTION
A lovely home with a landscaped yard and view of the city below is the focal point of this retreat program, begun under the auspices of the Catholic Diocese of Honolulu but now interdenominational. In addition to providing "hospitality for those searching for a time and place for quiet prayer and soulful reflection and rest," the center offers directed retreats, time-out prayer days for clergy, workshops on spiritual direction and other topics, and theme retreats (such as centering prayer, healing, and reconciliation).

ACCOMMODATIONS AND RESERVATIONS
The retreat house, located away from the office address above, is at 2604 Liliha Street in upper Nuuanu, has one double bedroom, two single bedrooms, and a five-bed dormitory with shared baths. Linens and towels provided. Stays longer than two days require a $50 deposit. Meals available on request. Room rates range from $25 to $30 per night, not including meals.

POINTS OF INTEREST
Library. Ten minutes from downtown Honolulu (city bus stops at corner of retreat house).

(Retreat house is located at 2602 Liliha Street.) Plan ten minutes from downtown Honolulu or twenty minutes from the Windward side. From town (Hotel Street), take No. 13 city bus. From the Windward side, take the Pali Highway to exit at Wyllie Street. Take first right to Liliha Street. From airport take No. 19 or 20 bus to Aalaa Park and transfer to No. 13.

Nevada

228. Wellspring Retreat House and Conference Center
P.O. Box 60818
701 Park Place
Boulder City, NV 89006
702/293-4988
Fax 702/293-7208
Episcopal/Sisters of Charity

DESCRIPTION

This oasis of flower beds, pine trees, and cacti offers views of surrounding mountains and Lake Mead. The building itself was once a hospital that served workers on the Hoover Dam. It is now on the National Register of Historic Places.

The Sisters of Charity live under the rule of Saint Vincent de Paul, taking three religious vows: poverty, chastity, and obedience. "Here in a quiet space," the brochure says, "people are able to find God and discover the place within themselves where that encounter occurs." The retreat house,

while a place of quiet, is a five-minute walk from
the historic town center. The staff say, "There are
spacious grounds with pleasant views on every side."
Individuals may accompany the sisters in the daily
prayer offices.

ACCOMMODATIONS AND RESERVATIONS
Most rooms contain two beds. The Sisters of Charity provide meals for up to fifty people (special dietary needs can
be accommodated). $40 suggested donation for an over-
night stay with two meals; $46 donation for an overnight
stay with three meals. The sisters suggest a contribution of
$80 for a weekend stay (includes five meals).

POINTS OF INTEREST
The center houses a religious library consisting of some
2,500 works. The chapel, which the center makes available to
visiting groups, offers a gorgeous view of Lake Mead. Hoover
Dam, Read Rock Canyon, and the west rim of the Grand
Canyon are nearby.

LOCATION
Boulder City is southeast of Las Vegas just off Interstate 515.
Call for further directions.

New Mexico

 229. Ghost Ranch Conference Center
HC 77, Box 11
Abiquiu, NM 87510
505/685-4333
Fax 505/685-4519
Presbyterian Church (USA)

DESCRIPTION

Ghost Ranch dates back to a Spanish land grant given to Pedro Serrano and his family in 1766. In the 1930s Mr. and Mrs. Arthur Pack bought a part of the original land and some years thereafter donated the ranch to the Presbyterian Church. Now, the staff say, "Ghost Ranch hosts people of diverse faiths, racial, and cultural origins, who come to the natural beauty of northern New Mexico to study a wide range of topics." Topics include paleontology, music, theology, social issues, and conversational Spanish. The ranch offers a spiritual retreat facility, as well as summer programs for youth and college students.

ACCOMMODATIONS AND RESERVATIONS

Ghost Ranch accommodates as many as 350 visitors. The dining hall serves up to 300 guests three times a day. Double occupancy (includes overnight accommodations and three meals): $60 for private bath, $55 for semiprivate bath, $44 for dorm-style bath. Children fourteen and younger are half of the adult price; children four and under stay free of charge. Family-style rooms, meeting rooms available.

POINTS OF INTEREST

The ranch is a Registered Natural Landmark, since fossil remains of the earliest known dinosaur were found there. The ranch features both the Florence Hawley Ellis Museum of Anthropology and the Ruth Hall Museum of Paleontology. The center is committed to several environmental projects. During the summer, visitors may have access to a supervised swimming pool. Horseback rides available. Hiking trails. Library open twenty-four hours a day. Campfires. Trading post. Coin-operated laundry machines.

Northern New Mexico. North of Santa Fe, south and east of Chama. East of Interstate 84 (watch for sign between mileposts 224 and 225).

 230. Glorieta Baptist Conference Center
Reservations Department
P.O. Box 8
Glorieta, NM 87535
800/797-4222
Fax 505/757-6149
Southern Baptist

DESCRIPTION
The center, which is set on a 2,400-acre valley, is owned and operated by LifeWay Christian Resources. The center sits in the Santa Fe National Forest, a 380,000-acre tract, most of which remains as wilderness. For the past few years Glorieta has drawn in an annual average of some fifty-four thousand guests, a little more than half of which have visited in the summer. Many groups, including both Southern Baptists and non-Baptist church groups, use the facilities throughout the course of a year. The conference center has Ski Bible conferences during the winter months and regular Elderhostels. Individual retreatants are welcome.

ACCOMMODATIONS AND RESERVATIONS
Sixty-seven conference rooms take up twenty-eight thousand square feet of space. Forty-four hotel rooms have private baths. Cottages, seventy private apartments, five dormitories, and a camp with forty-eight RV spaces (each space has full hookups) and areas for tents provide a number of accommodation options.

Ten preschool rooms, day camp, prayer garden. Softball fields, tennis, volleyball court, various trails for hikers of all abilities, biking, basketball, Ping-Pong, soccer, miniature golf.

LOCATION
Eighteen miles from Santa Fe on Interstate 25 in the Sangre de Cristo Mountains (at 7,500 feet). From 25 north take exit 299 to Glorieta. Turn left from ramp, left at sign for the center. Follow to entrance (one half mile).

231. Monastery of Christ in the Desert
Abiquiu, NM 87510
505/470-4515
Catholic/Benedictine

DESCRIPTION
Retreatants interested in a rugged approach may appreciate the craggy, isolated beauty of this monastic guest house, nestled amid desert mountains. The chapel, eating area, and guest house are constructed of adobe and stone, perched in a canyon 6,500 feet above sea level. The summer months of July and August can be quite wet. Snow is common in winter and mud in spring. In winter the rooms are heated with wood-burning stoves, for which chopped wood is provided. Only portions of the buildings have electricity and kerosene lamps provide light elsewhere. There are areas for hiking.

ACCOMMODATIONS AND RESERVATIONS
Believing it takes time to disengage from normal life's pace and to adjust to a monastic rhythm, the monastery requires a minimum stay of two days and two nights. (Maximum

stay is two weeks in the summer and three in the winter.) Accommodations allow for men and women to be on private retreat. The monks are not equipped to give directed retreats, nor regular spiritual direction.

Write or phone (505) 470–4515 for reservations well in advance (two to three months for the summer and autumn months). Please specify the dates you wish to make a retreat. If you leave a message, leave a number where the call can be returned collect.

POINTS OF INTEREST
Carson National Forest and Santa Fe National Forest are close at hand.

LOCATION
The monastery is about 135 miles from the closest major airport in Albuquerque, New Mexico, 75 miles north of Santa Fe, and about 53 miles south of Chama, off of US Route 84. You will need to provide your own transportation to and from the monastery (contact the monastery for further directions). There is a bus service from the airport in Albuquerque to Santa Fe. Cars can be rented at the Albuquerque airport and in Santa Fe. The road to the monastery is winding, steep, and narrow at some points.

 232. Pecos Benedictine Monastery
Monks of Our Lady of Guadalupe Abbey
Sisters of Mother of Mercy and Peace Monastery
P.O. Box 1080
Pecos, NM 87552
505/757-6415, ext. 254
Fax 505/757-2285
http://www.pecosabbey.org
Catholic/Benedictine

The monastery, a thousand-acre tract of valleys and hills, is seated at an altitude of seven thousand feet. The air is clear and dry, and most days are sunny. Year-round the center offers retreats for large groups as well as private and directed retreats. Visitors join Benedictine monks and sisters at Eucharist and prayer. The monastery has frequent workshops, addressing such themes as Pentecostal renewal in the Holy Spirit, healing ministry, finding God in silence, the way to health, and hope for the coming millennium. A distinguishing feature of the monastery, its Web site says, is that "in 1969 four monks from Benet Lake came to Pecos with the vision of establishing a charismatic Benedictine way of life. The vision soon blossomed into reality with the monastery becoming a worldwide center for charismatic renewal." In this tradition the monastery also offers a monthlong School for Charismatic Spiritual Directors.

ACCOMMODATIONS AND RESERVATIONS
Directed and nondirected retreats, suggested donation of $60 per day (additional free will offering for directed retreats). Hermitage stays, suggested donation of $65 per day. Reservations must be confirmed in writing, along with a $50 deposit. Weekend retreats end Sunday afternoon. Various prices for workshops.

POINTS OF INTEREST
Four self-contained hermitages are available, all of which have been open since 1997. Several miles away is the Pecos National Historical Park, which features an ancient Indian pueblo and the site of a Civil War battle. Santa Fe, rich in

culture and in adobe architecture, is some twenty-five miles to the west of the monastery.

LOCATION
The monastery borders the Pecos River. From Santa Fe, take Interstate 25 North to exit 299 (Glorieta). Follow signs to Pecos. Route 63 North to Pecos Benedictine Monastery.

 233. The Spiritual Renewal Center, Inc.
2348 Pajarito Road, SW (soon to be 6400 Coors Road, NW)
Albuquerque, NM 87105
505/877-4211
Fax 505/877-1413
domreths@swcp.com
Catholic/Dominican Sisters

DESCRIPTION
Formerly known as Dominican Retreat House, this center hosts both private and group retreats. The center, which is currently set on over four acres of farmland, is in the process of expanding into a larger and more comfortable setting. According to one of the center's brochures, the sisters are striving to provide a place where people can "come, find peace, grow in their spiritual lives, and deepen their relationship with God." Weekend retreats address such topics as centering prayer, spiritual exercises of Saint Ignatius, healing the generations, self-esteem, and dealing with anxiety.

ACCOMMODATIONS AND RESERVATIONS
Air-conditioned rooms. Capacity for twenty-five to thirty-one people overnight and forty to sixty for day or evening events. With the expansion forty private bedrooms will be

offered. Weekend retreats, $75 offering ($25 deposit required). Days of reflection, $12. Evenings of reflection, $15. Private retreat, $35 per day (includes private room, one meal), minimum stay of two days. Some financial assistance available.

POINTS OF INTEREST
Lounge. Chapel. Small farms to the east and west, with a view of the Sandia Mountains. Days of reflection offered in English and Spanish.

LOCATION
Call for up-to-date directions.

234. Tres Rios Christian Growth Center
1159 Black River Village Road
Carlsbad, NM 88220
505/785-2361
Fax 505/785-2348
Christian Church (Disciples of Christ)

DESCRIPTION
Covering well over three hundred acres of land, this desert oasis near Carlsbad Caverns is designed largely to accommodate the needs and interests of large groups, which are normally responsible for planning their own programs. Individual and family retreats are also available and a hermitage allows for solitude.

ACCOMMODATIONS AND RESERVATIONS
Rooms are air-conditioned. Two living units house as many as forty-nine guests. Living units consist of family units with a common room between bedroom areas. Each unit has a kitchenette for small groups. Dining room for groups over

twenty. Reservation deposit required for each living center unit used. Lodging, $20 per person per night, single room. $15 per person per night, double occupancy. Other fees apply (for example, linens are $4.50 per set; meals are $4 to $6 each). Lodging and meals are free to children five and under.

POINTS OF INTEREST

Year-round availability. Fishing, meeting rooms, hiking trails, RV and camping sites. Swimming pools, hot tub, Ping-Pong tables, multipurpose sports area. Arrangements can be made for guided tours of Carlsbad Caverns, potash mines, the Guadalupe Mountains, and the Living Desert State Park. The area is rich in New Mexico history.

LOCATION

Just north of the Texas-New Mexico border near Carlsbad Caverns. West of 285, east of Whites City.

Oklahoma

 235. Saint Gregory's Abbey
1900 West MacArthur Drive
Shawnee, OK 74801
405/878-5490
Catholic/Benedictine

DESCRIPTION

Situated forty miles from Oklahoma City on a wooded plain at an abbey and university with a Tudor Gothic building called by local residents "the Castle," this retreat center offers summer weekend "preached" retreats. Private (self-directed) retreats are available year-round.

ACCOMMODATIONS AND RESERVATIONS
Facilities are air-conditioned. The abbey houses retreatants for preached retreats in college residence halls with semiprivate baths (and makes available wheelchair-accessible bathrooms). The usual fee for summer weekend retreats is $55, plus a self-determined offering for the retreat master. Those making self-directed retreats stay in abbey guest rooms. The suggested offering there is $25 per day.

POINTS OF INTEREST
The Mabee-Gerrer Museum on the abbey grounds has collections of medieval and Renaissance art, Hudson River School and other American art of the early twentieth century, and an extensive Native American collection.

LOCATION
The abbey and university lie south of Interstate 40. From Oklahoma City, take Interstate 40 East to the first Shawnee exit. Follow Highway 177 South for about two miles, then turn left (east) on MacArthur Drive. After about one and a half miles a tree-lined drive comes into view, which is the entrance to Saint Gregory's.

Texas

236. Benedictine Retreat Center
Corpus Christi Abbey
HCR#2 Box 6300
Sandia, TX 78383
512/547-3257

Fax 512/547-5184
Catholic/Benedictine

DESCRIPTION

Fifty miles north of Corpus Christi and twenty miles from Mathis, Texas, on the shores of Lake Corpus Christi, the Benedictine Retreat Center provides a quiet place where people "can come to be spiritually refreshed through prayer, contemplation, and silence" while enjoying almost one hundred lakeside acres. Quiet weekend retreats, and private and spiritually directed retreats are available for individuals or couples.

ACCOMMODATIONS AND RESERVATIONS

Rooms are private and semiprivate, and air-conditioned. Linens and private baths provided. Expect warm temperatures. Retreatants give what they can monetarily "as God has given to them."

POINTS OF INTEREST

Gift shop, library, chapel. The lake contains largemouth bass, crappie, shad, and catfish. Nearby is Lake Corpus Christi State Park. Also within driving distance are Padre Island National Seashore, the Art Museum of South Texas and the Corpus Christi Museum of Science and History.

LOCATION

About 150 miles southwest of San Antonio, the center nears the southernmost region of Texas. Traveling north of Corpus Christi on Interstate 37, take Exit 34 to Texas-359 South for about ten miles. Watch for signs to abbey at turn at FM-534.

237. Christ the King Retreat Center

802 Ford Street
San Angelo, TX 76905
915/651-5352
Catholic

DESCRIPTION

Designed to be a "Christ-centered environment where people of all denominations and walks of life can come to find time away and space away," this center is found on the southeast side of San Angelo on nineteen acres bordering the Concho River. A secluded walkway winds along the north edge of the property and the riverbank. What the center calls "personally directed retreats" allows for "quiet open time [for] paying attention to your own experience and becoming aware of God's presence there." Usually lasting for five to eight days (although a shorter period is possible), the retreatant and director meet daily to reflect on one's experience of living and prayer, "listening for the inner rhythms of life, listening for the nudges and nuances of God."

ACCOMMODATIONS AND RESERVATIONS

Two dorms contain fifty-one rooms, a chapel, library, dining room, kitchen, and conference rooms.

POINTS OF INTEREST

San Angelo State Park offers camping, picnicking, hiking, mountain biking, and horseback riding. Also lake swimming and wading, fishing, boating, and bird and wildlife observation. Other nearby attractions include Fort Concho, a restored historic fort; Concho Avenue, which has a historic shopping district.

415

LOCATION
East of Texas 277 and west of State 306 Loop in the southwest side of San Angelo. San Angelo is some 200 miles west
of Dallas.

 238. Christian Renewal Center
1515 Hughes Road
P.O. Box 635
Dickinson, TX 77539
281/337-1312
Catholic/Missionary Oblates of Mary Immaculate

DESCRIPTION
Fifty secluded acres along Dickinson Bayou midway
between Houston and Galveston has allowed this
center to provide a wide range of programs of spiritual formation for thirty years. While the center
offers programs to the public and serves as a host
facility for outside workshops, it honors requests for
individual private retreats based on room availability. Wooded and waterfront trails provide a scenic
environment, and priests and staff provide personal
direction and private retreat guidance. Program foci
include Hispanic families in transition and spiritual
formation for adults and youth. Private and directed
retreatants welcome.

ACCOMMODATIONS AND RESERVATIONS
Single and double rooms are available, as well as dormlike
cabin lodges. Suggested donation for private or directed retreats is $40 per day.

POINTS OF INTEREST
Eucharistic meditation chapel and main chapel. Outdoor
swimming pool, sand volleyball court, and recreation fields.

One mile east of Interstate 45, thirty minutes from downtown Houston and twenty minutes from Houston's Hobby
Airport.

239. Laity Lodge

P.O. Box 670
Kerrville, TX 78029
830/792-1230
Fax 830/257-3137
http://www.hebuttfoundation.org
Protestant/Interdenominational

DESCRIPTION

The word "laity" in the name comes from the
Greek word sometimes translated "people of God"
and often used to refer to laypersons. Laity Lodge is
an "ecumenical Christian retreat center . . . dedicated to our common quest to know Christ and
what that means in the ordinary secular relationships of our lives." It nestles along the Frio River
amid scenery of striking, rugged beauty. It is part of
the larger H. E. Butt Foundation (headquartered in
Kerrville, Texas), which has for decades provided
retreats and youth and family camps on a 1,900-acre
ranch sixty miles west of Kerrville.

Group retreats often enlist noted writers and
speakers. Some programs combine theology, psychology, and management, others focus on artistic
creativity or provide opportunities for contemplation and Bible study. Customized private retreats
offer direction through the director of the lodge.

ACCOMMODATIONS AND RESERVATIONS

While Laity Lodge has a wide range of lodge rooms (air-conditioned and some with private baths), those wanting a private retreat will be especially interested in the Wayfarer's Cottage (also known as the Quiet House), a beautifully designed stone cottage built on a hilltop and hidden amid cedars and oaks. It is designed for contemplative retreats for one or two people. "Gladly acknowledging our debt to the Catholic monastic tradition and its heritage of silent retreats," a brochure relates, "we strive to synthesize that multifaceted legacy and its marvelous riches with [a] more historically Protestant emphasis." Lengths of stays at Wayfarer's Cottage typically range from two to six days. Each guest at Wayfarer's is responsible for food preparation. Basic food staples are provided, but guests should bring fresh foods. Bedding and linens are furnished. Married couples are encouraged to use the house for relationship building. Cost is $50 per night per person; $60 for a couple.

POINTS OF INTEREST

Canoeing, paddleboats, tennis, a walk along the Frio River, and other outdoor activities are all available, as is a well-stocked bookstore.

LOCATION

Two and a half hours northwest of San Antonio. Coming northwest from San Antonio take Interstate 10 West and proceed eighteen miles past Kerrville. Take Exit 490 (Highway 41/Mountain Home/Rocksprings). Turn left and go about twenty-five miles to Highway 83. Turn left and go south approximately fifteen miles to the H. E. Butt Foundation entrance on the left. Coming southwest from San Antonio take Highway 90 Southwest through Hondo to Sabinal. Follow signs to Garner State Park via Highways 187, 127, and 83, through Leakey and twelve miles north of Leakey on Highway 83 to the Foundation Camp sign (on right) marking the camp entrance, a half mile north of the roadside picnic area.

From Austin (approximately three and a half hours travel time) take Highway 290 through Johnson City to Fredericksburg. Turn left in Fredericksburg at Highway 16 South toward Kerrville. At Kerrville, take Interstate 10 West eighteen miles to Exit 490. Turn left on Highway 41 and proceed to the intersection with Highway 83 (about twenty-five miles). Turn left on Highway 83. Go south about fifteen miles to the H. E. Butt Foundation entrance (on left).

240. Montserrat Jesuit Retreat House
P.O. Box 398
Lake Dallas, TX 75065
940/321-6020 or 321-6030
Fax 940/321-6040
Catholic/Jesuit

DESCRIPTION

The relaxed, prayerful atmosphere at Montserrat is described in its brochure: "Everything is voluntary—except silence." The retreat house is on twenty-eight acres on Lake Dallas. The gracious, secluded setting, which has a small pier into the water, offers guests deep silence, individual counseling, and time for quiet reflection.

Three retreat masters are on the staff to direct retreats. They and another Jesuit specially trained in the Spiritual Exercises of Ignatius of Loyola are available for consultations and confessions throughout the retreat.

ACCOMMODATIONS AND RESERVATIONS

The air-conditioned and handicapped-accessible retreat house has fifty private rooms with private baths. Sixteen rooms have two single beds. All linens, towels, and soap are provided. The retreat house has a dining room building, a chapel, and a library, each of which seats seventy-five.

There is no set fee for a retreat. The center asks that guests give what they can afford. The suggested cost for a three-day retreat is $195.

POINTS OF INTEREST
If guests wish to spend the time reading, there is an excellent collection of books in the library, which looks out over the lake. The high spot of each day is the liturgy celebrated in the chapel, enhanced by the sun filtering through the stained glass windows.

LOCATION
Montserrat is about thirty miles from downtown Dallas and twenty-five minutes from Dallas-Fort Worth Airport. On Interstate 35 East take the Swisher exit east to Shady Shores Road. Take a left turn. The retreat house is on the right.

241. Mount Carmel Center
4600 W. Davis Street
Dallas, TX 75211
214/331-6224
Fax 214/330-0844
http://www.professionalwebs.com/mtcarmel
Catholic/Carmelite

DESCRIPTION
On thirty hilltop acres overlooking the city of Dallas, Mount Carmel Center envisions itself as an informal institute of Christian spirituality, a contemplative center operated by the Discalced Carmelite Friars of the Southwestern (Saint Thérèse) Province since 1974. In the tradition of sixteenth-century spiritual leaders Saint Teresa of Ávila and Saint John of

the Cross, this center "seeks to foster among the Christian community the contemplative dimension—an openness to transcendence—a disposition to commune with the infinite mystery of God." Liturgical prayer, to which retreatants are invited, is offered regularly through the day.

Private retreatants are welcome to spend hours of one day or a number of days in private prayer and reflection, enjoying the peace and quiet of the center and its solitary acres.

ACCOMMODATIONS AND RESERVATIONS
The dormitory called the House of Silence offers simple, rustic accommodations, and a small guest house is available. There is air-conditioning and some rooms have private baths. Summer study retreats include classes, private counseling, a contemplative celebration of the Eucharist, and participation in the Liturgy of the Hours. There is time and space for solitude and private prayer.

Suggested donation: for some hours, a freewill offering; for some days, $30 a night; for directed retreats, $40 a night.

POINTS OF INTEREST
A small Byzantine oratory and a larger contemporary chapel are always available and the wooded grounds are spacious. Nearby are Old City Park (museum) and the city's monument to President Kennedy.

LOCATION
Off of Interstate 35 take Texas Road 180 (Davis Road) West to the center.

242. Moye Center

600 London Street
Castroville, TX 78009

830/931-2233
Fax 830/931-2227
moyecenter@aol.com
Catholic/Sisters of Divine Providence

DESCRIPTION

This center, run by an order with French roots and centuries of service, sees retreats as opening "opportunities for prayer, reflection, learning, and sharing . . . challenging oppression and reconciling tensions . . . [and providing] a gathering place for women and men from varied backgrounds and beliefs." This, the sisters believe, will providentially allow retreatants to find "empowerment and transformation." The historic buildings, with ample rooms, have served through the years as a private school for girls, a seminary for priests exiled from Mexico, a high school and military academy for boys, and a convent. Picturesque, open grounds allow retreatants space for reflective walks. In addition to workshops and conferences, Moye Center offers private retreats and opportunities for spiritual direction.

ACCOMMODATIONS AND RESERVATIONS

Quiet surroundings join with several buildings, including dorms and private and semiprivate rooms (all with shared baths).

POINTS OF INTEREST

Large chapel. The town is located in the bend of the Medina River, and known as the Little Alsace of Texas, Castroville has historic homes, distinctive architecture, handicrafts, antique shops, and parks.

Twenty-two miles west of San Antonio. Take Highway 90 West to Castroville/Mexico Street. Go north on Mexico Street and then turn right onto PR 4779.

243. Oblate Renewal Center

5700 Blancó Road
San Antonio, TX 78216-6615
210/349-4173
Fax 210/349-4281
orcsa@express-news.net
Catholic/Missionary Oblates of Mary

DESCRIPTION

A secluded, peaceful setting is created by the new stucco and tin-roofed buildings of the retreat center and its forty-one acres of wooded landscape that includes plants and flowers native to South Texas. Despite its convenient location, the conference, workshop, and retreat center located on the campus of the Oblate School of Theology is set apart.

Retreat groups and individuals may have ongoing spiritual direction from retreat directors who provide both listening and support. Those wishing to make private retreats must first meet for an interview with center staff.

ACCOMMODATIONS AND RESERVATIONS
The recently completed fifty-thousand-square-foot renewal center's large, graceful windows frame the beautiful surroundings. Spacious lodging facilities have fifty-nine private rooms with two twin beds for overnight stays. All bathrooms are private. Linens and towels are provided.

The dining room is circled by bay windows. Meals are

provided for private retreatants. A sheltered arcade connects the buildings. The center is handicapped accessible and air-conditioned.

POINTS OF INTEREST

A Perpetual Admiration Chapel and the Renewal Center Chapel are the worship facilities available to conference or retreat participants. The Lourdes Grotto and Shrine adjoins the center property. Also, the center has a library, a swimming pool, and ample meandering walkways.

San Antonio, a bilingual, multicultural city, offers many opportunities to experience diversity and cultural exchange.

LOCATION

The renewal center is next to the Oblate School of Theology main campus. It is located in North Central San Antonio, near the International Airport and one mile south of Northwest Interstate 410.

 244. Omega Center

Benedictine Retreat & Spirituality Center
216 West Highland
Boerne, TX 78006
830/249-3894
Catholic/Benedictine

DESCRIPTION

Set on forty-seven shaded acres on a scenic hilltop, the center offers an environment of Benedictine hospitality, stewardship, serenity, and prayer in the beautiful Texas hill country.

Staff members are available to direct private retreats and to design and facilitate group retreats. Omega ministers to individuals, families, and groups by sharing and designing services that enable guests to listen, discover, and experience.

ACCOMMODATIONS AND RESERVATIONS
There is comfortable air-conditioned lodging for sixty-seven overnight guests. Two private retreat rooms have private baths. Linen and towels are furnished for private retreatants. Pillows are furnished. Lodging is $20 per person per night, with a $20 deposit for a private retreat. A minimum of fifteen guests are required for meal service. Breakfast is $5; lunch, supper, and brunch are $6.

POINTS OF INTEREST
A quiet and peaceful chapel. A spacious park area has a barbecue pit, and there are many paths and roads for walking and jogging as well as scattered sheltered and open seating areas for rest and relaxation. The center has a heated Junior Olympic–size swimming pool.

LOCATION
From San Antonio take IH 10 West to Boerne Business exit. Approximately one and a half miles from exit, turn left on West Highland Street. From Austin take IH 35 to New Braunfels. Take Boerne Exit H 46. Come forty-five miles on H 46 to Boerne. In Boerne, turn left on Main Street, then right on West Highland.

U t a h

245. Retreat House

Abbey of the Holy Trinity
1250 South 9500 East
Huntsville, UT 84317
801/745-3784 or 801/745-3931
Fax 801/745-6430

hta@xmission.com
Catholic/Cistercians of the Strict Observance (Trappist)

DESCRIPTION

Twenty-five monks live in this abbey eighteen miles
east of Ogden near the base of Mount Ogden. There
is a stark beauty of sagebrush and clear, high-elevation air. The Trappist Abbey of Gethsemani in Kentucky founded this monastery in 1947, partly in response to the influx of monks to Gethsemani,
where Thomas Merton's increasingly popular books
on monastic life and spirituality were attracting
overflow numbers. At the time, the only readily
available building structures were Quonset huts,
which a contractor expanded and adapted for monastic use. The original quadrangle of large Quonset
buildings was intended to be temporary, but the
rugged steel and concrete structures still serve the
monks well.

The monks see their mission as that of "a hidden, austere, simple life of prayer and manual labor
inspired by the Gospel of Jesus Christ." Their labor
(and income) center around creamed and liquid
honey (sold at the gate house and by mail order), a
poultry department, and beef cattle. About 750 acres
of irrigated fields produce alfalfa, barley, wheat, and
pasturage. A bakery produces whole wheat and rai-
sin bread from the wheat.

The monks pray in the sevenfold choral celebration of what is called the Divine Office. Retreatants
(men only) are welcome.

ACCOMMODATIONS AND RESERVATIONS

The retreat house (for men only) occupies one wing of the monastic quadrangle. Eleven private rooms with shared bath (one with private bath) are available. Food and linens are provided. Reservations may be made for a few days or a maximum of one week. No suggested donation, but offerings are gratefully received.

POINTS OF INTEREST

Library and periodical collection.

LOCATION

Fifty miles north of Salt Lake City. From points south and north take Interstate 15 to the Ogden exit east. In Ogden get onto Route 39. Take Route 39 toward Huntsville. Just before the town, turn right at the sign for the monastery.

Canada

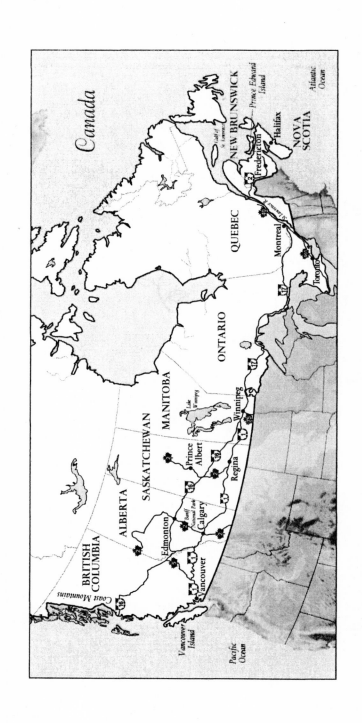

246. King's Fold

Box 758
Cochrane, AL T0L 0W0
403/932-3174
Fax 403/932-9531
Kingsfoldretreat@cadvision.com
Interdenominational

DESCRIPTION

Sitting in the foothills in full view of the Canadian Rockies on 160 forested acres, this interdenominational retreat center promises to be a "place for rest, renewal, and spiritual discovery in the context of the Christian faith." In addition to accommodations for up to thirty people in single and double beds, the center offers two cabins apart from the main facility for those wanting a solitary place for fasting and prayer.

ACCOMMODATIONS AND RESERVATIONS

A dining room with a spacious fireplace exhibits a spectacular view of the mountain range. Most rooms come with private baths. Information on affordable rates available upon request.

POINTS OF INTEREST

Rests on the banks of the Ghost River. Large book and tape library.

LOCATION

About an hour's drive northwest of Calgary, thirty-five kilometers (just under twenty-two miles) northwest of Cochrane. Follow Highway 1A West through Cochrane for thirteen kilometers (just over eight miles). Turn north (right) onto Highway 40 (Forresty Trunk Road). Transportation from Calgary can be arranged for a fee.

 247. Star of the North Retreat Center
3A Saint Vital Avenue
Saint Albert, AL T8N 1K1
403/459-5511
Catholic/Missionary Oblates of Mary Immaculate

DESCRIPTION
Three miles from Edmonton, this hill-perched center overlooks the Sturgeon Valley and the scenic city of Saint Albert. In addition to workshops, the center provides silent preached retreats (individual guidance available) and individual retreats (spiritual direction and shared prayer available). Retreatants can also visit the Genesis Room, filled with art supplies, where they can explore creative expression.

ACCOMMODATIONS AND RESERVATIONS
Twenty-eight double and thirty-four single private bedrooms (shared baths) and four private suites, each with attached bath.

POINTS OF INTEREST
Located on a historic site next door to the Vital Grandin Museum and Saint Albert Church. A walkway along the Sturgeon River and Lacombe Park is nearby.

LOCATION
Take Highway 2 North from Edmonton to Saint Albert. Turn west (left) at Saint Vital Avenue.

248. Queenswood House

2494 Arbutus Road
Victoria, BC V8N 1V8
250/477-3822
Fax 250/477-3891
Catholic/Sisters of Saint Ann

DESCRIPTION

Fifteen naturally wooded acres encompass Queenswood. Ample open areas provide retreatants places to walk or sit among flowers and trees. The house accommodates both large or small groups and individuals seeking a private or directed retreat. Queenswood welcomes members of all faiths and denominations. One guest has said the grounds "offer the blessing of peace and the balm of beauty." Workshops cover themes such as freedom and wholeness, spiritual journey and dreams, healing the inner child, Christian meditation, learning from conflict, contemplative monk and author Thomas Merton, and studies in awareness.

ACCOMMODATIONS AND RESERVATIONS

Overnight accommodations (mostly single-occupancy bedrooms) for twenty-five to thirty. Cafeteria-style dining room.

Spiritual direction is $20–$50 per session. A fee is suggested for retreats, and it varies from program to program. However, the staff want to "serve all people regardless of ability to pay."

Library. Indoor swimming pool. Chapel. There is a beach within walking distance.

LOCATION
From Victoria Airport or Swartz Bay head south on Provincial Highway 17, then east on Trans-Canada Highway 1 past McKenzie and Finnerty to Arbutus.

Manitoba

 249. Saint Benedict's Retreat and Conference Centre
225 Masters Avenue
Winnipeg, MB R4A 2A1
204/339-1705
Fax 204/334-8840
stbens@mb.sympatico.ca
http://www.retreatsonline.com/can/goto/stbens.htm
Catholic/Benedictine

DESCRIPTION
Saint Benedict's Monastery and Centre is located on seventy-two acres of wooded grounds along the Red River. There are bicycle and walking paths and acres of land to roam. Offered is a wide range of programs, including silent, private, and directed retreats.

ACCOMMODATIONS AND RESERVATIONS
Some private and some shared bathrooms available (the six private baths are usually reserved for private retreatants). Meals are provided, and vegetarian food is available on re-

quest at time of booking. The House of Peace is a five-bedroom house on the grounds for individual or small group retreats. Guests from the United States are asked to pay in Canadian funds with an international money order. While no one is turned away from lack of funds, suggested rates of donation are (in Canadian dollars) $20 per day for room and lunch, $25 per day for room and lunch and supper), $40 per twenty-four-hour period. Directed retreat is $45–$50 per twenty-four-hour period, depending on length of stay.

POINTS OF INTEREST
Winnipeg is a thriving metropolitan area. The center lies in driving distance of provincial forests, Lake Winnipeg, and other lakes.

LOCATION
Twenty minutes north of downtown Winnipeg, three and a quarter kilometers (two miles) north of Perimeter Highway 101, just off of Main Street (Route 9).

250. Villa Maria Renewal Centre
100 Place Villa Maria
Winnipeg, MB (Saint Norbert) R3V 1A9
204/269-2114
Fax 204/269-2119
Catholic/Oblates of Mary Immaculate

DESCRIPTION
Groomed lawns and wooded walkways surround this center within minutes from downtown Winnipeg in the suburb of Saint Norbert. "Since 1960," states the mission statement, "Villa Maria Renewal Centre has been a place where men and women have been welcomed to take time apart to experi-

ence the love of God in their lives. It has been a house for the nurturing of spiritual values in the everyday." While Villa Maria hosts a wide range of group retreats on topics such as marriage and family life, twelve-step spirituality, and cultivating a personal spiritual life, private retreatants are also welcomed.

ACCOMMODATIONS AND RESERVATIONS
Private rooms with shared baths (each room has its own sink). Meals provided. Call for rates and for more information about spiritual direction.

POINTS OF INTEREST
Chapel and meditation room. Cultural attractions in nearby downtown Winnipeg.

LOCATION
Twenty minutes from downtown Winnipeg, just off the Pembina Highway (which begins in the United States as Highway 75).

Nova Scotia

 251. Bethany Center
Antigonish, NS B2G 2G6
902/863-4726
Fax 902/863-9439
Catholic/Sisters of Saint Martha

DESCRIPTION
Located in serene hilly farmland on the outskirts of town, the "Bethany" in the center's name refers to

the village, mentioned in the Gospel of John, where Jesus spent time with Martha and her sister and Lazarus. The center's mission has to do with providing "a space of hospitality, solitude, and spiritual nourishment which will support the activity of God in individuals, communities, and the whole of creation." Guided, directed, and topical retreats are offered. It is open to "all seeking spiritual nourishment." The acreage of the grounds provides ample opportunity for walks amid forested lake and farm country.

ACCOMMODATIONS AND RESERVATIONS
Single and double rooms provide ample space. Retreat fees are $40 per day (Canadian). A six-day retreat is $240. Inability to pay the full cost need not be a deterrent to attending.

POINTS OF INTEREST
Antigonish hosts a historical museum. The retreat center, located on the motherhouse grounds of the Sisters of Saint Martha, is within walking distance of Saint Francis Xavier University.

LOCATION
Take Exit 33 off of the Trans-Canada Highway. Proceed to Antigonish's Main Street and turn right. Follow the road over a railroad track and bear left to Saint Martha's Regional Hospital on the left, cresting a hill. Watch for a large brick building on the left with a sign for Bethany Center and the Motherhouse of the Sisters of Saint Martha.

252. Seton Spirituality Center
Terence Bay Post Office
Terence Bay, NS B3T 2C6
902/852-4212

Fax 902/852-1252
setonctr@supercity.ns.ca
Catholic/Sisters of Charity

DESCRIPTION
The mission of the center is to enable persons to
discover the creative action of God in their lives.
The sisters strive to offer an "atmosphere of hospitality and quiet that is conducive to prayer." As the
center is "rooted in Gospel values and characterized
by holistic spirituality, it fosters the integration of
faith and justice." A setting of natural beauty overlooking Terence Bay (and a short distance from Halifax) assists in this, as does the center's homey,
country-style atmosphere. The staff provides group
and private retreats, along with a variety of personal
and spiritual-growth development programs. The
facility owes its name to Saint Elizabeth Seton, wife,
mother, widow, and foundress of the Sisters of
Charity.

ACCOMMODATIONS AND RESERVATIONS
Programs are carried out at three locations. Please direct all
inquiries to the center at Terence Bay. Six comfortable single
bedrooms, a dining area, and one suite are available. Bedrooms are on the second floor; there is no elevator. Additional overnight accommodation (two double rooms) is
available at the nearby rectory. A nonrefundable deposit
must accompany each reservation.

POINTS OF INTEREST
The center has ocean frontage, spacious grounds, two meeting rooms, a library, and a chapel. Nearby metropolitan

Nova Scotia is the business, educational, and cultural center of Maritime Canada. It has galleries, museums, universities, along with beaches, parks, walking trails, and restored waterfronts. Historic churches, houses, and fortifications attract many tourists. The twin cities of Halifax and Dartmouth are strategically placed on opposite sides of one of the world's finest harbors. Two toll bridges, the Angus L. Macdonald and the A. Murray MacKay, span the harbor, and a regular passenger ferry service connects the two downtown areas.

LOCATION
From Halifax, via Armdale Rotary, take Saint Margaret's Bay Road to Route 333 (Prospect Road/Peggy's Cove). Travel fifteen and a half kilometers (just over nine and a half miles) along Route 333, turning left at the Petro Canada gas station at White's Lake. Follow this road about nine kilometers (five and a half miles) to Seton Spirituality Center.

From Truro or Halifax via Highway 102 take Exit 1A, then Exit 2B following Peggy's Cove signs to Route 333. Take a left at the Petro Canada gas station at White's Lake. Follow this road about nine kilometers (about five and a half miles) to Seton Spirituality Center.

Ontario

253. Loyola House/Guelph Centre of Spirituality

P.O. Box 245, Station Main
Guelph, ON N1H 6J9
519/824-1250
Fax 519/767-0994
http://www.jesuits.ca/guelph/index.html
Catholic/Jesuit

Loyola House opened in June of 1964 as a retreat house for men. Since 1969, Loyola House has offered personally directed retreats for women and men, and the directed retreat experience continues to be at the heart and foundation of most of the programs. Programs aim at personal growth in prayer and awareness. More specialized programs assist participants in their capacity to guide others spiritually. The spirituality of Ignatius of Loyola, born in Spain in 1491, provides the spiritual underpinnings for much of the spiritual direction, as do his *Spiritual Exercises,* a text that allows retreatants to follow Jesus and seek God and God's will in every circumstance. Loyola House/Guelph Centre offers thirty-day Ignatian directed retreats along with weeklong and weekend directed retreats. (A full directed forty-day retreat based on the *Spiritual Exercises* is offered three times a year.) Loyola House is known around the world as a center for training those involved in spiritual direction.

The typical retreat day is simple: three meals, the Eucharist, a daily meeting with a spiritual director. The rest of the day is free for prayer and reflection, either in the chapel, private bedroom, lounge, or outdoors. "People spend a lot of their free time wandering around the property letting God speak to them," notes the center's brochure, "in the hope of a sunrise, in the tranquillity of a sunset, in the activity of the farm, in the gentle movement of the creek, in the teeming life of the wet land, in a ponderous walk along a shaded path. In the daily interview with a spiritual director the retreatant is aided in noticing where God has been present, comes to trust what has been noticed, and looks at the next steps in prayer."

ACCOMMODATIONS AND RESERVATIONS
Air-conditioned, handicapped-accessible rooms all have private baths. Rates vary. A weekend directed retreat, for example, is $105 (US dollars). The Forty-Day Spiritual Exercises Institute Retreat is $1,700 (US). Other retreats are $50 (US) for the first night; $45 thereafter.

POINTS OF INTEREST
A pool allows for swimming in the summer and the surrounding acres provide a setting for cross-country skiing in the winter. The center shares grounds with Loyola House and Ignatius College.

LOCATION
From Toronto or Windsor on Highway 401 take Exit 295; this is a bypass around Guelph. Follow the signs for Highway 6 North. The center is on Highway 6. Look for signs for Guelph Centre for Spirituality just past Marymount Cemetery. From Niagara Falls and Hamilton drive north on QEW and take Highway 403 West (Hamilton/Brantford) to Highway 6 North and to Highway 401. Go west on 401 to Exit 295 and follow instructions as above.

254. Marguerite Centre
700 Mackay Street
Pembroke, ON K8A 1G6
613/732-9925
Fax 613/732-2408
marguerite@renc.igs.net
http://www.renc.igs.net/~marguerite
Catholic/Grey Sisters of the Immaculate Conception

DESCRIPTION

Although the center is located in the middle of the city, it is on a large piece of property with hills and many trees and gardens. Guests will be drawn to the unique geographical beauty of the Ottawa Valley. The Ottawa River flows through the city, and nearby Algonquin Park has a wide variety of recreational opportunities.

The center is a contemplative, nurturing place for those who desire spiritual and personal growth through retreats, community gatherings, and educational programs. Private retreats and spiritual direction are offered on an ongoing basis by individual arrangement.

ACCOMMODATIONS AND RESERVATIONS

Attractive rooms accommodate up to forty-six overnight guests. Linen and towels are provided. A modern kitchen and dining facility (the full-time kitchen staff has thirteen members, including a baker) provides nutritious, home-cooked meals. Overnight fees for retreatants are variable (the norm is about $25 [Canadian]).

POINTS OF INTEREST

Two chapels, one large and one that accommodates forty. The library has about five hundred volumes as well as many current periodicals.

LOCATION

The center is two hours northeast of Ottawa on Highway 17. It is approximately four hours from Toronto (401 East to Highway 41, then 41 North to Pembroke).

255. Saint Joseph's Centre of Spirituality

Box 155, L.C.D.
Hamilton, ON L8L 7V7
905/528-0138
Fax 905/528-8883
Catholic/Sisters of Saint Joseph of Hamilton

DESCRIPTION
Much of the mission of the sisters who sponsor this center is "to heal broken relationships and to reconcile and unite people with God." A four-story wing of the order's motherhouse serves as a guest house amid spacious grounds. While a number of group retreats are offered through the year, private retreats of a day or more, with or without a director, can be arranged.

ACCOMMODATIONS AND RESERVATIONS
Thirty-three single bedrooms with modest but attractive furnishings and shared baths. A modest nonrefundable deposit is required. The buildings are mostly handicapped accessible.

POINTS OF INTEREST
The city of Hamilton rests in "Golden Horseshoe" against the Niagara Escarpment and manifests social, cultural, economic, and industrial diversity. A distinctive Hamilton Landmark built in 1933, the Cathedral of Christ the King is a fine example of Gothic architecture, with Italian marble and eighty-two stained glass windows in Renaissance style.

LOCATION
Located at the crossroads of Dundas, Burlington, and Hamilton at Highway 6 and Highway 403 on Northcliffe Avenue.

From Hamilton take Highway 403 North to Highway 6 and turn left (northeast). Turn left on Northcliffe Avenue and proceed to the center.

$Quebec$

 256. Abbaye Saint-Benoit
Saint-Benoit-Du-Lac, QC J0B 2M0
819/843-0480
Catholic/Benedictine

DESCRIPTION

Castlelike French Gothic Revival buildings stand amid a stunning setting of dense woods and pasturelands. The monastery guest house opens its doors to those seeking God in silence and recollection (it is not intended to be a hostel or inexpensive bed-and-breakfast, say the monks). Guests may share in the monastic community's prayer, said eight times a day. A private chapel in the guest house also accommodates private prayer. Guests are asked to keep silence in the guest house, especially after 9 P.M. Modest attire is requested. The monks take seriously the words of Saint Benedict, the spiritual father of this monastery (as for other Benedictine houses), when he urges monks to host guests: "All guests will be welcome as Christ Himself, for He is going to say, 'I have asked for hospitality and you have received me.'"

ACCOMMODATIONS AND RESERVATIONS
Each guest has a private room with sink and towels. Retreat times run from Monday until Thursday at noon or from

Friday until Sunday at noon. The monastery hosts men retreatants; a guest house for women attended by Sisters of the Presentation of Mary stands nearby (Villa Sainte-Scholastique, Saint Benoit-du-Lac, J0B 2M0, 819/843–2340. A donation of $35 (Canadian) per day is suggested.

The monks are known for their Gregorian chant (of which recordings are sold in the abbey shop) and for the cheeses and applesauce they produce and sell. Lake Mephremagog and mountains stand nearby.

From New York or other northeast areas, take Interstate 89 from Burlington, Vermont, toward Saint Albans to Route 105. Take 105 East to Richford, then take Route 243 (it eventually merges with 245). In Boulton Center watch for signs for the abbey.

Saskatchewan

257. Franciscan Forest Sanctuary
Box 85, Site 1, R.R. 1
Christopher Lake, SK S0J 0N0
306/982-3663
Fax 306/982-4799
Catholic/Franciscan Sisters

The sisters have just created this center within forty acres of boreal forest to provide a "quiet refuge for reflection and prayer." "Our location," writes one, "is perhaps the biggest drawing card since we are in the forest, [and] we are small; there is nothing institutional about the place." The sisters vow to welcome "all to experience the peace and healing of nature, sharing our home, meals, conversation, and prayer so that each person will benefit from [his or her] stay and leave refreshed in mind, body, and spirit."

ACCOMMODATIONS AND RESERVATIONS
Dining room with fireplace, large and small decks overlooking gardens and forest, four seasonally decorated rooms with twin bed and bathroom.

POINTS OF INTEREST
Groomed walking trails, small chapel. Library. Located approximately a half mile (one kilometer) from Lakeland Art Gallery, with walking trails and children's play area, ten minutes to the beach at Christopher Lake.

LOCATION
Traveling north of Prince Albert on Highway 2, proceed seven kilometers (nearly four and a half miles) past the Christopher Lake turnoff (Highway 262) to Forest Gate Road and turn right (east). The center is half a kilometer (a third of a mile) on the left.

Glossary

daily office Certain prayers to be recited at fixed hours of the day or night. The office (sometimes also called "Divine Office") usually includes recital or chanting (singing) of the Psalms, as well as readings from other biblical passages and prayers. Sometimes used interchangeably with the term "Liturgy of the Hours" (see below).

directed retreat A retreat in which the retreatant meets (usually daily) with a spiritual guide for counsel, suggestions on how and what to pray, and help in dealing with spiritual (sometimes emotional) issues that may arise during the retreat.

Eucharist With roots in the word "thanksgiving," Eucharist refers to the ancient Christian practice of partaking of bread and wine in commemoration of Jesus' broken body and shed blood. In many Christian traditions it is called a sacrament, a term reserved for acts or aspects of the church that mediate in some way the grace or presence of God.

friary   A monastery for friars, i.e., members of what are traditionally considered mendicant orders (living from donations) such as the Franciscans or Dominicans.

guided retreat   A retreat where input is given to a group by a spiritual leader, but in which there is time for personal, individual reflection and prayer.

hermitage   A cabin or other building set apart from more peopled areas to facilitate deeper solitude. Hermitages are typically self-contained and often have kitchen facilities.

lectio divina   (often called "divine, or spiritual, reading") is a meditative way to read the Bible (or other writings). It stresses soaking in a given passage's truths and staying open to insight relevant to one's daily life or spiritual growth. Typically a fourfold pattern is suggested: reading (slowly and alertly and with attention to a passage or phrase or biblical character that "leaps out"), meditating (reflecting on the selected passage or phrase), praying (using the passage or insight as a basis for prayer), and contemplating (gently resting in God's presence, ready to receive from God any blessings from his presence).

liturgy   A pattern of worship and prayer, often rooted in ancient practice and tradition. Liturgy may be quite detailed in Catholic, Lutheran, and Episcopal churches, and tends to be more informal in nonliturgical Protestant churches (such as Baptist churches, for example).

Liturgy of the Hours   The daily prayer cycle of the Catholic Church and other liturgical churches, based in part on psalms that speak of praying at certain times of the day (Psalm 119:164, for example, declares, "seven times a day I praise you"). The frequency and format of prayers vary, but seven times within a twenty-four-hour period is not unusual. The "hours" each have names. As they range in duration from ten to forty-five minutes, the term is something of a misnomer. Here are names and times as practiced at the Abbey of Gethsemani in Kentucky:

Vigils (3:15 A.M.)

Lauds (5:45 A.M.)

Terce (7:30 A.M.)

Sext (12:15 P.M.)

None (2:15 P.M.)

Vespers (5:30 P.M.)

Compline (7:30 P.M.)

Mass   A liturgy in which the Eucharist (see definition above) is "celebrated." This term, typically used in the Catholic tradition, is rarely used in Protestant contexts.

monastery   A religious community where monks live, work, worship, and pray. Whereas a community of women used to be called a "convent" or "nunnery," the modern tendency is to use the term "monastery" inclusively for either male or female communities.

oratory   A place or house for prayer.

preached retreat   A retreat, almost always with a group of others, in which a presenter gives talks, usually on designated themes or topics, that serve as a basis for the retreat.

private retreat   A retreat in which the guest is largely on his or her own; interaction with others at the retreat center is expected to be kept at a minimum to guard the retreatant's solitude.

spiritual direction; spiritual director   The practice of giving spiritual counsel and prayer to someone who wants to grow spiritually. A director is a person, usually with special training, who can help the "directee" understand dynamics of the spiritual life, interact with insights from the Bible, and discern signs of God's movement or leading in everyday life.

Stations of the Cross   A series of fourteen representations of successive events in Jesus' life as he journeyed to the Cross. These are often found in churches or outside and are intended as aids for devotion and prayer.

$\mathcal{A}lphabetic$ $\mathcal{L}ist$ of
$\mathcal{R}etreat$ $\mathcal{C}enters$

* *Note:* Where two retreat centers share the same name, the location has been included to distinguish one from the other and aid identification.

Afterword

Please feel free to share any comments you have about your experience on retreats. Also, any corrections or additions to the directory of retreat centers will be gladly considered. You may write me at:

P.O. Box 968
Nolensville, TN 37135

End Notes

INTRODUCTION
In Search of Quiet Places
1. Tamala M. Edwards, "Get Thee to a Monastery,"
Time, August 3, 1998.

CHAPTER 1
A Vacation for the Soul
1. Tamala M. Edwards, "Get Thee to a Monastery,"
Time, August 3, 1998.
2. Emilie Griffin, *Wilderness Time* (San Francisco:
Harper San Francisco, 1997), 7.

CHAPTER 2
Reasons to Go
1. Thomas Merton, *The Wisdom of the Desert* (New
York: New Directions, 1960), 3.
2. Philip Zaleski, *The Recollected Heart* (San Francisco:
Harper San Francisco, 1995), 11.
3. Quoted in Tamala M. Edwards, "Get Thee to a
Monastery," *Time,* August 3, 1998.

4. Frances Irene Taber, *Come Aside and Rest Awhile* (Wallingford, Penn.: Pendle Hill, 1997), 21.

5. Quoted in ibid., 21–22.

6. John Mogabgab, "Seeking the Quiet Places," *Weavings*, November/December 1986, 40.

7. Thomas Merton, *Thoughts in Solitude* (New York: Farrar, Straus and Giroux, 1956), 4.

8. Ibid., xii–xiii.

9. Richard Ford, *Independence Day* (New York: Alfred A. Knopf, 1995), 9.

10. Robert Benson, *Living Prayer* (New York: Jeremy P. Tarcher/Putnam, 1998), 97.

11. Geoffrey Cowley and Anne Underwood, "Memory," *Newsweek*, June 15, 1998, 52–53.

12. Kathleen Norris, *Amazing Grace* (New York: Riverhead, 1998), 16–17.

13. Beth J. Lueders, "A Great Escape," *Clarity*, October/November 1998, 9.

14. Thomas Merton, *Raids on the Unspeakable* (New York: New Directions, 1966), 9.

15. Marya Smith, "Getting Away from It All," *Chicago Tribune*, November 6, 1994.

16. Herman Melville, *Moby-Dick* (New York: Penguin, 1851), 393–94.

CHAPTER 3

Three to Get Ready

1. Richard J. Foster, "Growing Edges," *Renovaré Perspective*, April 1997, 1.

2. Quoted in *Reader's Digest*, November 1998, 165.

3. Lewis H. Lapham, "A Juggernaut of Words," *Harper's*, June 1979, 16.

4. C. S. Lewis, *Studies in Medieval and Renaissance Litera-*

ture, quoted in Ray Ashford, *The Quiet Life* (Canada: Northstone, 1992), 61.

5. Esther de Waal, *The Celtic Way of Prayer* (New York: Doubleday, 1997), 2–3.

6. C. S. Lewis, *Mere Christianity* (New York: Macmillan, 1960), 174–75.

CHAPTER 4

When It's Time to Go

1. Emilie Griffin, *Wilderness Time* (San Francisco: Harper San Francisco, 1997), 7.

2. Philip Zaleski, *The Recollected Heart* (San Francisco: Harper San Francisco, 1995), 63–64.

3. Anne Morrow Lindbergh, *Gift from the Sea* (New York: Pantheon, 1955), 115.

4. Emilie Griffin, *Wilderness Time* (San Francisco: Harper San Francisco, 1995), 14–15.

5. Eugene H. Peterson, *The Message* (Colorado Springs, Colo.: NavPress, 1993), 475.

CHAPTER 5

Packing and Other Fine (but Crucial) Points

1. Catherine de Hueck Doherty, *Poustinia* (Notre Dame, Ind.: Ave Maria, 1975), 22.

2. Philip Zaleski, *The Recollected Heart* (San Francisco: Harper San Francisco, 1995), 48.

CHAPTER 6

What Do I Do There?

1. Philip Zaleski, *The Recollected Heart* (San Francisco, Harper San Francisco, 1995), 5–6, 10.

1. Elizabeth O'Connor, *Call to Commitment* (New York: Harper & Row, 1963), 67–68.

2. Andrew Murr, "Alone at Last," *Newsweek,* July 27, 1998, 45.

Printed in the United States
1399200002B/258

9 780385 491587